ABOUT THIS PUBLICATION

FOR SERVICE ASSISTANCE

Customer Service
1.704.898.0770

North Carolina General Statues is published by The Muliti-Media Group of Greater Charlotte in Charlotte, North Carolina. Copyright 2015 by the Multi-Media Group of Greater Charlotte. This book or parts thereof may not be reproduced in any form, stored in a retrieval system, or transmitted in any form by any means—electronic, mechanical, photocopy, recording or otherwise—without prior written permission of the publisher, except as provided by United States of America copyright law.

The records required by U.S. Code 2257(a) through (c) and the pertinent regulations 28 C.F.R. Cli. 1, Part 75 with respect to this publication and all materials associated with such records are maintained by The Multi-Media Group of Greater Charlotte, Publisher and available for review by Attorney General.

www.visionbooks.org

Copyright © 2015 by MMGGC
All rights reserved!

TID: 5072101
ISBN (10) digit: 150299030X
ISBN (13) digit: 978-1502990303

123-4-56789-01239-Paperback
123-4-56789-01239-Hardback

First Edition

090520140547

Printed in the United States of America

2015 EDITION

North Carolina Criminal Law And Procedure-Pamphlet # 63

Printed In conjunction with the Administration of the Courts

North Carolina Criminal Law and Procedure
Pamphlet Reference Guide

Chapters	Pamphlet
Chapter 1 Civil Procedure	1
Chapter 1 Civil Procedure (Continue)	2
Chapter 1A Rules of Civil Procedure	2
Chapter 1B Contribution.	2
Chapter 1C Enforcement of Judgments.	2
Chapter 1D Punitive Damages.	2
Chapter 1E Eastern Band of Cherokee Indians.	2
Chapter 1F North Carolina Uniform Interstate Depositions and Discovery Act.	2
Chapter 2 - Clerk of Superior Court [Repealed and Transferred.]	3
Chapter 3 - Commissioners of Affidavits and Deeds [Repealed.]	3
Chapter 4 - Common Law	3
Chapter 5 - Contempt [Repealed.]	3
Chapter 5A - Contempt	3
Chapter 6 - Liability for Court Costs	3
Chapter 7 - Courts [Repealed and Transferred.]	3
Chapter 7A – Judicial Department	3
Chapter 7A – Continuation (Judicial Department)	4
Chapter 7A – Continuation (Judicial Department)	5
Chapter 7B - Juvenile Code	5
Chapter 8 - Evidence	6
Chapter 8A - Interpreters for Deaf Persons [Recodified.]	6
Chapter 8B - Interpreters for Deaf Persons	6
Chapter 8C - Evidence Code	6
Chapter 9 - Jurors	6
Chapter 10 - Notaries [Repealed.]	6
Chapter 10A - Notaries [Recodified.]	6
Chapter 10B - Notaries	6
Chapter 11 - Oaths	6
Chapter 12 - Statutory Construction	6
Chapter 13 - Citizenship Restored	6
Chapter 14 - Criminal Law	7
Chapter 14 –Criminal Law (Continuation)	8
Chapter 15 - Criminal Procedure	9
Chapter 15A - Criminal Procedure Act (Continuation)	10
Chapter 15A - Criminal Procedure Act (Continuation)	11
Chapter 15B - Victims Compensation	11
Chapter 15C - Address Confidentiality Program	11
Chapter 16 - Gaming Contracts and Futures	11
Chapter 17 - Habeas Corpus	11

Chapter 17A - Law-Enforcement Officers [Recodified.]	11
Chapter 17B - North Carolina Criminal Justice Education and Training System [Recodified.] Chapter 17C - North Carolina Criminal Justice Education and Training Standards Commission	11 11
Chapter 17D - North Carolina Justice Academy	11
Chapter 17E - North Carolina Sheriffs' Education and Training Standards Commission	11
Chapter 18 - Regulation of Intoxicating Liquors [Repealed.]	12
Chapter 18A - Regulation of Intoxicating Liquors [Repealed.]	12
Chapter 18B - Regulation of Alcoholic Beverages	12
Chapter 18C - North Carolina State Lottery	12
Chapter 19 - Offenses against Public Morals	12
Chapter 19A - Protection of Animals	12
Chapter 20 - Motor Vehicles	13
Chapter 20 - Motor Vehicles (Continuation)	14
Chapter 20 - Motor Vehicles (Continuation)	15
Chapter 20 - Motor Vehicles (Continuation)	16
Chapter 21 - Bills of Lading	17
Chapter 22 - Contracts Requiring Writing	17
Chapter 22A - Signatures	17
Chapter 22B - Contracts Against Public Policy	17
Chapter 22C - Payments to Subcontractors	17
Chapter 23 - Debtor and Creditor	17
Chapter 24 – Interest	17
Chapter 25 – Uniform Commercial Code	18
Chapter 25 – Uniform Commercial Code (Continuation)	19
Chapter 25A – Retail Installment Sales Act	20
Chapter 25B - Credit	20
Chapter 25C - Sales of Artwork	20
Chapter 26 - Suretyship	20
Chapter 27 - Warehouse Receipts [Repealed.]	20
Chapter 28 - Administration [Repealed.]	20
Chapter 28A - Administration of Decedents' Estates	20
Chapter 28B - Estates of Absentees in Military Service	20
Chapter 28C - Estates of Missing Persons	20
Chapter 29 - Intestate Succession	21
Chapter 30 - Surviving Spouses	21
Chapter 31 - Wills	21
Chapter 31A - Acts Barring Property Rights	21
Chapter 31B - Renunciation of Property and Renunciation of Fiduciary Powers Act	21
Chapter 31C - Uniform Disposition of Community Property Rights at Death Act	21
Chapter 32 - Fiduciaries	21
Chapter 32A - Powers of Attorney	21
Chapter 33 - Guardian and Ward [Repealed and Recodified.]	21

Chapter 33A - North Carolina Uniform Transfers to Minors Act	21
Chapter 33B - North Carolina Uniform Custodial Trust Act	21
Chapter 34 - Veterans' Guardianship Act	22
Chapter 35 - Sterilization Procedures	22
Chapter 35A - Incompetency and Guardianship	22
Chapter 36 - Trusts and Trustees [Repealed.]	22
Chapter 36A - Trusts and Trustees	22
Chapter 36B - Uniform Management of Institutional Funds Act [Repealed.]	22
Chapter 36C - North Carolina Uniform Trust Code	22
Chapter 36D - North Carolina Community Third Party Trusts, Pooled Trusts	23
Chapter 36E - Uniform Prudent Management of Institutional Funds Act	23
Chapter 37 - Allocation of Principal and Income [Repealed.]	23
Chapter 37A - Uniform Principal and Income Act	23
Chapter 38 - Boundaries	23
Chapter 38A - Landowner Liability	23
Chapter 39 - Conveyances	23
Chapter 39A - Transfer Fee Covenants Prohibited	23
Chapter 40 - Eminent Domain [Repealed.]	23
Chapter 40A - Eminent Domain	23
Chapter 41 - Estates	23
Chapter 41A - State Fair Housing Act	23
Chapter 42 - Landlord and Tenant	23
Chapter 42A - Vacation Rental Act	23
Chapter 43 - Land Registration	23
Chapter 44 - Liens	24
Chapter 44A - Statutory Liens and Charges	24
Chapter 45 - Mortgages and Deeds of Trust	24
Chapter 45A - Good Funds Settlement Act	24
Chapter 46 - Partition	24
Chapter 47 - Probate and Registration	25
Chapter 47A - Unit Ownership	25
Chapter 47B - Real Property Marketable Title Act	25
Chapter 47C - North Carolina Condominium Act	25
Chapter 47D - Notice of Settlement Act [Expired.]	25
Chapter 47E - Residential Property Disclosure Act	25
Chapter 47F - North Carolina Planned Community Act	25
Chapter 47G - Option to Purchase Contracts	25
Chapter 47H - Contracts for Deed	25
Chapter 48 - Adoptions +	26
Chapter 48A - Minors	26
Chapter 49 - Bastardy	26
Chapter 49A - Rights of Children	26
Chapter 50 - Divorce and Alimony	26
Chapter 50A - Uniform Child-Custody Jurisdiction and	

Enforcement Act	26
Chapter 50B - Domestic Violence	26
Chapter 50C - Civil No-Contact Orders	26
Chapter 51 - Marriage	26
Chapter 52 - Powers and Liabilities of Married Persons	27
Chapter 52A - Uniform Reciprocal Enforcement of Support Act [Repealed.]	27
Chapter 52B - Uniform Premarital Agreement Act	27
Chapter 52C - Uniform Interstate Family Support Act	27
Chapter 53 - Banks	27
Chapter 53A - Business Development Corporations and North Carolina Capital Resource Corporations	28
Chapter 53B - Financial Privacy Act	28
Chapter 54 - Cooperative Organizations	28
Chapter 54A - Capital Stock Savings and Loan Associations [Repealed.]	28
Chapter 54B - Savings and Loan Associations	29
Chapter 54C - Savings Banks	29
Chapter 55 - North Carolina Business Corporation Act	30
Chapter 55A - North Carolina Nonprofit Corporation Act	31
Chapter 55B - Professional Corporation Act	31
Chapter 55C - Foreign Trade Zones	31
Chapter 55D - Filings, Names, and Registered Agents for Corporations, Nonprofit Corporations, and Partnerships	31
Chapter 56 - Electric, Telegraph and Power Companies [Repealed.]	31
Chapter 57 - Hospital, Medical and Dental Service Corporations [Recodified.]	31
Chapter 57A - Health Maintenance Organization Act [Recodified.]	31
Chapter 57B - Health Maintenance Organization Act [Recodified.]	31
Chapter 57C - North Carolina Limited Liability Company Act.	31
Chapter 58 - Insurance.	32
Chapter 58 - Insurance (Continuation)	33
Chapter 58 - Insurance (Continuation)	34
Chapter 58 - Insurance (Continuation)	35
Chapter 58 - Insurance (Continuation)	36
Chapter 58 - Insurance (Continuation)	37
Chapter 58 - Insurance (Continuation)	38
Chapter 58A - North Carolina Health Insurance Trust Commission [Recodified.]	38
Chapter 59 - Partnership.	39
Chapter 59B - Uniform Unincorporated Nonprofit Association Act.	39
Chapter 60 - Railroads and Other Carriers [Repealed and Transferred.]	39
Chapter 61 - Religious Societies	39
Chapter 62 - Public Utilities	39

Chapter 62 - Public Utilities (Continuation)	40
Chapter 62A - Public Safety Telephone Service And Wireless Telephone Service	40
Chapter 63 - Aeronautics	40
Chapter 63A - North Carolina Global TransPark Authority	40
Chapter 64 - Aliens	40
Chapter 65 – Cemeteries	40
Chapter 66 - Commerce and Business	41
Chapter 67 - Dogs	41
Chapter 68 - Fences and Stock Law	41
Chapter 69 - Fire Protection	41
Chapter 70 - Indian Antiquities, Archaeological Resources and Unmarked Human Skeletal Remains Protection	42
Chapter 71 - Indians [Repealed.]	42
Chapter 71A - Indians	42
Chapter 72 - Inns, Hotels and Restaurants	42
Chapter 73 - Mills	42
Chapter 74 - Mines and Quarries	42
Chapter 74A - Company Police [Repealed.]	42
Chapter 74B - Private Protective Services Act [Repealed.]	42
Chapter 74C - Private Protective Services	42
Chapter 74D - Alarm Systems	42
Chapter 74E - Company Police Act	42
Chapter 74F - Locksmith Licensing Act	42
Chapter 74G - Campus Police Act	42
Chapter 75 - Monopolies, Trusts and Consumer Protection	42
Chapter 75A - Boating and Water Safety	43
Chapter 75B - Discrimination in Business	43
Chapter 75C - Motion Picture Fair Competition Act	43
Chapter 75D - Racketeer Influenced and Corrupt Organizations	43
Chapter 75E - Unlawful Activities in Connection With Certain Corporate Transactions	43
Chapter 76 - Navigation	43
Chapter 76A - Navigation and Pilotage Commissions	43
Chapter 77 - Rivers, Creeks, and Coastal Waters	43
Chapter 78 - Securities Law [Repealed.]	43
Chapter 78A - North Carolina Securities Act	43
Chapter 78B - Tender Offer Disclosure Act [Repealed.]	43
Chapter 78C - Investment Advisers	43
Chapter 78D - Commodities Act	43
Chapter 79 - Strays [Repealed.]	43
Chapter 80 - Trademarks, Brands, etc.	44
Chapter 81 - Weights and Measures [Recodified.]	44
Chapter 81A - Weights and Measures Act of 1975.	44
Chapter 82 - Wrecks [Repealed.]	44
Chapter 83 - Architects [Recodified.]	44

Chapter 83A - Architects	44
Chapter 84 - Attorneys-at-Law	44
Chapter 84A - Foreign Legal Consultants	44
Chapter 85 - Auctions and Auctioneers [Repealed.]	44
Chapter 85A - Bail Bondsmen and Runners [Recodified.]	44
Chapter 85B - Auctions and Auctioneers	44
Chapter 85C - Bail Bondsmen and Runners [Recodified.]	44
Chapter 86 - Barbers [Recodified.]	44
Chapter 86A - Barbers	44
Chapter 87 - Contractors	44
Chapter 88 - Cosmetic Art [Repealed.]	44
Chapter 88A - Electrolysis Practice Act	44
Chapter 88B - Cosmetic Art	45
Chapter 89 - Engineering and Land Surveying [Recodified.]	45
Chapter 89A - Landscape Architects	45
Chapter 89B - Foresters	45
Chapter 89C - Engineering and Land Surveying	45
Chapter 89D - Landscape Contractors	45
Chapter 89E - Geologists Licensing Act	45
Chapter 89F - North Carolina Soil Scientist Licensing Act	45
Chapter 89G - Irrigation Contractors	45
Chapter 90 - Medicine and Allied Occupations	45
Chapter 90 - Medicine and Allied Occupations (Continuation)	46
Chapter 90 - Medicine and Allied Occupations (Continuation)	47
Chapter 90 - Medicine and Allied Occupations (Continuation)	48
Chapter 90A - Sanitarians and Water and Wastewater Treatment Facility Operators	48
Chapter 90B - Social Worker Certification and Licensure Act	48
Chapter 90C - North Carolina Recreational Therapy Licensure Act	48
Chapter 90D - Interpreters and Transliterators	48
Chapter 91 - Pawnbrokers [Repealed.]	48
Chapter 91A - Pawnbrokers Modernization Act of 1989	48
Chapter 92 - Photographers [Deleted.]	48
Chapter 93 - Certified Public Accountants	48
Chapter 93A - Real Estate License Law	49
Chapter 93B - Occupational Licensing Boards	49
Chapter 93C - Watchmakers [Repealed.]	49
Chapter 93D - North Carolina State Hearing Aid Dealers and Fitters Board.	49
Chapter 93E - North Carolina Appraisers Act	49
Chapter 94 - Apprenticeship	49
Chapter 95 - Department of Labor and Labor Regulations	49
Chapter 95 - Department of Labor and Labor Regulations (Continuation)	50
Chapter 96 - Employment Security	50
Chapter 97 - Workers' Compensation Act	50
Chapter 97 - Workers' Compensation Act (Continuation)	51

Chapter 98 - Burnt and Lost Records	51
Chapter 99 - Libel and Slander	51
Chapter 99A - Civil Remedies for Criminal Actions	51
Chapter 99B - Products Liability	51
Chapter 99C - Actions Relating to Winter Sports Safety and Accidents	51
Chapter 99D - Civil Rights	51
Chapter 99E - Special Liability Provisions	51
Chapter 100 - Monuments, Memorials and Parks	51
Chapter 101 - Names of Persons	51
Chapter 102 - Official Survey Base	51
Chapter 103 - Sundays, Holidays and Special Days	51
Chapter 104 - United States Lands	51
Chapter 104A - Degrees of Kinship	51
Chapter 104B - Hurricanes or Other Acts of Nature	51
Chapter 104C - Atomic Energy, Radioactivity and Ionizing Radiation [Repealed and Recodified.]	51
Chapter 104D - Southern States Energy Compact	51
Chapter 104E - North Carolina Radiation Protection Act	51
Chapter 104F - Southeast Interstate Low-Level Radioactive Waste Management Compact [Repealed]	51
Chapter 104G - North Carolina Low-Level Radioactive Waste Management Authority Act of 1987 [Repealed]	51
Chapter 105 - Taxation	51
Chapter 105 - Taxation (Continuation)	52
Chapter 105 - Taxation (Continuation)	53
Chapter 105 - Taxation (Continuation)	54
Chapter 105A - Setoff Debt Collection Act	55
Chapter 105B - Defaulted Student Loan Recovery Act	55
Chapter 106 - Agriculture	55
Chapter 106 - Agriculture (Continue)	56
Chapter 106 - Agriculture (Continue)	57
Chapter 107 - Agricultural Development Districts [Repealed.]	57
Chapter 108 - Social Services [Repealed and Recodified.]	57
Chapter 108A - Social Services	57
Chapter 108B - Community Action Programs	58
Chapter 108C Medicaid and Health Choice Provider Requirements.	58
Chapter 108D Medicaid Managed Care for Behavioral Health Services.	58
Chapter 109 - Bonds [Recodified.]	58
Chapter 110 - Child Welfare	58
Chapter 111 - Aid to the Blind	58
Chapter 112 - Confederate Homes and Pensions [Repealed.]	58
Chapter 113 - Conservation and Development	58
Chapter 113 - Conservation and Development (Continuation)	59

Chapter	Page
Chapter 113A - Pollution Control and Environment	59
Chapter 113A - Pollution Control and Environment (Continuation)	60
Chapter 113B - North Carolina Energy Policy Act of 1975	60
Chapter 114 - Department of Justice	60
Chapter 115 - Elementary and Secondary Education [Repealed.]	60
Chapter 115A - Community Colleges, Technical Institutes, and Industrial Education Centers [Repealed.]	60
Chapter 115B - Tuition and Fee Waivers	60
Chapter 115C - Elementary and Secondary Education	60
Chapter 115C - Elementary and Secondary Education (Continuation)	61
Chapter 115C - Elementary and Secondary Education (Continuation)	62
Chapter 115C - Elementary and Secondary Education (Continuation)	63
Chapter 115D - Community Colleges	63
Chapter 115E - Private Educational Facilities Finance Act [Recodified]	63
Chapter 116 - Higher Education	63
Chapter 116 - Higher Education (Continuation)	64
Chapter 116A - Escheats and Abandoned Property [Repealed.]	64
Chapter 116B - Escheats and Abandoned Property	64
Chapter 116C - Continuum of Education Programs	64
Chapter 116D - Higher Education Bonds	64
Chapter 117 - Electrification	64
Chapter 118 - Firemen's and Rescue Squad Workers' Relief and Pension Funds [Recodified.]	64
Chapter 118A - Firemen's Death Benefit Act [Repealed.]	64
Chapter 118B - Members of a Rescue Squad Death Benefit Act [Repealed.]	64
Chapter 119 - Gasoline and Oil Inspection and Regulation	64
Chapter 120 - General Assembly	65
Chapter 120 - General Assembly (Continuation)	66
Chapter 120 - General Assembly (Continuation)	67
Chapter 120C - Lobbying	67
Chapter 121 - Archives and History	67
Chapter 122 - Hospitals for the Mentally Disordered [Repealed.]	67
Chapter 122A - North Carolina Housing Finance Agency	67
Chapter 122B - North Carolina Agricultural Facilities Finance Act [Repealed.]	67
Chapter 122C - Mental Health, Developmental Disabilities, and Substance Abuse Act of 1985	67
Chapter 122C - Mental Health, Developmental Disabilities, and Substance Abuse Act of 1985 (Continuation)	68
Chapter 122D - North Carolina Agricultural Finance Act	68

Chapter 122E - North Carolina Housing Trust and Oil Overcharge Act	68
Chapter 123 - Impeachment	69
Chapter 123A - Industrial Development [Repealed.]	69
Chapter 124 - Internal Improvements	69
Chapter 125 - Libraries	69
Chapter 126 - State Personnel System	69
Chapter 127 - Militia [Repealed.]	69
Chapter 127A - Militia	69
Chapter 127B - Military Affairs	69
Chapter 127C - Advisory Commission on Military Affairs	69
Chapter 128 - Offices and Public Officers	69
Chapter 128 - Offices and Public Officers (Continuation)	70
Chapter 129 - Public Buildings and Grounds	70
Chapter 130 - Public Health [Repealed.]	70
Chapter 130A - Public Health	70
Chapter 130A - Public Health (Continuation)	71
Chapter 130A - Public Health (Continuation)	72
Chapter 130B - Hazardous Waste Management Commission [Repealed.]	72
Chapter 131 - Public Hospitals [Repealed.]	72
Chapter 131A - Health Care Facilities Finance Act	72
Chapter 131B - Licensing of Ambulatory Surgical Facilities [Repealed.]	72
Chapter 131C - Charitable Solicitation Licensure Act [Repealed.]	72
Chapter 131D - Inspection and Licensing of Facilities	72
Chapter 131E - Health Care Facilities and Services	72
Chapter 131E - Health Care Facilities and Services (Continuation)	73
Chapter 131F - Solicitation of Contributions	73
Chapter 132 - Public Records	73
Chapter 133 - Public Works	74
Chapter 134 - Youth Development [Recodified.]	74
Chapter 134A - Youth Services [Repealed.]	74
Chapter 135 - Retirement System for Teachers and State Employees; Social Security; Health Insurance Program for Children	74
Chapter 135 - Retirement System for Teachers and State Employees; Social Security; Health Insurance Program for Children	75
Chapter 136 - Transportation	75
Chapter 136 - Transportation (Continuation)	76
Chapter 137 - Rural Rehabilitation [Repealed.]	76
Chapter 138 - Salaries, Fees and Allowances	76
Chapter 138A - State Government Ethics Act	76
Chapter 139 - Soil and Water Conservation Districts	76

Chapter 140 - State Art Museum; Symphony and Art Societies	76
Chapter 140A - State Awards System	76
Chapter 141 - State Boundaries	76
Chapter 142 - State Debt	76
Chapter 143 - State Departments, Institutions, and Commissions	77
Chapter 143 - State Departments, Institutions, and Commissions (Continuation)	78
Chapter 143 - State Departments, Institutions, and Commissions (Continuation)	79
Chapter 143 - State Departments, Institutions, and Commissions (Continuation)	80
Chapter 143A - State Government Reorganization	80
Chapter 143B - Executive Organization Act of 1973	80
Chapter 143B - Executive Organization Act of 1973 (Continuation)	81
Chapter 143B - Executive Organization Act of 1973 (Continuation)	82
Chapter 143C - State Budget Act	83
Chapter 143D - The State Governmental Accountability and Internal Control Act	83
Chapter 144 - State Flag, Official Governmental Flags, Motto, and Colors	83
Chapter 145 - State Symbols and Other Official Adoptions.	83
Chapter 146 - State Lands	83
Chapter 147 - State Officers	83
Chapter 148 - State Prison System	84
Chapter 149 - State Song and Toast	84
Chapter 150 - Uniform Revocation of Licenses [Repealed.]	84
Chapter 150A - Administrative Procedure Act [Recodified.]	84
Chapter 150B - Administrative Procedure Act	84
Chapter 151 - Constables [Repealed.]	84
Chapter 152 - Coroners	84
Chapter 152A - County Medical Examiner [Repealed.]	84
Chapter 152A - County Medical Examiner [Repealed.] (Continuation)	85
Chapter 153 - Counties and County Commissioners [Repealed.]	85
Chapter 153A - Counties	85
Chapter 153B - Mountain Resources Planning Act	85
Chapter 153C - Uwharrie Regional Resources Act	85
Chapter 154 - County Surveyor [Repealed.]	85
Chapter 155 - County Treasurer [Repealed.]	85
Chapter 156 - Drainage	85
Chapter 156 – Drainage (Continuation)	86

Chapter 157 - Housing Authorities and Projects	86
Chapter 157A - Historic Properties Commissions [Transferred.]	86
Chapter 158 - Local Development	86
Chapter 159 - Local Government Finance	86
Chapter 159 - Local Government Finance (Continuation)	87
Chapter 159A - Pollution Abatement and Industrial Facilities Financing Act [Unconstitutional.]	87
Chapter 159B - Joint Municipal Electric Power and Energy Act	87
Chapter 159C - Industrial and Pollution Control Facilities Financing Act	87
Chapter 159D - The North Carolina Capital Facilities Financing Act	87
Chapter 159E - Registered Public Obligations Act	87
Chapter 159F - North Carolina Energy Development Authority [Repealed.]	87
Chapter 159G - Water Infrastructure	87
Chapter 159H - [Reserved.]	87
Chapter 159I - Solid Waste Management Loan Program and Local Government Special Obligation Bonds	87
Chapter 160 - Municipal Corporations [Repealed And Transferred.]	87
Chapter 160A - Cities and Towns	88
Chapter 160A - Cities and Towns (Continuation)	89
Chapter 160B - Consolidated City-County Act	89
Chapter 160C - Baseball Park Districts [Repealed.]	90
Chapter 161 - Register of Deeds	90
Chapter 162 - Sheriff	90
Chapter 162A - Water and Sewer Systems	90
Chapter 162B Continuity of Local Government in Emergency.	90
Chapter 163 Elections and Election Laws.	90
Chapter 163 Elections and Election Laws. (Continuation)	91
Chapter 164 Concerning the General Statutes of North Carolina.	92
Chapter 165 Veterans.	92
Chapter 166 Civil Preparedness Agencies [Repealed.]	92
Chapter 166A North Carolina Emergency Management Act.	92
Chapter 167 State Civil Air Patrol [Repealed.]	92
Chapter 168 Persons with Disabilities.	92
Chapter 168A Persons With Disabilities Protection Act.	92

§ 115C-501. Purposes for which elections may be called.

(a) To Vote a Supplemental Tax. - Elections may be called by the local tax-levying authority to ascertain the will of the voters as to whether there shall be levied and collected a special tax in the several local school administrative units, districts, and other school areas, including districts formed from contiguous counties, to supplement the funds from State and county allotments and thereby operate schools of a higher standard by supplementing any item of expenditure in the school budget. When supplementary funds are authorized by the carrying of such an election, such funds may be used to employ additional teachers other than those allotted by the State, to teach any grades or subjects or for kindergarten instruction, to establish and maintain approved summer schools, to make the contribution to the Teachers' and State Employees' Retirement System of North Carolina for such teachers, or for any object of expenditure: Provided, that elections may be called to ascertain the will of the voters of an entire county, as to whether there shall be levied and collected a special tax on all the taxable property within the county for the purposes enumerated in this subsection. In such event, the supplemental tax shall be apportioned among the local school administrative units in the county pursuant to G.S. 115C-430.

(b) To Increase a Supplemental Tax Rate. - Elections may be called in any school area which has previously voted a supplemental tax of less than the maximum for the purpose of increasing the rate of tax previously voted but not to exceed the maximum.

(c) To Enlarge City Administrative Units. - Elections may be called in any districts, or other school areas, of a county administrative unit to ascertain the will of the voters in such districts or other school areas, as to whether an adjoining city administrative unit shall be enlarged by consolidating such districts, or other school areas, with such city administrative unit, and whether after such enlargement of the city administrative unit there shall be levied in such other districts, or other school area or areas, so consolidated with the city administrative unit the same school taxes as shall be levied in the other portion of the city administrative unit.

(d) To Supplement and Equalize Educational Advantages. - Elections may be called in any area of a county administrative unit which is enclosed in one common boundary line to ascertain the will of the voters as to whether there shall be levied and collected a special tax to supplement and equalize the standards on which the schools in such areas are operated, and at the same time repeal any special taxes heretofore voted by any parts of such area.

(e) To Abolish a Special School Tax. - Elections may be called in any local school administrative unit, district or other school area which has previously voted a supplemental tax, to ascertain the will of the people as to whether such tax shall be abolished.

(f) To Vote School Bonds. - Boards of county commissioners are authorized as provided by law to call elections to ascertain the will of the voters as to whether bonds for school purposes may be issued.

(g) To Provide a Supplemental Tax on a Countywide Basis after Petition for Consolidation of City or County Administrative Units. - Elections may be called for an entire county on the question of a special tax to supplement the funds from State and county allotments and thereby operate schools of a higher standard by supplementing any item of expenditure in the school budget, where the boards of education of all the city administrative units in said county have petitioned the county board of education for a consolidation with the county administrative unit pursuant to the provisions of the first paragraph of G.S. 115C-70(a) and prior to the approval of said petitions by the county and State boards of education. In which event, and provided the petitions so specify, if said election for a countywide supplemental tax fails to carry, said petitions may be withdrawn and any existing supplemental tax theretofore voted in any of the city administrative units involved or in the county administrative unit shall not be affected. If the vote for the countywide supplemental tax carries, said tax shall not be levied unless and until the consolidation of the units involved shall be completed according to the requirements of the first paragraph of G.S. 115C-70(a).

(h) To Annex or Consolidate Areas or Districts from Contiguous Counties and to Provide a Supplemental School Tax in Such Annexed Areas or Consolidated Districts. - An election may be called in any districts or other school areas, from contiguous counties, as to whether the districts in one county shall be enlarged by annexing or consolidating therewith any adjoining districts, or other school area or areas from an adjoining county, and if a special or supplemental school tax is levied and collected in the districts of the county to which the territory is to be annexed or consolidated, whether upon such annexation or consolidation there shall be levied and collected in the territory to be annexed or consolidated the same special or supplemental tax for schools as is levied and collected in the districts in the other county. If such election carries, the said special or supplemental tax shall be collected pursuant to G.S. 115C-511 and remitted to the local school administrative unit on whose behalf such special and supplemental tax is already levied.

(i) To Vote School Bonds and Taxes in Certain Merged School Administrative Units. - Elections for the purpose of authorizing the levy of certain taxes and the issuance of bonds shall be called by a merged school administrative unit described in G.S. 115C-513 with the consent of the boards of county commissioners of both counties in which the merged unit is located. The election shall be conducted and the results canvassed by the boards of elections of both counties. The boards of elections shall certify the results of the election to the board of education of the merged school administrative unit. The board of education shall certify and declare the result of the election, which shall be determined on an aggregate basis from the results certified by the boards of elections. The board of education shall publish a statement of the result once as provided in the Local Government Bond Act, Article 4 of Chapter 159 of the General Statutes.

(j) All elections called under this section shall be conducted in accordance with G.S. 163-287. (1955, c. 1372, art. 14, s. 1; 1957, c. 1066; c. 1271, s. 1; 1959, c. 573, s. 9; 1961, c. 894, s. 2; c. 1019, s. 1; 1975, c. 437, ss. 2-4; 1981, c. 423, s. 1; 1991, c. 325, s. 2; 2013-381, ss. 10.16, 10.17.)

§ 115C-502. Maximum rate and frequency of elections.

(a) A tax for supplementing the public school budget shall not exceed fifty cents (50¢) on the one-hundred-dollar ($100.00) value of property subject to taxation by the local school administrative unit: Provided, that in any local school administrative unit, district, or other school area having a total population of not less than 100,000 said local annual tax that may be levied shall not exceed sixty cents (60¢) on one-hundred-dollars ($100.00) valuation of said property.

(b) If a majority of those who vote in any election called pursuant to the provisions of this Article do not vote in favor of the purpose for which such election is called, another election for the same purpose shall not be called for and held in the same local school administrative unit, district, or area until the lapse of six months after the prior election. However, the foregoing time limitation shall not apply to any election held in a local school administrative unit, district, or other school area which is larger or smaller than the local school administrative unit, district, or area in which the prior election was held, or to any election held for a different purpose than the prior election. (1955, c. 1231; c. 1372, art. 14, s. 2; 1957, c. 1271, s. 2; 1959, c. 573, s. 10; 1975, c. 437, s. 5; 1981, c. 423, s. 1.)

§ 115C-503. Who may petition for election.

Local boards of education may petition the board of county commissioners for an election in their respective local school administrative units or for any school areas therein.

A majority of the qualified voters who have resided for the preceding 12 months in an area which is adjacent to a city administrative unit may petition the county board of education for an election on the question of annexing such area to the city administrative unit. For any of the other purposes enumerated in G.S. 115C-501, twenty-five percent (25%) of the qualified voters who reside in a local school administrative unit may petition the local board of education for an election. (1955, c. 1372, art. 14, s. 3; 1961, c. 1019, s. 2; 1981, c. 423, s. 1; 1985 (Reg. Sess., 1986), c. 975, s. 7.)

§ 115C-504. Necessary information in petitions.

The petition for an election shall contain such of the following information as may be pertinent to the proposed election:

(1) Purpose for calling the proposed election.

(2) A legally sufficient description of the area, by metes and bounds or otherwise, in which the election is requested.

(3) The maximum rate of tax which is proposed to be levied. This subdivision shall not apply to a petition for an election to enlarge a city administrative unit.

(4) If the petition is for an election to enlarge a city administrative unit, it shall state therein that, if a majority of those who shall vote in the area proposed to be consolidated with the city administrative unit shall vote in favor of such enlargement, such area shall be consolidated with the city administrative unit, effective July 1 next following such election, and that there shall thereafter be levied in such area so consolidated with the city administrative unit the same school taxes as shall be levied in the other portions of the city administrative unit, including any tax to provide for the payment of school bonds theretofore issued by or for such city administrative unit or for all or some part of the school

area annexed to such city administrative unit, unless payment of such bonds has otherwise been provided for.

(5) If the petition for an election is to supplement and equalize educational advantages, and if any school districts in the area in which it is proposed to vote such a tax have heretofore voted a supplementary tax, the petition and the notice of election shall state that in the event such election is carried, it will repeal all local taxes heretofore voted in any district except those in effect for debt service in any district, unless such debt service obligation is assumed by the county or otherwise provided for. (1955, c. 1372, art. 14, s. 4; 1957, c. 1271, ss. 3-5; 1981, c. 423, s. 1.)

§ 115C-505. Boards of education must consider petitions.

The board of education to whom the petition requesting an election is addressed shall receive the petition and give it due consideration. If, in the discretion of the board of education, the petition for an election shall be approved, it shall be endorsed by the chairman and the secretary of the board and a record of the endorsement shall be made in the minutes of the board. Petitions for an election to enlarge a city administrative unit shall be subject to the approval and endorsement of both county and city boards of education which are therein affected.

Local boards of education shall have no discretion in granting an election to abolish a special school tax in any local school administrative unit, or district, or other school area, which has previously voted a supplemental tax, whenever a majority of the qualified voters residing in said local school administrative unit, district or school area shall petition for an election. When such a petition, showing the proper number of names of qualified voters, is presented to a board of education, it is hereby made mandatory that such petition shall be granted and the election held. If at the election a majority of those in the district who have voted thereon have voted "against local tax," the tax shall be deemed revoked and shall not be levied: Provided, that in Alexander, Anson, Beaufort, Buncombe, Carteret, Catawba, Chatham, Chowan, Cleveland, Craven, Currituck, Davidson, Duplin, Franklin, Gates, Greene, Henderson, Hoke, Hyde, Iredell, Jackson, Johnston, Lenoir, Martin, Mecklenburg, Moore, Nash, Onslow, Pamlico, Pitt, Randolph, Richmond, Robeson, Rockingham, Transylvania, Vance, Wake, Warren and Wilkes Counties, petition of twenty-five percent (25%) of the number of voters in the election creating said special tax district, said petition to be signed by qualified voters residing in such special tax district, shall be sufficient.

The provisions of this section as to abolishing local tax districts shall not be applied when such local tax district is in debt in any sum whatever, or has obligated or committed its resources in any contractual manner: Provided, that no election for revoking a local tax in any local tax district shall be ordered and held in the district within less than one year from the date of the election at which the tax was voted and the district established, nor at any time within less than one year after the date of the last election on the question of revoking the tax in the district; and no petition seeking to revoke a school tax shall be approved by a board of education more often than once a year. (1955, c. 1372, art. 14, s. 5; 1957, c. 1100; 1981, c. 423, s. 1; 1985 (Reg. Sess., 1986), c. 975, s. 24.)

§ 115C-506. Action of board of county commissioners or governing body of municipality.

Petitions requesting special school elections and bearing the approval of the board of education of the local school administrative unit shall be presented to the board of county commissioners, and it shall be the duty of said board of county commissioners to call an election and fix the date for the same: Provided, that the board of education requesting the election may, for any reason deemed sufficient by said board which shall be specified and recorded in the minutes of the board, withdraw the petition by the twenty-fifth day before the election, and if the petition be so withdrawn, the election shall not be held unless by some other provision of law the holding of such election is mandatory. In the case of a city administrative unit in any incorporated city or town and formed from portions of contiguous counties, said petition shall be presented to the governing body of the city or town situated within, coterminous with, or embracing such city administrative unit, and the election shall be ordered by said governing body, and said governing body shall perform all the duties pertaining to said election performed by the board of county commissioners in elections held under this Article. (1955, c. 1372, art. 14, s. 6; 1959, c. 72; 1981, c. 423, s. 1; 1993 (Reg. Sess., 1994), c. 762, s. 9.)

§ 115C-507. Rules governing elections.

All elections under this Chapter shall be held and conducted by the appropriate county board of elections.

If the purpose of the election is to enlarge a city administrative unit, the notice of election shall include the following: a statement of the purpose of the election; a legal description of the area within which the election is to be held; and a statement that if a majority of those who shall vote in the area proposed to be consolidated with the city administrative unit shall vote in favor of such enlargement such area shall be consolidated with the city administrative unit, effective July 1 next following such election, and there shall thereafter be levied in such area so consolidated with the city administrative unit the same school taxes as shall be levied in the other portions of the city administrative unit, including any tax levy to provide for the payment of school bonds theretofore issued by or for such city administrative unit or for all or some part of the school area annexed to such city administrative unit, unless payment of such bonds has otherwise been provided for.

The notice of the election shall be given as provided in G.S. 163-33(8) and in addition include a legal description of the area within which the election is to be held, and, if any additional tax is proposed to be levied, the maximum rate of tax to be levied which shall not exceed the maximum prescribed by this Article, and the purpose of the tax.

No new registration of voters is required, but the board of elections, in its discretion, may use either Method A or Method B set forth in G.S. 163-288.2 in activating the voters in the territory.

The ballot in such election shall contain the words "FOR local tax and AGAINST local tax" except when the election is held under subsection (c) of G.S. 115C-501, in which case the ballots shall contain the words "FOR enlargement of the _____ City Administrative Unit and school tax of the same rate," and "AGAINST enlargement of the _____ City Administrative Unit and school tax of the same rate."

The elections shall be held in accordance with the applicable provisions of Chapter 163 and the expense of the election shall be paid by the board of education of the administrative unit in which the election is held, provided that when territory is proposed to be added to a city administrative unit, that unit shall bear the expense.

No election held under this Article shall be open to question except in an action or proceeding commenced within 30 days after the board of elections has certified the results. (1955, c. 1372, art. 14, s. 7; 1957, c. 1271, ss. 6, 7; 1981, c. 423, s. 1; 2011-31, s. 11.)

§ 115C-508. Effective date; levy of taxes.

(a) If, in any election authorized by this Article, a majority of the voters voting in such election vote in favor of the enlargement of a city administrative unit, such enlargement shall become effective July 1 next following such election; and thereafter there shall be levied and collected in the area consolidated with the city administrative unit the same school taxes as shall be levied in the other portions of the city administrative unit.

(b) If, in any election authorized by this Article, a majority of the voters voting in such election vote in favor of a supplemental tax, or in favor of the increase of a supplemental tax, or in favor of a tax to supplement and equalize educational advantages, the tax so authorized shall be levied and collected beginning with the fiscal year commencing July 1 next following such election. (1957, c. 1271, s. 8; 1981, c. 423, s. 1.)

§ 115C-509. Conveyance of school property upon enlargement of city administrative unit.

Before any election is called to enlarge a city administrative unit, if any school property is located in the area proposed to be consolidated with the city administrative unit, the board of education of such city administrative unit and the board of education of the county administrative unit concerned shall agree with each other as to the school property to be conveyed and transferred to the board of education of the city administrative unit if a majority of the voters voting in the election vote in favor of such enlargement. And, if such enlargement is authorized by such election, the board of education of the county administrative unit shall, within 10 days after July 1 next following such election, convey and transfer to the board of education of the city administrative unit the property so agreed to be conveyed and transferred. (1957, c. 1271, s. 8; 1981, c. 423, s. 1.)

§ 115C-510. Elections in districts created from portions of contiguous counties.

Districts already created and those that may be created from portions of two or more contiguous counties may hold elections under this Article to be incorporated or to vote a special local tax therein for the purposes enumerated in G.S. 115C-501.

Elections for either purpose must be initiated by petitions from the portion of each county included in the district, or the proposed district. In districts already created or proposed to be created, the petition must be signed by fifteen percent (15%) of the registered voters who reside in the area. When the petitions shall have been approved by each of the boards of education of such contiguous counties, they shall then be presented by each of said boards of education to their respective boards of county commissioners.

The boards of commissioners of each of the contiguous counties, in compliance with the provisions of this Article relating to the conduct of local tax elections, then shall call upon the county board of elections to hold an election in that portion of the proposed district lying in its county. Election returns shall be made from each portion of the proposed district to the board of commissioners ordering the election in that portion, and the returns shall be canvassed and recorded as required in this Article for local tax districts.

If a majority of the voters who vote thereon in each of the counties shall vote in favor of the tax, or for incorporation, the election shall be determined to have carried in the whole district, and shall be so recorded in the records of the board of county commissioners in each county in which the district is located.

If the proposition submitted to the voters in the election is a question of incorporating the district, the ballots for this election shall have printed thereon the words "For Incorporation" and "Against Incorporation." If the election for incorporation is carried, the district is thereby incorporated and shall possess all the authority of incorporated districts.

In case the election carried in each portion of the proposed district, the several county boards of education concerned shall each pass a formal order consolidating the territory into one joint local tax district, which shall be and become a body corporate by the name and style of "_____Joint Local Tax School District of _____Counties." The county board of education having the largest school census and the largest area in the part of the joint local tax district lying in its county shall determine the location of the schoolhouse; but if the largest census and largest area do not both lie in the same county, then the county boards shall jointly select the site for the building; and in case of a disagreement they shall submit the question to a board of arbitration consisting of three members, one member to be named by each board of education if three counties are concerned, or if there are but two counties, then each board shall choose one member and the two so named shall select the third member. The decision of this board of arbitration shall be binding on all county boards of education concerned.

The building of all schoolhouses in such joint local tax districts shall be effected by the county board of education of the county in which the building is to be located under authority of law governing the erection of school buildings by county boards of education. It shall be lawful for the boards of education in the other county or counties to contribute to the cost of the building in proportion to the number of children shown by the official census to be resident within that part of the joint district lying within each county respectively. If the building is to be erected from moneys borrowed from the State Literary Fund or from county taxation, then each county board of education shall contribute to its construction in the proportion set out above and pay over its contribution to the treasurer of the county board having control of the erection of the building: Provided, it shall be lawful for the county board that controls the erection of the building to borrow from the State and lend to the district the full amount of the cost of the building in cases where the entire amount, or part of the amount, is to repaid by the district from district funds.

All district funds of a joint local tax district shall be kept distinct from all other funds, placed to the credit of the district, and expended as other local tax or district bond funds are lawfully disbursed.

The county board of education and county superintendent of schools of the county in which the schoolhouse is located shall have as full and ample control over the joint school and the district as it has in the case of other local tax districts, subject only to the limitations of this section.

All districts formed from portions of contiguous counties before the ratification of this Article are hereby authorized and empowered to exercise all the powers and privileges conferred by this Article. (1955, c. 1372, art. 14, s. 8; 1981, c. 423, s. 1; 1985 (Reg. Sess., 1986), c. 975, ss. 8, 24.)

§ 115C-511. Levy and collection of taxes.

(a) If a local school administrative unit or district has voted a tax to operate schools of a higher standard than that provided by State and county support, the board of county commissioners of each county in which the local school administrative unit is located is authorized to levy a tax on all property having a situs in the local school administrative unit for the purpose of supplementing the local current expense fund, the capital outlay fund, or both.

(b) Before April 15 of each year, the tax supervisor of each county in which the local school administrative unit is located shall certify to the superintendent of schools an estimate of the total assessed value of property in the county subject to taxation on behalf of the local school administrative unit and any districts therein pursuant to this Article. The board of education, in the budget it submits to the board of county commissioners, shall request the rate of ad valorem tax it wishes to have levied on its behalf as a school supplemental tax, not in excess of the rate approved by the voters. The board of county commissioners may approve or disapprove this request in whole or in part, and may levy such rate of supplemental tax as it may find to be in the best interests of the taxpayers and the public schools, not in excess of the rate requested by the board of education. Upon approving a supplemental tax levy pursuant to this section, the board of county commissioners shall cause the school supplemental tax to be computed for all property subject thereto. The taxes thus computed shall be shown separately on the county tax receipts for the fiscal year, and the county shall collect the school supplemental tax in the same manner that county taxes are collected. Collections shall be remitted to the local school administrative unit within 10 days after the close of each calendar month. Partial payments shall be proportionately divided between the county and the local school administrative unit. The board of county commissioners may, in its discretion, deduct from the proceeds of the school supplemental tax the actual additional cost to the county of levying, computing, billing, and collecting the tax.

(c) It shall be unlawful for any part of a tax levied pursuant to this Article to be used for any purpose other than those purposes authorized by the election in the unit or district. (1955, c. 1372, art. 14, s. 9; 1965, c. 584, s. 12; 1975, c. 437, s. 6; 1981, c. 423, s. 1.)

§ 115C-512. Expansion of existing supplemental school tax area pursuant to merger of school administrative units in certain counties.

(a) This section applies to:

(1) Counties that have three school administrative units located entirely within the county, only one of which units has a supplemental school tax in effect that is levied exclusively by the elected school board of the administrative unit.

(2) Counties that have three school administrative units, two of which are entirely within the county and one of which is located in more than one county.

(b) If a school administrative unit in a county to which this section applies merges with another school administrative unit in the county, and one of the merging units has previously voted a supplemental school tax that is in effect prior to and at the time of the merger, then the geographic area subject to the supplemental school tax in effect prior to the merger shall be expanded to include the entire geographic area encompassed by the new school administrative unit resulting from the merger. The levy and collection of and the expenditure of revenues from the tax shall be expanded as herein provided without approval of the voters of the geographic area directly affected by the merger, and shall be used for purposes provided in G.S. 115C-501(a).

(b1) If legislation is enacted providing for the merger of two school administrative units located entirely within a county described in subdivision (a)(2), and one of the merging units has previously voted a supplemental school tax that is in effect, then from July 1, 1991, and for two years following the effective date of the merger, the board of commissioners of the county in which the units are located may create a special tax district pursuant to this Article consisting of one of the merging units and may levy a supplemental school tax in that district at a rate that is different from the rate levied in the remainder of the merged unit. The tax levied in the special district may be levied without approval of the voters of the district but may not exceed the amount of the supplemental school tax previously voted in one of the merged units. The supplemental school tax levied pursuant to this subsection may be used for any purpose for which a board of education may budget funds under Article 31 of Chapter 115C of the General Statutes.

(c) Notwithstanding levying authority in existence prior to the merger, the board of county commissioners shall, upon merger of the administrative units, have the exclusive authority to levy the supplemental tax expanded in accordance with this section, provided that the tax shall be levied at a rate not to exceed the rate of the supplemental school tax in effect prior to the merger of the school administrative units. (1989, c. 768, s. 1; 1991, c. 325, s. 1.)

§ 115C-513. Special tax for certain merged school administrative units.

(a) Scope. - This section applies to a merged school administrative unit that consists of one entire county and part of a second county and is composed of two merging units, one of which is located within one county and one of which is located partly in the same county as the first unit and partly in a second county. A merged school administrative unit to which this section applies may levy taxes as provided in this section to be applied to the payment of notes, bonds, or refunding bonds issued to finance capital costs of school facilities as described in G.S. 159-48.

(b) Issuance of Bonds. - The board of education of a merged school administrative unit may issue notes, bonds, or refunding bonds at one time or from time to time to pay the capital costs of school facilities as described in G.S. 159-48. The bonds shall be issued and maintained in accordance with the provisions of Articles 1, 4, 5A, 7, 9, 10, and 11 of Chapter 159 of the General Statutes, except as modified by this section.

The board of education of a merged school administrative unit shall call for a referendum authorizing the issuance of notes, bonds, and refunding bonds and the levy of a tax to pay amounts relating to these notes, bonds, or refunding bonds. The referendum may be called only with the consent of the boards of commissioners of both counties in which the merged school administrative unit is located. The referendum shall be held in the merged school administrative unit and only those qualified voters who reside in the unit may vote. The board of commissioners of each county shall have the referendum conducted by the board of elections of its county.

After issuance of the approved bonds, the merged school administrative unit shall make timely payments of principal and interest on the bonds after receipt of notification of its debt service obligation pursuant to G.S. 159-35. The provisions of G.S. 159-36 govern a failure by the merged school administrative unit to levy taxes or otherwise provide for payment of the debt.

Bonds, notes, and refunding bonds issued under this section shall be exempt from all State, county, and municipal taxation and assessment, direct or indirect, general or special, whether imposed for the purpose of general revenue or otherwise, excluding inheritance and gift taxes, income taxes on the gain from the transfer of bonds, notes, and refunding bonds, and franchise taxes. The interest on bonds, notes, and refunding bonds is not subject to taxation as income.

Article 9 of the North Carolina Uniform Commercial Code, Chapter 25 of the General Statutes, does not apply to any security interest created in connection with the issuance of bonds under this section.

(c) Tax. - If a majority of the qualified voters of a merged school administrative unit voting on the question approve the issuance of bonds and levy of a tax as provided in this section, the board of education of the merged school administrative unit may levy a tax on all property having a situs in the merged school administrative unit for the purpose of retiring bonds issued by the unit under this section. Taxes levied pursuant to this section may be levied prior to the issuance of notes or bonds. The authority of a merged school administrative unit to levy a tax pursuant to this section terminates after all of the related notes, bonds, and refunding bonds are discharged or paid.

Before April 15 of each year, the tax assessor of each county in which the merged school administrative unit is located shall certify to the superintendent of schools an estimate of the total assessed value of property in the county subject to taxation on behalf of the merged school administrative unit pursuant to this Article. The board of education of the merged school administrative unit, in the budget it submits to each board of county commissioners, shall set the rate of ad valorem tax it levies as a tax under this section. The levy under this section shall be at the rate necessary to provide for payment of interest on and principal of outstanding notes, bonds, and refunding bonds issued by the merged school administrative unit.

Each county in which the merged school administrative unit is located shall compute and collect this tax in the same manner that county taxes are collected. The tax shall be shown separately on the tax receipts for the fiscal year. Collections shall be remitted to the merged school administrative unit within 10 days after the close of each calendar month. Partial payments shall be proportionally divided between the county collecting the tax and the merged school administrative unit. The board of commissioners of each county collecting the tax levied under this section may, in its discretion, deduct from the proceeds of the tax the actual additional cost to the county of computing, billing, and collecting the tax. (1991, c. 325, s. 3; 1995, c. 46, s. 4.)

§ 115C-514. Reserved for future codification purposes.

§ 115C-515. Reserved for future codification purposes.

§ 115C-516. Reserved for future codification purposes.

SUBCHAPTER IX. PROPERTY.

Article 37.

School Sites and Property.

§ 115C-517. Acquisition of sites.

Local boards of education may acquire suitable sites for schoolhouses or other school facilities either within or without the local school administrative unit; but no school may be operated by a local school administrative unit outside its own boundaries, although other school facilities such as repair shops, may be operated outside the boundaries of the local school administrative unit. Whenever any such board is unable to acquire or enlarge a suitable site or right-of-way for a school, school building, school bus garage or for a parking area or access road suitable for school buses or for other school facilities by gift or purchase, condemnation proceedings to acquire same may be instituted by such board under the provisions of Chapter 40A of the General Statutes, and the determination of the local board of education of the land necessary for such purposes shall be conclusive. (1955, c. 1335; c. 1372, art. 15, s. 1; 1957, c. 683; 1969, c. 516; 1971, c. 290; 1981, c. 423, s. 1; c. 1127, s. 78; 1995, c. 199, s. 1.)

§ 115C-518. Disposition of school property; easements and rights-of-way.

(a)   When in the opinion of any local board of education the use of any building site or other real property or personal property owned or held by the board is unnecessary or undesirable for public school purposes, the local board of education may dispose of such according to the procedures prescribed in General Statutes, Chapter 160A, Article 12, or any successor provisions thereto. Provided, when any real property to which the board holds title is no longer suitable or necessary for public school purposes, the board of county commissioners for the county in which the property is located shall be afforded the first opportunity to obtain the property. The board of education shall offer the property to the board of commissioners at a fair market price or at a price negotiated between the two boards. If the board of commissioners does not choose to obtain the property as offered, the board of education may dispose of such property according to the procedure as herein provided. Provided that no State or federal regulations would prohibit such action. For the purposes of this section references in Chapter 160A, Article 12, to the "city," the "council," or a specific city official are deemed to refer, respectively, to the school administrative unit, the board of education, and the school administrative official who most nearly performs the same duties performed by the specified city official. A local board of education may also sell any property other than real property through the facilities of the North Carolina Department of Administration. The proceeds of any sale of real property or from any lease for a term of over one year shall be applied to reduce the county's bonded indebtedness for the school administrative unit disposing of such real property or for capital outlay purposes.

(b) In addition to the foregoing, local boards of education are hereby authorized and empowered, in their sound discretion, to grant easements to any public utility, municipality or quasi-municipal corporations to furnish utility services, with or without compensation except the benefits accruing by virtue of the location of the said public utility, and to dedicate portions of any lands owned by such boards as rights-of-way for public streets, roads or sidewalks, with or without compensation except the benefits accruing by virtue of the location or improvement of such public streets, roads or sidewalks.

(c) Any sale, exchange or lease of real or personal property by any local board of education prior to June 18, 1982, and pursuant to the authority of G.S. 115-126 is hereby validated, ratified and confirmed. (1955, c. 1372, art. 15, s. 2; 1959, c. 324; c. 573, s. 11; 1961, c. 395; 1975, c. 264; c. 879, s. 46; 1977, c. 803; 1981, c. 423, s. 1; 1981 (Reg. Sess., 1982), c. 1216; 1983, c. 731; 1985 (Reg. Sess., 1986), c. 975, s. 22.)

§ 115C-519. Deeds to property.

All deeds to school property shall, after registration, be delivered to the superintendent of the local school administrative unit in which the property is located and he shall provide a safe place for preserving all such deeds. (1955, c. 1372, art. 15, s. 3; 1981, c. 423, s. 1.)

§ 115C-520. Vehicles owned by boards of education.

All school buses, trucks, automobiles and other motor vehicles owned by local boards of education and used for transporting pupils to and from school or used by other school personnel in the performance of their work, shall be exempt from taxation, but all such vehicles shall be duly registered in the Division of Motor Vehicles as provided in G.S. 20-84. (1955, c. 1372, art. 15, s. 4; 1975, c. 716, s. 5; 1981, c. 423, s. 1.)

§ 115C-521. Erection of school buildings.

(a) It shall be the duty of local boards of education to provide classroom facilities adequate to meet the requirements of G.S. 115C-47(10) and 115C-301. Local boards of education shall submit their long-range plans for meeting school facility needs to the State Board of Education by January 1, 1988, and every five years thereafter. In developing these plans, local boards of education shall consider the costs and feasibility of renovating old school buildings instead of replacing them.

(b) It shall be the duty of the boards of education of the several local school administrative school units of the State to make provisions for the public school term by providing adequate school buildings equipped with suitable school furniture and apparatus. The needs and the cost of those buildings, equipment, and apparatus, shall be presented each year when the school budget is submitted to the respective tax-levying authorities. The boards of commissioners shall be given a reasonable time to provide the funds which they, upon investigation, shall find to be necessary for providing their respective units with buildings suitably equipped, and it shall be the duty of the several boards of county commissioners to provide funds for the same.

Upon determination by a local board of education that the existing permanent school building does not have sufficient classrooms to house the pupil enrollment anticipated for the school, the local board of education may acquire and use as temporary classrooms for the operation of the school, relocatable or mobile classroom units, whether built on the lot or not, which units and method of use shall meet the approval of the School Planning Division of the State Board of Education, and which units shall comply with all applicable requirements of the North Carolina State Building Code and of the local building and electrical codes applicable to the area in which the school is located. These units shall also be anchored in a manner required to assure their structural safety in severe weather. The acquisition and installation of these units shall be subject in all respects to the provisions of Chapter 143 of the General Statutes. The provisions of Chapter 87, Article 1, of the General Statutes, shall not apply to persons, firms or corporations engaged in the sale or furnishing to local boards of education and the delivery and installation upon school sites of classroom trailers as a single building unit or of relocatable or mobile classrooms delivered in less than four units or sections.

(c) The building of all new school buildings and the repairing of all old school buildings shall be under the control and direction of, and by contract with, the board of education for which the building and repairing is done. If a board of education is considering building a new school building to replace an existing school building, the board shall not invest any construction money in the new building unless it submits to the State Superintendent and the State Superintendent submits to the North Carolina Historical Commission an analysis that compares the costs and feasibility of building the new building and of renovating the existing building and that clearly indicates the desirability of building the new building. No board of education shall invest any money in any new building until it has (i) developed plans based upon a consideration of the State Board's facilities guidelines, (ii) submitted these plans to the State Board for its review and comments, and (iii) reviewed the plans based upon a consideration of the comments it receives from the State Board. No local board of education shall contract for more money than is made available for the erection of a new building. However, this subsection shall not be construed so as to prevent boards of education from investing any money in buildings that are being constructed pursuant to a continuing contract of construction as provided for in G.S. 115C-441(c). All contracts for buildings shall be in writing and all buildings shall be inspected, received, and approved by the local superintendent and the architect before full payment is made therefor. Nothing in this subsection shall prohibit boards of education from repairing and altering buildings with the help of janitors and other regular employees of the board.

In the design and construction of new school buildings and in the renovation of existing school buildings that are required to be designed by an architect or engineer under G.S. 133-1.1, the local board of education shall participate in the planning and review process of the Energy Guidelines for School Design and Construction that are developed and maintained by the Department of Public Instruction and shall adopt local energy-use goals for building design and operation that take into account local conditions in an effort to reduce the impact of operation costs on local and State budgets. In the design and construction of new school facilities and in the repair and renovation of existing school facilities, the local board of education shall consider the placement and design of windows to use the climate of North Carolina for both light and ventilation in case of power shortages. A local board shall also consider the installation of solar energy systems in the school facilities whenever practicable.

In the case of any school buildings erected, repaired, or equipped with any money loaned or granted by the State to any local school administrative unit, no board of education shall invest any money until it has (i) developed plans based upon a consideration of the State Board's facilities guidelines, (ii) submitted these plans to the State Board for its review and comments, and (iii) reviewed the plans based upon a consideration of the comments it receives from the State Board.

(c1) No local board of education shall apply for a certificate of occupancy for any new middle or high school building until the plans for the science laboratory areas of the building have been reviewed and approved to meet accepted safety standards for school science laboratories and related preparation rooms and stockrooms. The review and approval of the plans may be done by the State Board of Education or by any other entity that is licensed or authorized by the State Board to do so.

(d) Local boards of education shall make no contract for the erection of any school building unless the site upon which it is located is owned in fee simple by the board: Provided, that the board of education of a local school administrative unit, with the approval of the board of county commissioners, may appropriate funds to aid in the establishment of a school facility and the operation thereof in an adjoining local school administrative unit when a written agreement between the boards of education of the administrative units involved has been reached and the same recorded in the minutes of the boards, whereby children from the administrative unit making the appropriations shall be entitled to attend the school so established.

In all cases where title to property has been vested in the trustees of a special charter district which has been abolished and has not been reorganized, title to the property shall be vested in the local board of education of the county embracing the former special charter district.

(e) The State Board of Education shall establish within the Department of Public Instruction a central clearinghouse for access by local boards of education that may want to use a prototype design in the construction of school facilities. The State Board shall compile necessary publications and a computer database to distribute information on prototype designs to local school administrative units. All architects and engineers registered in North Carolina may submit plans for inclusion in the computer database and these plans may be accessed by any person. The original architect of record or engineer of record shall retain ownership and liability for a prototype design. The State Board may adopt rules it considers necessary to implement this subsection.

(f) A local board of education may use prototype designs from the clearinghouse established under subsection (e) of this section that is a previously approved and constructed project by the School Planning Division of the State Board of Education, and other appropriate review agencies. The local board of education may contract with the architect of record to make changes and upgrades as necessary for regulatory approval.

(g) For prototype schools under this section, local boards of education shall be exempt from the designer selection procedure in Article 3D of Chapter 143 of the General Statutes and may enter into an agreement with the original design professional of the prototype to supply design services for future construction of the prototype school. (1955, c. 1372, art. 15, ss. 5-7; 1969, c. 1022, s. 1; 1981, c. 423, s. 1; c. 638, s. 1; 1983, c. 761, s. 93; 1985, c. 783, s. 3; 1987, c. 622, s. 14; 1993, c. 416, s. 1; c. 465, s. 1; 1993 (Reg. Sess., 1994), c. 775, s. 6; 1995, c. 8, s. 1; 1996, 2nd Ex. Sess., c. 18, ss. 18.17(c), (d); 1997-222, s. 3; 1997-236, s. 1; 2009-59, s. 3; 2013-401, s. 7.)

§ 115C-521.1. Building standards for preschool students.

A public school that voluntarily applies for a child care facility license may use an existing or newly constructed classroom in a public school for three- and four-year-old preschool students without modifications to the classroom or building if the classroom:

(1) Has at least one toilet and one sink for hand washing;

(2) Meets kindergarten standards for overhead light fixtures;

(3) Meets kindergarten standards for floors, walls, and ceilings; and

(4) Has floors, walls, and ceilings that are free from mold, mildew, and lead hazards.

A public school that voluntarily applies for a child care facility license shall meet all other requirements for child care facility licensure. (2009-123, s. 1.)

§ 115C-522. Provision of equipment for buildings.

(a) It shall be the duty of local boards of education to purchase or exchange all supplies, equipment, and materials, and these purchases shall be made in accordance with Article 8 of Chapter 143 of the General Statutes. These purchases may be made from contracts made by the Department of Administration. Title to instructional supplies, office supplies, fuel and janitorial supplies, enumerated in the current expense fund budget and purchased out of State funds, shall be taken in the name of the local board of education which shall be responsible for the custody and replacement: Provided, that no contracts shall be made by any local school administrative unit for purchases unless provision has been made in the budget of the unit to pay for the purchases, unless surplus funds are on hand to pay for the purchases, or unless the contracts are made pursuant to G.S. 115C-47(28) and G.S. 115C-528 and adequate funds are available to pay in the current fiscal year the sums obligated for the current fiscal year. The State Board of Education shall adopt rules regarding equipment standards for supplies, equipment, and materials related to student transportation. The State Board may adopt guidelines for any commodity that needs safety features. If a commodity that needs safety features is available on statewide term contract, any guidelines adopted by the State Board must at a minimum meet the safety standards of the statewide term contract. Compliance with Article 8 of Chapter 143 of the General Statutes is not mandatory for the purchase of published books, manuscripts, maps, pamphlets, and periodicals.

(1) Where competition is available, local school administrative units may utilize the:

a. E-Quote service of the NC E-Procurement system as one means of solicitation in seeking informal bids for purchases subject to the bidding requirements of G.S. 143-131; and

b. Division of Purchase and Contract's electronic Interactive Purchasing System as one means of advertising formal bids on purchases subject to the bidding requirements of G.S. 143-129 and applicable rules regarding advertising. This sub-subdivision does not prohibit a local school administrative unit from using other methods of advertising.

(2) In order to provide an efficient transition of purchasing procedures, the Secretary of the Department of Administration and the local school administrative units shall establish a local school administrative unit purchasing user group. The user group shall be comprised of a proportionate number of representatives from the Department of Administration and local school administrative unit purchasing and finance officers. The user group shall examine any issues that may arise between the Department of Administration and local school administrative units, including the new relationship between the Department and the local school administrative units, the appropriate exchange of information, the continued efficient use of E-Procurement, appropriate bid procedures, and any other technical assistance that may be necessary for the purchase of supplies and materials.

(b) It shall be the duty of the local boards of education to provide suitable school furniture and apparatus, as provided in G.S. 115C-521(b).

(c) It shall be the duty of local boards of education and tax-levying authorities to provide suitable supplies for the school buildings under their jurisdictions. These shall include, in addition to the necessary instructional supplies, proper window shades, blackboards, reference books, library equipment, maps, and equipment for teaching the sciences.

Likewise, it shall be the duty of said boards of education and boards of county commissioners to provide every school with a good supply of water, approved by the Department of Environment and Natural Resources, and where such school cannot be connected to water-carried sewerage facilities, there shall be provided sanitary privies for the boys and for the girls according to specifications of the Commission for Public Health. Such water supply and sanitary privies shall be considered an essential and necessary part of the equipment of each public school and may be paid for in the same manner as desks and other essential equipment of the school are paid for. (1955, c. 1352, art. 5, s. 35; art. 15, s. 8; 1965, c. 840; 1973, c. 476, s. 128; 1981, c. 423, s. 1; 1985, c. 436, s. 2; 1989, c. 727, s. 219(33); 1995 (Reg. Sess., 1996), c. 716, s. 13; 1997-443, s. 11A.51; 1998-194, s. 2; 2003-147, s. 1; 2004-199, s. 29(a); 2004-203, s. 72(b); 2007-182, s. 2.)

§ 115C-522.1: Repealed by Session Laws 2003-147, s. 2, effective for a local school administrative unit when the unit is certified as being E-Procurement compliant, or April 1, 2004, whichever is first.

§ 115C-523. Care of school property.

It shall be the duty of every teacher and principal in charge of school buildings to instruct the children in the proper care of public property, and it is their duty to exercise due care in the protection of school property against damage, either by defacement of the walls and doors or any breakage on the part of the pupils, and if they shall fail to exercise a reasonable care in the protection of property during the day, they may be held financially responsible for all such damage, and if the damage is due to carelessness or negligence on the part of the teachers or principal, the superintendent may hold those in charge of the building responsible for the damage, and if it is not repaired before the close of a term, a sufficient amount may be deducted from their final vouchers to repair the damage for which they are responsible.

Notwithstanding any other provision of law, the parents or legal guardians of any minor are liable for any gross negligence or willful damage or destruction of school property by that minor to the extent of five thousand dollars ($5,000). The Board of Education shall make written demand upon the parent or legal guardian as a prerequisite to bringing suit.

It shall be the duty of all principals to report immediately to their respective superintendents any unsanitary condition, damage to school property or needed repair. (1955, c. 1372, art. 17, s. 7; 1981, c. 423, s. 1; 1985, c. 581, s. 4.)

§ 115C-524. Repair of school property; use of buildings for other than school purposes.

(a)   Repair of school buildings is subject to the provisions of G.S. 115C-521(c) and (d).

(b)   It shall be the duty of local boards of education and tax-levying authorities, in order to safeguard the investment made in public schools, to keep all school buildings in good repair to the end that all public school property shall be taken care of and be at all times in proper condition for use. It shall be the duty of all principals, teachers, and janitors to report to their respective boards of education immediately any unsanitary condition, damage to school property, or needed repair. All principals, teachers, and janitors shall be held responsible for the safekeeping of the buildings during the school session and all breakage and damage shall be repaired by those responsible for same, and where any principal or teacher shall permit damage to the public school buildings by lack of proper discipline of pupils, such principal or teacher shall be held responsible for such damage: Provided, principals and teachers shall not be held responsible for damage that they could not have prevented by reasonable supervision in the performance of their duties.

Notwithstanding the provisions of G.S. 115C-263 and 115C-264, local boards of education may adopt rules and regulations under which they may enter into agreements permitting non-school groups to use school real and personal property, except for school buses, for other than school purposes so long as such use is consistent with the proper preservation and care of the public school property. No liability shall attach to any board of education, individually or collectively, for personal injury suffered by reason of the use of such school property pursuant to such agreements. (1955, c. 1372, art. 15, s. 9; 1957, c. 684; 1963, c. 253; 1981, c. 423, s. 1; 1985 (Reg. Sess., 1986), c. 975, s. 23; 1991 (Reg. Sess., 1992), c. 900, s. 79(a).)

§ 115C-525. Fire prevention.

(a) Duty of Principal Regarding Fire Hazards. - The principal of every public school in the State shall have the following duties regarding fire hazards during periods when he is in control of a school:

(1) Every principal shall make certain that all corridors, halls, and tower stairways which are used for exits shall always be kept clear and that nothing shall be permitted to be stored or kept in corridors or halls, or in, on or under stairways that could in any way interfere with the orderly exodus of occupants. The principal shall make certain that all doors used for exits shall be kept in good working condition. During the occupancy of the building or any portion thereof by the public or for school purposes, the principal shall make certain that all doors necessary for prompt and orderly exodus of the occupants are kept unlocked.

(2) Every principal shall make certain that no electrical wiring shall be installed within any school building or structure or upon the premises and that no alteration or addition shall be made in any existing wiring, except with the authorization of the superintendent. Any such work shall be performed by a licensed electrical contractor, or by a maintenance electrician regularly employed by the board of education and approved by the Commissioner of Insurance.

(3) Every principal shall make certain that combustible materials necessary to the curriculum and for the operation of the school shall be stored in a safe and orderly manner.

(4) Every principal shall make certain that all supplies, such as oily rags, mops, etc., which may cause spontaneous combustion, shall be stored in an orderly manner in a well-ventilated place.

(5) Every principal shall make certain that all trash and rubbish shall be removed from the school building daily. No trash or rubbish shall be permitted to accumulate in a school attic, basement or other place on the premises.

(6) Every principal shall cooperate in every way with the authorized building inspector, electrical inspector, county fire marshal or other designated person making the inspections required by G.S. 115C-525(b).

It shall further be the duty of the principal to bring to the attention of the local superintendent of schools the failure of the building inspector, electrical inspector, county fire marshal, or other person to make the inspections required by G.S. 115C-525(b). It shall further be the duty of the principal to call to the attention of the superintendent of schools all recommendations growing out of the inspections, in order that the proper authorities can take steps to bring about the necessary corrections.

(b) Inspection of Schools for Fire Hazards; Removal of Hazards. - Every public school building in the State shall be inspected a minimum of two times during the year in accordance with the following plan: Provided, that the periodic inspections herein required shall be at least 120 days apart:

(1) Each school building shall be inspected to make certain that none of the fire hazards enumerated in G.S. 115C-525(a)(1) through (5) exist, and to ensure that the building and all heating, mechanical, electrical, gas, and other equipment and appliances are properly installed and maintained in a safe and

serviceable manner as prescribed by the North Carolina Building Code. Following each inspection, the persons making the inspection shall furnish to the principal of the school a written report of conditions found during inspection, upon forms furnished by the Commissioner of Insurance, and the persons making the inspection shall also furnish a copy of the report to the superintendent of schools; the superintendent shall keep such copy on file for a period of three years. In addition to the periodic inspections herein required, any alterations or additions to existing school buildings or to school building utilities or appliances shall be inspected immediately following completion.

(2) The board of county commissioners of each county shall designate the persons to make the inspections and reports required by subdivision (1) of this subsection. The board may designate any city or county building inspector, any city or county fire prevention bureau, any city or county electrical inspector, the county fire marshal, or any other qualified persons, but no person shall make any inspection unless he shall be qualified as required by G.S. 153A-351.1 and Section 7 of Chapter 531 of the 1977 Session Laws. Nothing in this section shall be construed as prohibiting two or more counties from designating the same persons to make the inspections and reports required by subdivision (1) of this subsection. The board of county commissioners shall compensate or provide for the compensation of the persons designated to make all such inspections and reports. The board of county commissioners may make appropriations in the general fund of the county to meet the costs of such inspections, or in the alternative the board may add appropriations to the school current expense fund to meet the costs thereof: Provided, that if appropriations are added to the school current expense fund, such appropriations shall be in addition to and not in substitution of existing school current expense appropriations.

(3) It shall be the duty of the Commissioner of Insurance, the Superintendent of Public Instruction, and the State Board of Education to prescribe any additional rules and regulations which they may deem necessary in connection with such inspections and reports for the reduction of fire hazards and protection of life and property in public schools.

(4) It shall be the duty of each principal to make certain that all fire hazards called to his attention in the course of the inspections and reports required by subdivision (1) of this subsection are immediately removed or corrected, if such removal or correction can be accomplished by the principal. If such removal or correction cannot be accomplished by the principal, it shall be the duty of the principal to bring the matter to the attention of the superintendent.

(5) It shall be the duty of each superintendent of schools to make certain that all fire hazards called to his attention in the course of the inspections and reports required by subdivision (1) of this subsection and not removed or corrected by the principals as required by subdivision (4) of this subsection are removed or corrected, if such removal or correction can be brought about within the current appropriations available to the superintendent. Where any removal or correction of a hazard will require the expenditure of funds in excess of current appropriations, it shall be the duty of the superintendent to bring the matter to the attention of the appropriate board of education, and the board of education in turn shall bring the same to the attention of the board of county commissioners, in order that immediate steps be taken, within the framework of existing law, to remove or correct the hazard.

(c) Liability for Failure to Perform Duties Imposed by G.S. 115C-288(d) and 115C-525(a) or 115C-525(b). - Any person willfully failing to perform any of the duties imposed by G.S. 115C-288(d), 115C-525(a) or 115C-525(b) shall be guilty of a Class 3 misdemeanor and shall only be fined not more than five hundred dollars ($500.00) in the discretion of the court. (1957, c. 844; 1959, c. 573, s. 14; 1981, c. 423, s. 1; 1989, c. 681, s. 12; 1993, c. 539, s. 892; 1994, Ex. Sess., c. 24, s. 14(c); 2009-570, s. 40.)

§ 115C-526. Reward for information leading to arrest of persons damaging school property.

Local boards of education are authorized and empowered to offer and pay rewards in an amount not exceeding three hundred dollars ($300.00) for information leading to the arrest and conviction of any persons who willfully deface, damage, destroy or commit acts of vandalism or larceny of, the property belonging to the public school system under the jurisdiction of and administered by any local board of education. (1967, c. 369; 1973, c. 1216; 1975, c. 437, s. 7; 1981, c. 423, s. 1.)

§ 115C-527. Use of schools and other public buildings for political meetings.

The governing authority having control over schools or other public buildings which have facilities for group meetings, or where polling places are located, is hereby authorized and directed to permit the use of such buildings without charge, except custodial and utility fees, by political parties, as defined in G.S. 163-96, for the express purpose of annual or biennial precinct meetings and county and district conventions: Provided, that the use of such buildings by political parties shall not be permitted at times when school is in session or which would interfere with normal school activities or functions normally carried on in such school buildings, and such use shall be subject to reasonable rules and regulations of the school boards and other governing authorities. (1975, c. 465; 1981, c. 423, s. 1; 1983, c. 519, ss. 1, 2.)

§ 115C-528. Lease purchase and installment purchase contracts for certain equipment.

(a) Local boards of education may purchase or finance the purchase of automobiles; school buses; mobile classroom units; food service equipment, photocopiers; and computers, computer hardware, computer software, and related support services by lease purchase contracts and installment purchase contracts as provided in this section. Computers, computer hardware, computer software, and related support services purchased under this section shall meet the technical standards specified in the North Carolina Instructional Technology Plan as developed and approved under G.S. 115C-102.6A and G.S. 115C-102.6B.

(b) A lease purchase contract under this section creates in the local board the right to possess and use the property for a specified period of time in exchange for periodic payments and shall include either an obligation or an option to purchase the property during the term of the contract. The contract may include an option to upgrade the property during the term. A local board may exercise an option to upgrade without rebidding the contract.

(c) An installment purchase contract under this section creates in the property purchased a security interest to secure payment of the purchase price to the seller or to an individual or entity advancing moneys or supplying financing for the purchase transaction.

(d) The term of a contract entered into under this section shall not exceed the useful life of the property purchased. An option to upgrade shall be considered in determining the useful life of the property.

(e) A contract entered into under this section shall be considered a continuing contract for capital outlay and subject to G.S. 115C-441(c1).

(f) A contract entered into under this section is subject to Article 8 of Chapter 159 of the General Statutes, except for G.S. 159-148(a)(4) and (b)(2). For purposes of determining whether the standards set out in G.S. 159-148(a)(3) have been met, only the five hundred thousand dollar ($500,000) threshold shall apply.

(g) Subsections (e) and (f) of this section shall not apply to contracts entered into under this section so long as the term of each contract does not exceed three years and the total amount financed during any three-year period is no greater than two hundred fifty thousand dollars ($250,000) or is no greater than three times the local board's annual State allocation for classroom materials, equipment, and instructional supplies, whichever is less. The local board shall submit information, including the principal and interest paid and the amount of outstanding obligation, concerning these contracts as part of the annual budget it submits to its board of county commissioners under Article 31 of this Chapter.

(h) No contract entered into under this section may contain a nonsubstitution clause that restricts the right of a local board to:

(1) Continue to provide a service or activity; or

(2) Replace or provide a substitute for any property financed or purchased by the contract.

(i) No deficiency judgment may be rendered against any local board of education or any unit of local government, as defined in G.S. 160A-20(h), in any action for breach of a contractual obligation authorized by this section, and the taxing power of a unit of local government is not and may not be pledged directly or indirectly to secure any moneys due under a contract authorized by this section. (1995 (Reg. Sess., 1996), c. 716, s. 14; 1997-236, s. 4; 2007-519, s. 1.)

§ 115C-529. Useful life guidelines.

The State Office of Information Technology Services shall develop and annually revise guidelines for determining the useful life of computers purchased under G.S. 115C-528. The Division of Purchase and Contract shall develop and periodically revise guidelines for determining the useful life of automobiles, school buses, and photocopiers purchased under G.S. 115C-528. The Local Government Commission shall develop and periodically revise guidelines for determining the useful life of mobile classroom units purchased under G.S. 115C-528. Guidelines for computers and photocopiers shall include provisions for upgrades during the term of the contract. The State Office of Information Technology Services, the Division of Purchase and Contract, and the Local Government Commission shall provide their respective guidelines to the State Board of Education by November 1, 1996. The State Board of Education shall provide the guidelines to local boards of education by January 1, 1997. (1995 (Reg. Sess., 1996), c. 716, s. 15; 2004-129, s. 34.)

§ 115C-530. Operational leases of school buildings and school facilities.

(a) Local boards of education may enter into operational leases of real or personal property for use as school buildings or school facilities. Operational leases for terms of less than three years shall not be subject to the approval of the board of county commissioners. Operational leases for terms of three years or longer, including periods that may be added to the original term through the exercise of options to renew or extend, are permitted if all of the following conditions are met:

(1) The budget resolution includes an appropriation authorizing the current fiscal year's portion of the obligation.

(2) An unencumbered balance remains in the appropriation sufficient to pay in the current fiscal year the sums obligated by the lease for the current fiscal year.

(3) The leases are approved by a resolution adopted by the board of county commissioners. If an operational lease is approved by the board of county commissioners, in each year the county commissioners shall appropriate sufficient funds to meet the amounts to be paid during the fiscal year under the lease.

(4) Any construction, repair, or renovation of the property is in compliance with the requirements of G.S. 115C-521(c) relating to energy guidelines.

For purposes of this section, an operational lease is defined according to generally accepted accounting principles and may be for new or existing buildings.

(b) Local boards of education may enter into contracts for the construction, repair, or renovation of leased property if (i) the budget resolution includes an appropriation authorizing the obligation, (ii) an unencumbered balance remains in the appropriation sufficient to pay in the current fiscal year the sums obligated by the transaction for the current fiscal year, and (iii) the construction, repair, or renovation is in compliance with the requirements of G.S. 115C-521(c) relating to energy guidelines. Construction, repair, or renovation work undertaken or contracted by a private developer is subject to the requirements of Article 8 of Chapter 143 of the General Statutes. Contracts for new construction and renovation that are subject to the bidding requirements of G.S. 143-129(a) and which do not constitute continuing contracts for capital outlay must be approved by the board of county commissioners.

(c) Operational leases and contracts entered into under this section are subject to approval by the Local Government Commission under Article 8 of Chapter 159 of the General Statutes if they meet the standards set out in G.S. 159-148(a)(1), 159-148(a)(2), and 159-148(a)(3). For purposes of determining whether the standards set out in G.S. 159-148(a)(3) have been met, only the five hundred thousand dollar ($500,000) threshold shall apply. (1997-236, s. 2; 2010-196, s. 3.)

§ 115C-531. (Repealed effective July 1, 2015) Capital leases of school buildings and school facilities.

(a) Definitions. - The following definitions apply in this section:

(1) Capital lease. - A capital lease as defined by generally accepted accounting principles, regardless of how the parties describe the agreement.

(2) Private developer. - The entity with which the school board enters into a capital lease or build-to-suit lease under the provisions of this section.

(b) Authorization. - Local boards of education may enter into capital leases of real or personal property for use as school buildings or school facilities. The capital lease may relate to an existing building or a new school building to be constructed. The term of any capital lease, including any renewal periods, shall not exceed 40 years from the expected date that the local board of education will take occupancy of the property that is the subject of a capital lease. Subdivisions (c) and (d) of G.S. 115C-521 do not apply to a capital lease entered into under this section.

(c) Construction, Repairs, and Renovation. - The provisions of G.S. 115C-530(b) apply to a capital lease under this section. A capital lease entered into under this section may provide that the private developer is responsible for providing, or contracting for, construction, repair, or renovation work. Construction, repair, or renovation work undertaken or contracted by a private developer is not subject to the requirements of Article 8 of Chapter 143 of the General Statutes. Construction, repair, or renovation work undertaken or contracted by the private developer involving the estimated expenditure of three hundred thousand dollars ($300,000) or more is subject to the provisions of G.S. 115C-532.

(d) Nonsubstitution Clause. - A capital lease may not contain a nonsubstitution clause that restricts the right of a local board to continue to provide a service or activity or to replace or provide a substitute for any property financed or purchased by the capital lease.

(e) No Deficiency Judgment; No Pledge of Taxing Power. - No deficiency judgment may be rendered against any local board of education or any unit of local government, as defined in G.S. 160A-20(h), in any action for breach of a contractual obligation authorized by this section, and the taxing power of a unit is not and may not be pledged directly or indirectly to secure any moneys due under a contract authorized by this section. A capital lease shall state that it does not constitute a pledge of the taxing power or full faith and credit of the local board of education or board of county commissioners.

(f) Budgetary Accounting. - A capital lease entered into under this section shall be considered a continuing contract for capital outlay and is subject to G.S. 115C-441(c1); provided, however, notwithstanding any provision of G.S. 115C-441(c1) or G.S. 115C-426, in each fiscal year the appropriation of funds by the county for the payment of amounts due under the capital lease shall be at the discretion of the board of county commissioners.

(g) Local Government Commission Approval. - Capital leases entered into under this section are subject to approval by the Local Government Commission under Article 8 of Chapter 159 of the General Statutes if they meet the standards set out in G.S. 159-148(a)(1), 159-148(a)(2), and 159- 148(a)(3). For purposes of determining whether the standards set out in G.S. 159-148(a)(3) have been met, only the five-hundred-thousand-dollar ($500,000) threshold applies.

(h) No Agreements on Student Assignment. - A capital lease may not contain any provision with respect to the assignment of specific students or students from a specific area to any specific school.

(i) Lien Laws Not Affected. - All laws relating to liens on private property apply to private property interests in a capital lease project undertaken under this section. (2006-232, s. 1; 2006-259, s. 54(a); 2011-234, s. 1.)

§ 115C-532. (Repealed effective July 1, 2015) Additional provisions applicable to build-to-suit capital leases.

(a) Definitions. - The definitions of G.S. 115C-531 apply in this section. In addition, for the purposes of this section, the following definitions apply:

(1) Build-to-suit capital lease. - A capital lease that provides for the construction of new facilities or the renovation of existing facilities by the private developer, the cost of which is estimated to be greater than three hundred thousand dollars ($300,000).

(2) Prime contractor. - A contractor who contracts directly with the private developer or the private developer's construction manager at risk, if any, for construction, repair, or renovation work under this section.

(b) Contract Provisions. - A build-to-suit capital lease may include contractual provisions by the private developer regarding the provision of products, services, and guaranties related to a facility that is the subject of a capital lease. A local board of education may also enter into a separate agreement or series of related agreements regarding the provision of products, services, and guaranties related to a facility that is the subject of a capital lease; provided all agreements are approved by the board of county commissioners in connection with the approval of the build-to-suit capital lease.

(c) Approval by Local Board of Education. - Before entering into a build-to-suit capital lease pursuant to this section, the local board of education shall adopt a resolution as provided in this subsection. Before adopting the resolution required by this subsection, the local board of education shall publish a notice of its intent to enter into a build-to-suit capital lease at least 10 days in advance of the date of the meeting at which the action is contemplated and in a newspaper having general circulation within the geographic area served by the local board of education. The notice shall include, at a minimum, the date, time, and place of the meeting, a description in brief and general terms of the subject of the lease, the name of the other party to the lease, and an indication of the board's intent to take action to authorize the lease at the indicated meeting. The resolution shall provide the following:

(1) That entering into the build-to-suit capital lease for one or more specified buildings or facilities is in the unit's best interests under all the circumstances. In making this evaluation, the local board of education may consider the time, cost, and quality of design, engineering, and construction, including the time required to begin and the time required to complete a particular activity; occupancy costs, including lease payments, life-cycle maintenance, repair, and energy costs; and any other factors the board deems relevant.

(2) That the private developer is qualified to provide, either alone or in conjunction with other identified and associated persons, the products and services called for under the proposed capital lease and any related agreements. The local board of education shall make this determination taking into account any factors the local board deems relevant, including the knowledge, skill, and reputation of the provider and its associated persons, the goals and plans of providers for utilization of minority business enterprises, and the costs to be incurred by the local board of education.

(d) Additional Requirements Regarding Design Services. - All architectural, engineering, and survey services shall be procured in accordance with the provisions of Article 3D of Chapter 143 of the General Statutes. Required design and engineering services shall be performed by an engineer or a licensed architect, to the extent permitted under G.S. 83A-13(b). Specifications for any new school building shall be consistent with the requirements of G.S. 143-128(a). All applicable requirements for the review or approval of design and specifications for school buildings by the Department of Public Instruction and the Department of Insurance apply to school buildings constructed, repaired, or renovated under a capital lease authorized under this section.

(e) Additional Requirements Regarding Construction Services. - A private developer is required to seek competition and minority business participation in connection with all construction work under this section in accordance with the following provisions:

(1) A private developer shall either (i) solicit bids from prime contractors for all construction work under this section or (ii) select a construction manager at risk through a qualification based process in which case the selected construction manager at risk shall solicit bids from all of its prime contractors for all construction work under this section.

(2) The private developer or its construction manager at risk may prequalify contractors. The prequalification criteria, if any, shall be determined by the local board of education and the private developer to address quality, performance, the time specified in the bids for performance of the contract, the cost of construction oversight, time for completion, capacity to perform, and other factors deemed appropriate by the private developer and the local board of education.

(3) A private developer and its construction manager at risk, if any, shall comply with the requirements applicable to a public entity pursuant to G.S. 143-128.2, and prime contractors shall comply with the provisions of G.S. 143-128.2 applicable to contractors, except the private developer and its construction manager shall adopt the local board of education's minority participation goal. The local board of education shall require the private developer to submit its plan for compliance with G.S. 143-128.2 for approval by the local board of education prior to the private developer soliciting bids under this subsection.

(4) A private developer or its construction manager at risk shall publicly advertise at least 30 days in advance of the bid date in a newspaper having general circulation within the geographic areas served by the local board of education, shall open bids publicly, and shall award each contract to the lowest responsible, responsive, and prequalified bidder, taking into consideration quality, performance, the time specified in the bids for performance of the contract, the cost of construction oversight, time for completion, compliance with G.S. 143-128.2, and any other factors deemed appropriate by the private developer and the local board of education and included in the bid solicitation. A private developer or its construction manager at risk shall enter into the construction contracts directly with the successful bidder. After the award of a contract or contracts, the private developer or its construction manager at risk and any contractor may negotiate and reach agreement with the successful

bidder on modifications to all aspects of the contract, including the time for performance, the scope of the work, and the price to be paid.

(5) The local board of education, in its discretion, may require the private developer to provide a performance and payment bond for construction work in accordance with the provisions of Article 3 of Chapter 44A of the General Statutes and may require the private developer to provide a bond or other appropriate guarantee to cover any other guarantees, products, or services to be provided by the private developer.

(f) Predevelopment Agreements with Private Developer Authorized. - Local boards of education may enter into predevelopment agreements with a private developer in advance of entering into a build-to-suit capital lease. Predevelopment agreements with private developers shall be approved by the board of county commissioners. Predevelopment agreements may include provisions for each of the following:

(1) Site selection, land acquisition, and site preparation, including such services as wetlands delineation, archaeological review, and State and local government land-use permitting.

(2) Building programming and design, including both architectural and engineering services pursuant to subsection (d) of this section.

(g) Real Estate Transfer Authorized. - Notwithstanding any contrary provisions of law, a city, county, or local board of education may, pursuant to the procedures in G.S. 160A-267, sell, lease, or otherwise transfer real or personal property to any private developer for construction, repair, or renovation of a school facility under a build-to-suit capital lease entered into pursuant to this section. The conveying unit may subject the property to any covenants, conditions, or restrictions as the unit deems to be necessary to carry out the purposes of this section. The disposition of property pursuant to this subsection is not subject to the requirements of G.S. 115C-518. No transfer by a local board of education under this subsection shall occur unless it is approved by the board of county commissioners.

(h) Additional Permitted Lease Terms. - In recognition of the potential economic and technical utility of build-to-suit capital leases, which include in their scope combinations of design, construction, operation, management, and maintenance responsibilities over prolonged periods of time, and the potential desirability of a single point of responsibility for these matters in connection with build-to-suit capital leases, any build-to-suit capital lease may include provisions imposing responsibility on the private developer or any identified affiliated entity for any of the following matters:

(1)   Site selection, land acquisition, and site preparation, including wetlands delineation, archaeological review, and State and local government land-use permitting.

(2)   Facility programming, planning, and design, including both architectural and engineering services.

(3)   Qualification and prequalification of contractors and subcontractors.

(4)   Construction and construction management.

(5)   Financing.

(6)   Facility maintenance and repairs.

(7)   Energy usage guarantees.

(8)   Transfer of ownership of the leased property to a local government entity at the end of the lease term.

(9)   Any other guaranties, products, and services as the local board of education may determine.

(i)   Letter of Credit. - A private developer shall provide an irrevocable letter of credit for the benefit of laborers and materialmen in an amount not less than five percent (5%) of the total cost of the improvements which are the subject of the build-to-suit capital lease and shall maintain the letter of credit throughout the construction of the project and for the succeeding six-month period. (2006-232, s. 1; 2006-259, s. 54(b); 2011-234, s. 1.)

Article 38.

State Insurance of Public School Property.

§ 115C-533. Duty of State Board to operate insurance system.

The State Board shall have the duty to manage and operate a system of insurance for public school property. (1955, c. 1372, art. 2, s. 2; 1957, c. 541, s. 11; 1961, c. 969; 1963, c. 448, ss. 24, 27; c. 688, ss. 1, 2; c. 1223, s. 1; 1965, c. 1185, s. 2; 1967, c. 643, s. 1; 1969, c. 517, s. 1; 1971, c. 704, s. 4; c. 745; 1973, c. 476, s. 138; c. 675; 1975, c. 699, s. 2; c. 975; 1979, c. 300, s. 1; c. 935; 1981, c. 423, s. 1.)

§ 115C-534. Duty to insure property.

(a) The board of every local school administrative unit in the public school system of this State, in order to safeguard the investment made in public schools, shall:

(1) Insure and keep insured to the extent of not less than seventy-five percent (75%) of the current insurable value as determined by the insurer and the insured of each of its insurable buildings against fire, lightning and the perils embraced in extended coverage.

(2) Insure and keep insured adequately the equipment and contents of said building.

(b) The tax-levying authority for each local school administrative unit shall appropriate funds necessary for compliance with the provisions of subsection (a).

(c) Willful failure to comply with the provisions of (a) and (b) above, is declared a Class 3 misdemeanor. Every 24 hours without such insurance constitutes a separate offense. (1957, c. 1040; 1981, c. 423, s. 1; 1993, c. 539, s. 893; 1994, Ex. Sess., c. 24, s. 14(c).)

§ 115C-535. Authority and rules for organization of system.

The State Board of Education is hereby authorized, directed and empowered to establish a division to manage and operate a system of insurance for public school property. The Board shall adopt such rules and regulations as, in its discretion, may be necessary to provide all details inherent in the insurance of public school property. The Board shall employ a director, safety inspectors, engineers and other personnel with suitable training and experience, which in its opinion is necessary to insure and protect effectively public school property, and it shall fix their compensation with the approval of the Personnel Commission. (1955, c. 1372, art. 16, s. 1; 1981, c. 423, s. 1.)

§ 115C-536. Public School Insurance Fund; decrease of premiums when fund reaches five percent of total insurance in force.

There shall be set up in the books of the State Treasurer a fund to be known and designated as the "Public School Insurance Fund," which fund hereafter in G.S. 115C-535 to 115C-542 is referred to as "the Fund." In order to provide adequate reserves against losses which may be incurred on account of the risks insured against as provided in G.S. 115C-535 to 115C-542 and to provide payment for such losses as may be incurred therein, there is hereby appropriated to the Fund the sum of two million dollars ($2,000,000), which shall be paid from and charged to the State Literary Fund as set up and defined in this Chapter. When the reserves in the Fund shall be increased by the payment of premiums by the governing boards of local school administrative school units, or otherwise, to the extent of one million dollars ($1,000,000), there shall be transferred from the Fund back to the State Literary Fund the sum of one million dollars ($1,000,000) and when the Fund shall again be increased to the extent of another one million dollars ($1,000,000), there shall be transferred therefrom back to the State Literary Fund an additional sum of one million dollars ($1,000,000) in full reimbursement of the sum of two million dollars ($2,000,000), which is authorized to be transferred from the State Literary Fund by the provisions hereof. All funds paid over to the State Treasurer for premiums on insurance by the governing boards of local school administrative units and all money received from interest or from loans and deposits and from any other source connected with the insurance of the property hereinafter referred to shall be held by the State Treasurer in the Fund for the purpose of paying all fire, lightning, windstorm, hail and explosion losses for which the said Fund shall be liable and the expenses necessary for the proper conduct of the insurance of said property, together with such premiums for reinsurance of such part of said insurance as the State Board of Education may deem necessary to reinsure, as provided for in G.S. 115C-535 to 115C-542. The State Treasurer shall be the custodian of the Fund and shall invest its assets in accordance with the provisions of G.S. 147-69.2 and 147-69.3.

When the Fund herein provided for reaches the sum of five percent (5%) of the total insurance in force, then annually thereafter the State Board of Education shall proportionately decrease the premiums on insurance to an amount which will be sufficient to maintain the Fund at five percent (5%) of the total insurance in force, and in the event in the judgment of the State Board of Education the income from the investments of the Fund are sufficient to maintain the same at five percent (5%) of the total insurance in force, no premium shall be charged for the ensuing year: Provided, that no building or property insured shall cease to pay premiums until five annual payments of premiums have been made whether or not through such payments the Fund shall be increased beyond five percent (5%) of the total insurance in force, unless such building or property shall cease to be insurable within the meaning of G.S. 115C-535 to 115C-542 within such five-year period. (1955, c. 1372, art. 16, s. 2; 1981, c. 423, s. 1.)

§ 115C-537. Insurance of property by local boards; notice of election to insure and information to be furnished; outstanding policies.

All local boards of education may insure all property within their units against the direct loss or damage by fire, lightning, windstorm, hail or explosions resulting by reason of defects in equipment in public school buildings and other public school properties in the Fund hereinbefore set up and provided for. Any property covered by an insurance policy in effect on the date when the property of a unit is insured in the Fund shall be insured by the Fund as of the expiration of the policy. Each local board shall give notice of its election to insure in the Fund at least 30 days prior to such insurance becoming effective and shall furnish to the State Board of Education a full and complete list of all outstanding fire insurance policies, giving in complete detail the name of the insurers, the amount of the insurance and expirations thereof. While the said insurance policies remain in effect, the Fund shall act as coinsurer of the properties covered by such insurance to the same extent and in the same manner as is provided for coinsurance under the provisions of the standard form of fire insurance as provided by law, and in the event of loss shall have the same rights and duties as required by participating insurance companies. (1955, c. 1372, art. 16, s. 3; 1957, c. 686, s. 3; 1981, c. 423, s. 1.)

§ 115C-538. Inspections of insured public school properties.

The State Board of Education shall provide for periodic inspections of all public school properties in the State of North Carolina insured under the provisions hereof, the said inspections for safety of buildings and particularly school buildings, against the loss or damage from fire and explosions. The inspections shall be the basis for offering such engineering advice as may be thought to be necessary to safeguard the children in the public schools from death and injury from school fires or explosions and to protect said school properties from loss, and the local boards of education shall be required so far as possible, and reasonable, to carry out and put into effect such recommendations in respect thereto as may be made by the State Board of Education. (1955, c. 1372, art. 16, s. 4; 1981, c. 423, s. 1.)

§ 115C-539. Information to be furnished prior to insuring in Fund; providing for payment of premiums.

Local boards of education shall at least 30 days before insuring in the Fund, furnish to the State Board of Education a complete and detailed list of all school buildings and contents thereof and other insurable school property, together with an estimate of the present value of the said property. Valuation for purposes of insuring in the Fund shall be reached by agreement in accordance with the procedure hereinafter set up for adjustment of losses. Local boards of education and the tax-levying authority shall be required to provide for the payment of premiums for insurance on the school properties of each local school administrative unit, respectively, to the extent of not less than seventy-five percent (75%) of the current insurable value of the said properties, including the insurance in fire insurance companies and the insurance provided by the Fund as set out herein. (1955, c. 1372, art. 16, s. 5; 1981, c. 423, s. 1.)

§ 115C-540. Determination and adjustment of premium rates; certificate as to insurance carried; no lapse; notice as to premiums required, and payment thereof.

The State Board of Education shall determine the annual premium rate to be charged for insurance of school properties as herein provided, which said rate shall not, however, be in excess of the rates fixed by law for insurance of such properties in effect on May 31, 1948, and such rates shall be adjusted from time to time so as to provide insurance against damage or loss resulting from fires, lightning, windstorm, hail or explosions resulting from defects in equipment in public school buildings and properties for the local school administrative units at the lowest cost possible in keeping with the payment of cost of administration of G.S. 115C-535 to 115C-542, and the creation of adequate reserves to pay losses which may be incurred. The State Board of Education shall furnish to each local school administrative unit annually and, at such times as changes may require, a certificate showing the amount of insurance carried on each item of insurable property. The said insurance shall not lapse but shall remain in force until the local board of education requests that said insurance be canceled or until such property becomes uninsurable in the manner set out in G.S. 115C-542. From time to time the local board of education shall be notified as to the amount of the premiums required to be paid for said insurance and the amounts thereof shall be provided for in the annual budget of such schools. The tax-levying authorities shall provide by taxation or otherwise a sum sufficient to pay the required premiums thereon.

The local board of education shall within 30 days from notice thereof pay to the State Board of Education the premiums on such insurance, and in the event that there are no funds on hand at such time with which to make said payment, the same shall be paid out of the first funds available to such school board. Delayed payments shall bear interest at the rate of six percent (6%) per annum. (1955, c. 1372, art. 16, s. 6; 1981, c. 423, s. 1.)

§ 115C-541. Adjustment of losses; determination and report of appraisers; payment of amounts to treasurers of local school administrative units; disbursement of funds.

In the event of loss or damage by fire, lightning, windstorm, hail, or explosions resulting from defects in equipment in public school buildings and properties for the local school administrative units, the Fund shall pay the loss in the same proportion as the amount of insurance carried bore to the valuation of the property at the time it was insured, but not exceeding the amount which it would cost to repair or replace the property with material of like quality within a reasonable time after such loss, not in excess of the amount of insurance provided for said property, and not in excess of the amount of such loss which the Fund is required to pay in participation with fire insurance companies having policies of insurance in force on said properties at the time of the loss or damage, and the Fund shall not be liable for a greater proportion of any loss than the amount of insurance thereon shall bear to the whole insurance covering the property against the peril involved.

In the event of loss or damage by fire, lightning, windstorm, hail, or explosions resulting from defects in equipment in public school buildings and properties of the local school administrative units, to the property insured, when an agreement as to the extent of such loss or damage cannot be arrived at between the State Board of Education and the local officials having charge of the said property, the amount of such loss or damage shall be determined by three appraisers; one to be named by the State Board of Education, one by the local board of education having charge of the property, and the two so appointed shall select a third, all of whom shall be disinterested persons, and qualified from experience to appraise and value such property: Provided, however, if the appraisers appointed by the State Board of Education and the local board of education shall fail for 15 days to agree upon the third appraiser, then, on request of the State Board of Education or the local board of education having charge of the property, such third appraiser shall be selected by any regular resident superior court judge of the superior court district or set of districts as defined in G.S. 7A-41.1 in which the property is located. The appraisers so named shall file their written report with the State Board of Education and with the local board of education having such property in charge. The costs of the appraisal shall be paid by the Fund. Upon the determination of the loss by the appraisers, the State Board of Education shall pay the amount of such loss or damage to school property in the control of the local school administrative unit to its treasurer, upon proper warrant of the State Board of Education. Said funds shall be paid out by the treasurer of said units, as provided by this Chapter for the disbursement of the funds of such unit. (1955, c. 1372, art. 16, s. 7; 1981, c. 423, s. 1; 1987 (Reg. Sess., 1988), c. 1037, s. 110.)

§ 115C-542. Maintenance of inspection and engineering service; cancellation of insurance.

The State Board of Education is authorized and empowered to maintain an inspection and engineering service deemed by it appropriate and necessary to reduce the hazards of fire in public school buildings insured in the Fund as hereinbefore provided, and to expend for such purpose not in excess of ten percent (10%) of the annual premiums collected from the local school authorities. The State Board of Education is hereby authorized and empowered to cancel any insurance on any school property when, in its opinion, because of dilapidation and depreciation such property is no longer insurable. Before cancellation, the local board of education shall be given at least 30 days notice, and in the event said property can be restored to insurable condition, the State Board of Education may make such orders with respect to the continuance of such coverage as may be deemed proper: Provided, that the findings and results of the inspection of local school property by the agents of the Board shall be reported to local boards of education and to the board of county commissioners of such units as carry insurance with the State 30 days before budget-making time in order that all school property shall be properly taken care of and made safe from fire hazards. (1955, c. 1372, art. 16, s. 8; 1981, c. 423, s. 1.)

§ 115C-543. Other property insurance.

The State Board of Education may adopt rules for providing property insurance on property insured by the Fund against all risks of direct physical loss not otherwise insured against pursuant to this Article. Losses covered by this additional insurance shall be paid out of the Fund in the same manner as fire and extended coverage losses.

Each local school administrative unit that elects to purchase this additional insurance shall pay a premium in accordance with rates fixed by the Board. This additional insurance shall be subject to the provisions and stipulations on policy forms approved by the State Board. (1987, c. 312, s. 1.)

§§ 115C-544 through 115C-546. Reserved for future codification purposes.

Article 38A.

Public School Building Capital Fund.

§ 115C-546.1. Creation of Fund; administration.

(a)   There is created the Public School Building Capital Fund. The Fund shall be used to assist county governments in meeting their public school building capital needs.

(b)   Repealed by Session Laws 2013-316, s. 2.4(a), effective July 23, 2013.

(c)   The Fund shall be administered by the Department of Public Instruction. (1987, c. 622, s. 12; c. 813, s. 20; 1989 (Reg. Sess., 1990), c. 1066, s. 28(b); 1991, c. 689, s. 260; 1995 (Reg. Sess., 1996), c. 631, s. 15; 1996, 2nd Ex. Sess. c. 13, s. 2.2; 1997-221, s. 26; 2000-140, s. 93.1(a); 2001-424, s. 12.2(b); 2003-284, s. 7.33(b); 2013-316, s. 2.4(a); 2013-360, s. 6.11(a).)

§ 115C-546.2. Allocations from the Fund; uses; expenditures; reversion to General Fund; matching requirements.

(a)   Repealed by Session Laws 2013-316, s. 2.4(b), effective July 23, 2013.

(b)   Counties shall use monies previously credited to the Fund by the Secretary of Revenue pursuant to G.S. 115C-546.1(b) for capital outlay projects including the planning, construction, reconstruction, enlargement, improvement, repair, or renovation of public school buildings and for the purchase of land for public school buildings; for equipment to implement a local school technology plan; or for both. Monies used to implement a local school technology plan shall be transferred to the State School Technology Fund and allocated by that Fund to the local school administrative unit for equipment.

As used in this section, "public school buildings" only includes facilities for individual schools that are used for instructional and related purposes and does not include centralized administration, maintenance, or other facilities.

In the event a county finds that it does not need all or part of the funds allocated to it for capital outlay projects including the planning, construction, reconstruction, enlargement, improvement, repair, or renovation of public school buildings, for the purchase of land for public school buildings, or for equipment to implement a local school technology plan, the unneeded funds allocated to that county may be used to retire any indebtedness incurred by the county for public school facilities.

In the event a county finds that its public school building needs and its school technology needs can be met in a more timely fashion through the allocation of financial resources previously allocated for purposes other than school building needs or school technology needs and not restricted for use in meeting public school building needs or school technology needs, the county commissioners may, with the concurrence of the affected local Board of Education, use those financial resources to meet school building needs and school technology needs and may allocate the funds it receives under this Article for purposes other than school building needs or school technology needs to the extent that financial resources were redirected from such purposes. The concurrence described herein shall be secured in advance of the allocation of the previously unrestricted financial resources and shall be on a form prescribed by the Local Government Commission.

(c) Monies in the Fund previously credited to the Fund by the Secretary of Revenue pursuant to G.S. 115C-546.1(b) allocated for capital projects shall be matched on the basis of one dollar of local funds for every three dollars of State funds. Such monies in the Fund transferred to the State Technology Fund do not require a local match.

Revenue received from local sales and use taxes that is restricted for public school capital outlay purposes pursuant to G.S. 105-502 or G.S. 105-487 may be used to meet the local matching requirement. Funds expended by a county after July 1, 1986, for land acquisition, engineering fees, architectural fees, or other directly related costs for a public school building capital project that was not completed prior to July 1, 1987, may be used to meet the local match requirement.

(d) If funds are appropriated from the Education Lottery Fund to the Public School Building Capital Fund, such funds shall be allocated for school capital construction projects on a per average daily membership basis according to the average daily membership for the budget year as determined and certified by the State Board of Education.

(1), (2) Repealed by Session Laws 2013-360, s. 6.11(b), effective July 1, 2013.

(3) No county shall have to provide matching funds required under subsection (c) of this section.

(4) A county may use monies in this Fund to pay for school construction projects in local school administrative units and to retire indebtedness incurred for school construction projects.

(5) A county may not use monies in this Fund to pay for school technology needs.

(e) The State Board of Education may use up to one million five hundred thousand dollars ($1,500,000) each year of monies in the Fund to support positions in the Department of Public Instruction's Support Services Division. (1987, c. 622, s. 12; c. 813, ss. 18.1, 19.1, 21; 1991 (Reg. Sess., 1992), c. 1030, s. 30; 1997-221, s. 27; 2005-276, s. 31.1(hh); 2005-344, s. 15.2; 2006-66, s. 7.15; 2006-259, s. 8(i); 2008-107, s. 7.18(a), (b); 2011-145, s. 5.4(h); 2011-391, s. 4; 2013-316, s. 2.4(b); 2013-360, s. 6.11(b).)

SUBCHAPTER X. PRIVATE AND PROPRIETARY SCHOOLS.

Article 39.

Nonpublic Schools.

Part 1. Private Church Schools and Schools of Religious Charter.

§ 115C-547. Policy.

In conformity with the Constitutions of the United States and of North Carolina, it is the public policy of the State in matters of education that "No human authority shall, in any case whatever, control or interfere with the rights of conscience," or with religious liberty and that "religion, morality and knowledge being necessary to good government and the happiness of mankind . . . the means of education shall forever be encouraged." (1979, c. 505; 1981, c. 423, s. 1.)

§ 115C-548. Attendance; health and safety regulations.

Each private church school or school of religious charter shall make, and maintain annual attendance and disease immunization records for each pupil enrolled and regularly attending classes. Attendance by a child at any school to which this Part relates and which complies with this Part shall satisfy the requirements of compulsory school attendance so long as the school operates on a regular schedule, excluding reasonable holidays and vacations, during at least nine calendar months of the year. Each school shall be subject to reasonable fire, health and safety inspections by State, county and municipal authorities as required by law.

The Division of Nonpublic Education, Department of Administration, shall ensure that materials are provided to these schools so that they can provide parents and guardians with information about meningococcal meningitis and influenza and their vaccines at the beginning of every school year. This information may be provided electronically or on the Division's Web page. This information shall include the causes, symptoms, and how meningococcal meningitis and influenza are spread and the places where parents and guardians may obtain additional information and vaccinations for their children.

The Division of Nonpublic Education, Department of Administration, shall also ensure that materials are provided to these schools so that they can provide parents and guardians with information about cervical cancer, cervical dysplasia, human papillomavirus, and the vaccines available to prevent these diseases. This information may be provided electronically or on the Division's Web page. This information shall include the causes and symptoms of these diseases, how they are transmitted, how they may be prevented by vaccination, including the benefits and possible side effects of vaccination, and the places where parents and guardians may obtain additional information and vaccinations for their children.

The Division of Nonpublic Education, Department of Administration, shall also ensure that information is available to these schools so that they can provide information annually on the preventable risks for preterm birth in subsequent pregnancies, including induced abortion, smoking, alcohol consumption, the use of illicit drugs, and inadequate prenatal care.

The Division of Nonpublic Education, Department of Administration, shall also ensure that information is available to these schools so that they can provide information on the manner in which a parent may lawfully abandon a newborn baby with a responsible person, in accordance with G.S. 7B-500. (1979, c. 505; 1981, c. 423, s. 1; 2004-118, s. 4; 2007-59, s. 3; 2007-126, s. 3; 2013-307, s. 1.2.)

§ 115C-549. Standardized testing requirements.

Each private church school or school of religious charter shall administer, at least once in each school year, a nationally standardized test or other nationally standardized equivalent measurement selected by the chief administrative officer of such school, to all students enrolled or regularly attending grades three, six and nine. The nationally standardized test or other equivalent measurement selected must measure achievement in the areas of English grammar, reading, spelling and mathematics. Each school shall make and maintain records of the results achieved by its students. For one year after the testing, all records shall be made available, subject to G.S. 115C-174.13, at the principal office of such school, at all reasonable times, for annual inspection by a duly authorized representative of the State of North Carolina. (1979, c. 505; 1981, c. 423, s. 1; 1987, c. 738, s. 180(b); 2004-199, s. 30(a).)

§ 115C-550. High school competency testing.

To assure that all high school graduates possess those minimum skills and that knowledge thought necessary to function in society, each private church school or school of religious charter shall administer at least once in each school year, a nationally standardized test or other nationally standardized equivalent measure selected by the chief administrative officer of such school, to all students enrolled and regularly attending the eleventh grade. The nationally standardized test or other equivalent measurement selected must measure competencies in the verbal and quantitative areas. Each private church school or school of religious charter shall establish a minimum score which must be attained by a student on the selected test in order to be graduated from high school. For one year after the testing, all records shall be made available, subject to G.S. 115C-174.13, at the principal office of such school, at all reasonable times, for annual inspection by a duly authorized representative of the State of North Carolina. (1979, c. 505; 1981, c. 423, s. 1; 2004-199, s. 30(b).)

§ 115C-551. Voluntary participation in the State programs.

Any such school may, on a voluntary basis, participate in any State operated or sponsored program which would otherwise be available to such school, including but not limited to the high school competency testing and statewide testing programs. (1979, c. 505; 1981, c. 423, s. 1.)

§ 115C-552. New school notice requirements; termination.

(a) Any new school to which this Part relates shall send to a duly authorized representative of the State of North Carolina a notice of intent to operate, name and address of the school, and name of the school's owner and chief administrator.

(b) Any school to which this Part applies shall notify a duly authorized representative of the State of North Carolina upon termination of the school. (1979, c. 505; 1981, c. 423, s. 1.)

§ 115C-553. Duly authorized representative.

The duly authorized representative of the State of North Carolina to whom reports of commencing operation and termination shall be made and who may inspect certain records under this Part shall be designated by the Governor. (1979, c. 505; 1981, c. 423, s. 1.)

§ 115C-554. Requirements exclusive.

No school, operated by any church or other organized religious group or body as part of its religious ministry, which complies with the requirements of this Part shall be subject to any other provision of law relating to education except requirements of law respecting fire, safety, sanitation and immunization. (1979, c. 505; 1981, c. 423, s. 1.)

Part 2. Qualified Nonpublic Schools.

§ 115C-555. Qualification of nonpublic schools.

The provisions of this Part shall apply to any nonpublic school which has one or more of the following characteristics:

(1) It is accredited by the State Board of Education.

(2)   It is accredited by a national or regional accrediting agency.

(3)   It is an active member of the North Carolina Association of Independent Schools.

(4)   It receives no funding from the State of North Carolina. For the purposes of this Article, scholarship grant funds awarded pursuant to Part 2A of this Article to eligible students attending a nonpublic school shall not be considered funding from the State of North Carolina. (1979, c. 506; 1981, c. 423, s. 1; 2013-360, s. 8.29(c).)

§ 115C-556. Attendance; health and safety regulations.

Each qualified nonpublic school shall make, and maintain annual attendance and disease immunization records for each pupil enrolled and regularly attending classes. Attendance by a child at any school to which this Part relates and which complies with this Part shall satisfy the requirements of compulsory school attendance so long as the school operates on a regular schedule, excluding reasonable holidays and vacations, during at least nine calendar months of the year. Each school shall be subject to reasonable fire, health and safety inspections by State, county and municipal authorities as required by law.

The Division of Nonpublic Education, Department of Administration, shall ensure that materials are provided to each qualified nonpublic school so that the school can provide parents and guardians with information about meningococcal meningitis and influenza and their vaccines at the beginning of every school year. This information may be provided electronically or on the Division's Web page. This information shall include the causes, symptoms, and how meningococcal meningitis and influenza are spread and the places where parents and guardians may obtain additional information and vaccinations for their children.

The Division of Nonpublic Education, Department of Administration, shall also ensure that materials are provided to each qualified nonpublic school so that the school can provide parents and guardians with information about cervical cancer, cervical dysplasia, human papillomavirus, and the vaccines available to prevent these diseases. This information may be provided electronically or on the Division's Web page. This information shall include the causes and symptoms of these diseases, how they are transmitted, how they may be prevented by vaccination, including the benefits and possible side effects of vaccination, and the places where parents and guardians may obtain additional information and vaccinations for their children.

The Division of Nonpublic Education, Department of Administration, shall also ensure that information is available to each qualified nonpublic school so that the school can provide information annually on the preventable risks for preterm birth in subsequent pregnancies, including induced abortion, smoking, alcohol consumption, the use of illicit drugs, and inadequate prenatal care.

The Division of Nonpublic Education, Department of Administration, shall also ensure that information is available to each qualified nonpublic school so that the school can provide information on the manner in which a parent may lawfully abandon a newborn baby with a responsible person, in accordance with G.S. 7B-500. (1979, c. 506; 1981, c. 423, s. 1; 2004-118, s. 5; 2007-59, s. 4; 2007-126, s. 4; 2013-307, s. 1.3.)

§ 115C-557. Standardized testing requirements.

Each qualified nonpublic school shall administer, at least once in each school year, a nationally standardized test or other nationally standardized equivalent measurement selected by the chief administrative officer of such school, to all students enrolled or regularly attending grades three, six and nine. The nationally standardized test or other equivalent measurement selected must measure achievement in the areas of English grammar, reading, spelling and mathematics. Each school shall make and maintain records of the results achieved by its students. For one year after the testing, all records shall be made available, subject to G.S. 115C-174.13, at the principal office of such school, at all reasonable times, for annual inspection by a duly authorized representative of the State of North Carolina. (1979, c. 506; 1981, c. 423, s. 1; 1987, c. 738, s. 180(c); 2004-199, s. 30(c).)

§ 115C-558. High school competency testing.

To assure that all high school graduates possess those minimum skills and that knowledge thought necessary to function in society, each qualified nonpublic school shall administer at least once in each school year, a nationally standardized test or other nationally standardized equivalent measure selected by the chief administrative officer of such school, to all students enrolled and regularly attending the eleventh grade. The nationally standardized test or other equivalent measurement selected must measure competencies in the verbal and quantitative areas. Each qualified nonpublic school shall establish a minimum score which must be attained by a student on the selected test in order to be graduated from high school. For one year after the testing, all records shall be made available, subject to G.S. 115C-174.13, at the principal office of such school, at all reasonable times, for annual inspection by a duly authorized representative of the State of North Carolina. (1979, c. 506; 1981, c. 423, s. 1; 2004-199, s. 30(d).)

§ 115C-559. Voluntary participation in the State programs.

Any such school may, on a voluntary basis, participate in any State operated or sponsored program which would otherwise be available to such school, including but not limited to the high school competency testing and statewide testing programs. (1979, c. 506; 1981, c. 423, s. 1.)

§ 115C-560. New school notice requirements; termination.

(a) Any new school to which this Part relates shall send to a duly authorized representative of the State of North Carolina a notice of intent to operate, name and address of the school, and name of the school's owner and chief administrator.

(b) Any school to which this Part applies shall notify a duly authorized representative of the State of North Carolina upon termination of the school. (1979, c. 506; 1981, c. 423, s. 1.)

§ 115C-561. Duly authorized representative.

The duly authorized representative of the State of North Carolina to whom reports of commencing operation and termination shall be made and who may inspect certain records under this Part shall be designated by the Governor. (1979, c. 506; 1981, c. 423, s. 1.)

§ 115C-562. Requirements exclusive.

No qualifying nonpublic school, which complies with the requirements of this Part, shall be subject to any other provision of law relating to education except requirements of law respecting fire, safety, sanitation and immunization. (1979, c. 506; 1981, c. 423, s. 1.)

Part 2A. Scholarship Grants.

§ 115C-562.1. (For applicability, see Editor's note) Definitions.

The following definitions apply in this Part:

(1)   Authority. - The State Education Assistance Authority.

(2)   Division. - The Division of Nonpublic Education, Department of Administration.

(3)   Eligible students. - A student who has not yet received a high school diploma and who meets all of the following requirements:

a.   Meets one of the following criteria:

1.   Was a full-time student assigned to and attending a public school pursuant to G.S. 115C-366 during the previous semester.

2.   Received a scholarship grant during the previous school year.

3.   Is entering either kindergarten or the first grade.

4.   Is a child in foster care as defined in G.S. 131D-10.2(9).

5.   Is a child whose adoption decree was entered not more than one year prior to submission of the scholarship grant application.

b. Resides in a household with an income level not in excess of one hundred thirty-three percent (133%) of the amount required for the student to qualify for the federal free or reduced-price lunch program.

(4) Local school administrative unit. - A local school administrative unit, charter school, or regional school.

(5) Nonpublic school. - A school that meets the requirements of Part 1 or Part 2 of this Article as identified by the Division.

(6) Scholarship grants. - Grants awarded annually by the Authority to eligible students. (2013-360, s. 8.29(a).)

§ 115C-562.2. (For applicability, see Editor's note) Scholarship grants.

(a) The Authority shall make available no later than February 1 annually applications to eligible students for the award of scholarship grants to attend any nonpublic school. Information about scholarship grants and the application process shall be made available on the Authority's Web site. Beginning March 1, the Authority shall begin awarding scholarship grants according to the following criteria:

(1) First priority shall be given to eligible students who received a scholarship grant during the previous school year if those students have applied by March 1.

(2) After scholarship grants have been awarded to prior recipients as provided in subdivision (1) of this subsection, scholarships shall be awarded with remaining funds as follows:

a. At least fifty percent (50%) of the remaining funds shall be used to award scholarship grants to eligible students residing in households with an income level not in excess of the amount required for the student to qualify for the federal free or reduced-price lunch program.

b. No more than thirty-five percent (35%) of the remaining funds shall be used to award scholarship grants to eligible students entering either kindergarten or first grade.

c. Any remaining funds shall be used to award scholarship grants to all other eligible students.

(b) Scholarship grants awarded to eligible students residing in households with an income level not in excess of the amount required for the student to qualify for the federal free or reduced-price lunch program shall be for amounts of up to four thousand two hundred dollars ($4,200) per year. Scholarship grants awarded to eligible students residing in households with an income level in excess of the amount required for the student to qualify for the federal free or reduced-price lunch program shall be for amounts of not more than ninety percent (90%) of the required tuition and fees for the nonpublic school the eligible child will attend. Tuition and fees for a nonpublic school may include tuition and fees for books, transportation, equipment, or other items required by the nonpublic school. No scholarship grant shall exceed four thousand two hundred dollars ($4,200) per year per eligible student, and no scholarship grant shall exceed the required tuition and fees for the nonpublic school the eligible student will attend.

(c) The Authority shall permit an eligible student receiving a scholarship grant to enroll in a different nonpublic school and remain eligible. An eligible student receiving a scholarship grant who transfers to another nonpublic school during the year may be eligible to receive a pro rata share of any unexpended portion of the scholarship grant for tuition and fees at the nonpublic school to which the student transfers.

(d) The Authority shall establish rules and regulations for the administration and awarding of scholarship grants and may include in those rules a lottery process for selection of scholarship grant recipients within the criteria established by this section. (2013-360, s. 8.29(a).)

§ 115C-562.3. (For applicability, see Editor's note) Verification of eligibility.

(a) The Authority may seek verification of information on any application for scholarship grants from eligible students. The Authority shall select and verify a random sample of no less than six percent (6%) of applications annually. The Authority shall establish rules for the verification process and may use the federal verification requirements process for free and reduced-price lunch applications as guidance for those rules. If a household fails to cooperate with verification efforts, the Authority shall revoke the award of the scholarship grant to the eligible student.

(b) Household members of applicants for scholarship grants shall authorize the Authority to access information needed for verification efforts held by other State agencies, including the Department of Revenue, the Department of Health and Human Services, and the Department of Public Instruction. (2013-360, s. 8.29(a).)

§ 115C-562.4. (For applicability, see Editor's note) Identification of nonpublic schools and distribution of scholarship grant information.

(a) The Division shall provide annually by February 1 to the Authority a list of all nonpublic schools operating in the State that meet the requirements of Part 1 or Part 2 of this Article. The Division shall notify the Authority of any schools included in the list that the Division has determined to be ineligible within five business days of the determination of ineligibility.

(b) The Authority shall provide information about the scholarship grant program to the Division, including applications and the obligations of nonpublic schools accepting eligible students receiving scholarship grants. The Division shall ensure that information about the scholarship grant program is provided to all qualified nonpublic schools on an annual basis. (2013-360, s. 8.29(a).)

§ 115C-562.5. (For applicability, see Editor's note) Obligations of nonpublic schools accepting eligible students receiving scholarship grants.

(a) A nonpublic school that accepts eligible students receiving scholarship grants shall comply with the following:

(1) Provide to the Authority documentation for required tuition and fees charged to the student by the nonpublic school.

(2) Conduct a criminal background check for the staff member with the highest decision-making authority, as defined by the bylaws, articles of incorporation, or other governing document, to ensure that person has not been convicted of any crime listed in G.S. 115C-332.

(3) Provide to the parent or guardian of an eligible student, whose tuition and fees are paid in whole or in part with a scholarship grant, an annual written explanation of the student's progress, including the student's scores on standardized achievement tests.

(4) Administer, at least once in each school year, a nationally standardized test or other nationally standardized equivalent measurement selected by the chief administrative officer of the nonpublic school to all eligible students whose tuition and fees are paid in whole or in part with a scholarship grant enrolled in grades three and higher. The nationally standardized test or other equivalent measurement selected must measure achievement in the areas of English grammar, reading, spelling, and mathematics. Test performance data shall be submitted to the Authority by July 15 of each year. Test performance data reported to the Authority under this subdivision is not a public record under Chapter 132 of the General Statutes.

(5) Provide to the Authority graduation rates of the students receiving scholarship grants in a manner consistent with nationally recognized standards.

(6) Contract with a certified public accountant to perform a financial review, consistent with generally accepted accounting principles, for each school year in which the school accepts students receiving more than three hundred thousand dollars ($300,000) in scholarship grants awarded under this Part.

(b) A nonpublic school that accepts students receiving scholarship grants shall not require any additional fees based on the status of the student as a scholarship grant recipient.

(c) A nonpublic school enrolling more than 25 students whose tuition and fees are paid in whole or in part with a scholarship grant shall report to the Authority on the aggregate standardized test performance of eligible students. Aggregate test performance data reported to the Authority which does not contain personally identifiable student data shall be a public record under Chapter 132 of the General Statutes. Test performance data may be shared with public or private institutions of higher education located in North Carolina and shall be provided to an independent research organization selected by the Authority for research purposes as permitted by the Federal Education Rights and Privacy Act, 20 U.S.C. § 1232g.

(d) A nonpublic school accepting students receiving scholarship grants that fails to comply with the requirements of this section shall be ineligible to receive future scholarship grants if the Authority determines that the nonpublic school is not in compliance with the requirements of this section. The nonpublic school shall notify the parent or guardian of any enrolled student receiving a scholarship grant that the nonpublic school is no longer eligible to receive future scholarship grants. A nonpublic school may appeal for reconsideration of eligibility after one year. (2013-360, s. 8.29(a).)

§ 115C-562.6. (For applicability, see Editor's note) Scholarship endorsement.

The Authority shall remit, at least two times each school year, scholarship grant funds awarded to eligible students to the nonpublic school for endorsement by at least one of the student's parents or guardians. The parent or guardian shall restrictively endorse the scholarship grant funds awarded to the eligible student to the nonpublic school for deposit into the account of the nonpublic school. The parent or guardian shall not designate any entity or individual associated with the nonpublic school as the parent's attorney-in-fact to endorse the scholarship grant funds but shall endorse the scholarship grant funds in person at the site of the nonpublic school. A parent's or guardian's failure to comply with this section shall result in forfeit of the scholarship grant. A scholarship grant forfeited for failure to comply with this section shall be returned to the Authority to be awarded to another student. (2013-360, s. 8.29(a).)

§ 115C-562.7. (For applicability, see Editor's note) Authority reporting requirements.
(a) The Authority shall report to the Department of Public Instruction annually, no later than September 1, the number and names of students who have received scholarship grants for the current school year and who were enrolled the prior semester in a local school administrative unit by the previously attended local school administrative unit. By September 15 of each year, the State Board of Education shall determine the amount of the reduction for each local school administrative unit by multiplying the students who have received scholarship grants for the current school year and who were enrolled the prior semester in a local school administrative unit by the per pupil allocation for average daily membership from the local school administrative unit. Local school administrative units shall identify to the Department of Public Instruction the reductions to State General Fund appropriations for Opportunity Scholarships by October 1 of each year.

(b) The Authority shall report annually, no later than March 1, to the Joint Legislative Education Oversight Committee on the following:

(1) Total number, grade level, race, ethnicity, and sex of eligible students receiving scholarship grants.

(2) Total amount of scholarship grant funding awarded.

(3) Number of students previously enrolled in local school administrative units or charter schools in the prior semester by the previously attended local school administrative unit or charter school.

(4) Nonpublic schools in which scholarship grant recipients are enrolled, including numbers of scholarship grant students at each nonpublic school.

(5) Nonpublic schools deemed ineligible to receive scholarships.

(c) The Authority shall report annually, no later than December 1, to the Department of Public Instruction and the Joint Legislative Education Oversight Committee on the following:

(1) Learning gains or losses of students receiving scholarship grants. The report shall include learning gains of participating students on a statewide basis and shall compare, to the extent possible, the learning gains or losses of eligible students by nonpublic school to the statewide learning gains or losses of public school students with similar socioeconomic backgrounds, using aggregate standardized test performance data provided to the Authority by nonpublic schools and by the Department of Public Instruction.

(2) Competitive effects on public school performance on standardized tests as a result of the scholarship grant program. The report shall analyze the impact of the availability of scholarship grants on public school performance on standardized tests by local school administrative units to the extent possible, and shall provide comparisons of the impact by geographic region and between rural and urban local school administrative units.

This report shall be conducted by an independent research organization to be selected by the Authority, which may be a public or private entity or university. The independent research organization shall report to the Authority on the results of its research. The Joint Legislative Education Oversight Committee shall review reports from the Authority and shall make ongoing recommendations to the General Assembly as needed regarding improving administration and accountability for nonpublic schools accepting students receiving scholarship grants. (2013-360, s. 8.29(a).)

Part 3. Home Schools.

§ 115C-563. Definitions.

As used in this Part or Parts 1 and 2 of this Article:

(a) "Home school" means a nonpublic school consisting of the children of not more than two families or households, where the parents or legal guardians or members of either household determine the scope and sequence of academic instruction, provide academic instruction, and determine additional sources of academic instruction.

(b) "Duly authorized representative of the State" means the Director, Division of Nonpublic Education, or his staff. (1987 (Reg. Sess., 1988), c. 891, s. 1; 2013-57, s. 1.)

§ 115C-564. Qualifications and requirements.

A home school shall make the election to operate under the qualifications of either Part 1 or Part 2 of this Article and shall meet the requirements of the Part elected, except that any requirement related to safety and sanitation inspections shall be waived if the school operates in a private residence and except that testing requirements in G.S. 115C-549 and G.S. 115C-557 shall be on an annual basis. The persons providing academic instruction in a home school shall hold at least a high school diploma or its equivalent. (1987 (Reg. Sess., 1988), c. 891, s. 1.)

§ 115C-565. Requirements exclusive.

No school which complies with this Part shall be subject to any other provision of law relating to education except requirements of law respecting immunization.

The Division of Nonpublic Education, Department of Administration, shall provide to home schools information about meningococcal meningitis and influenza and their vaccines. This information may be provided electronically or on the Division's Web page. The information shall include the causes, symptoms, and how meningococcal meningitis and influenza are spread and the places where parents and guardians may obtain additional information and vaccinations for their children.

The Division of Nonpublic Education, Department of Administration, shall also provide to home schools information about cervical cancer, cervical dysplasia, human papillomavirus, and the vaccines available to prevent these diseases. This information may be provided electronically or on the Division's Web page. This information shall include the causes and symptoms of these diseases, how they are transmitted, how they may be prevented by vaccination, including the benefits and possible side effects of vaccination, and the places where parents and guardians may obtain additional information and vaccinations for their children.

The Division of Nonpublic Education, Department of Administration, shall also provide to home schools information on the preventable risks for preterm birth in subsequent pregnancies, including induced abortion, smoking, alcohol consumption, the use of illicit drugs, and inadequate prenatal care. This information may be provided electronically or on the Division's Web page.

The Division of Nonpublic Education, Department of Administration, shall also provide to home schools information on the manner in which a parent may lawfully abandon a newborn baby with a responsible person, in accordance with G.S. 7B-500. This information may be provided electronically or on the Division's Web page. (1987 (Reg. Sess., 1988), c. 891, s. 1; 2004-118, s. 6; 2007-59, s. 5; 2007-126, s. 5; 2013-307, s. 1.4.)

Part 4. Miscellaneous Requirements.

§ 115C-566. Driving eligibility certificates; requirements.

(a) The Secretary of Administration, upon consideration of the advice of the Division of Nonpublic Education in the Department of Administration and representatives of nonpublic schools, shall adopt rules for the procedures a person who is or was enrolled in a home school, in a nonpublic school that is not accredited by the State Board of Education, or in an educational program found by a court, prior to July 1, 1998, to comply with the compulsory attendance law, must follow and the requirements that person must meet to obtain a driving eligibility certificate. The procedures shall provide that the person who is required under G.S. 20-11(n) to sign the driving eligibility certificate must provide the certificate if he or she determines that one of the following requirements is met:

(1)   The person seeking the certificate is eligible for the certificate under G.S. 20-11(n)(1) and is not subject to G.S. 20-11(n1).

(2)   The person seeking the certificate is eligible for the certificate under G.S. 20-11(n)(1) and G.S. 20-11(n1).

The rules shall define exemplary student behavior, define what constitutes the successful completion of a drug or alcohol treatment counseling program, and provide for an appeal to an appropriate educational entity by a person who is denied a driving eligibility certificate. The Division of Nonpublic Education also shall develop policies as to when it is appropriate to notify the Division of Motor Vehicles that a person who is or was enrolled in a home school or in a nonpublic school that is not accredited by the State Board of Education no longer meets the requirements for a driving eligibility certificate.

(b)   The Secretary of Administration shall develop a form for parents, guardians, or emancipated juveniles, as appropriate, to provide their written, irrevocable consent for a school to disclose to the Division of Motor Vehicles that the student no longer meets the conditions for a driving eligibility certificate under G.S. 20-11(n)(1) or G.S. 20-11(n1), if applicable, in the event that this disclosure is necessary to comply with G.S. 20-11 or G.S. 20-13.2. Other than identifying under which statutory subsection the student is no longer eligible, no other details or information concerning the student's school record shall be released pursuant to this consent. This form shall be used for students enrolled in home schools or nonpublic schools.

(c)   In accordance with rules adopted by the Secretary under this section, persons who are required to sign driving eligibility certificates that meet the conditions established in G.S. 20-11 shall obtain the necessary written, irrevocable consent from parents, guardians, or emancipated juveniles, as appropriate, in order to disclose information to the Division of Motor Vehicles and shall notify the Division of Motor Vehicles when a student who holds a driving eligibility certificate no longer meets the conditions under G.S. 20-

11(n)(1) or G.S. 20-11(n1). (1997-507, s. 5; 1998-212, s. 9.21(d); 1999-243, s. 6; 2006-264, s. 59(a).)

§ 115C-566.1. Disclosure of student data and records by nonpublic schools.

A nonpublic school that discloses personally identifiable information in student data or records according to the terms of a written agreement with a State agency, local school administrative unit, community college, or constituent institution of The University of North Carolina, in compliance with the Family Educational Rights and Privacy Act, 20 U.S.C. § 1232g, shall not be liable for a breach of confidentiality, disclosure, use, retention, or destruction of the student data or records if the breach, disclosure, use, retention, or destruction results from actions or omissions of either (i) the State agency, local school administrative unit, community college, or constituent institution of The University of North Carolina to which the data was provided or (ii) persons provided access to the data or records by those entities. (2012-133, s. 2.)

§ 115C-567. Reserved for future codification purposes.

Article 40.

Proprietary Schools.

§§ 115C-568 through 115C-583: Recodified as §§ 115D-87 through 115D-97 by Session Laws 1987, c. 442, s. 2.

Chapter 115D.

Community Colleges.

Article 1.

General Provisions for State Administration.

§ 115D-1. Statement of purpose.

The purposes of this Chapter are to provide for the establishment, organization, and administration of a system of educational institutions throughout the State offering courses of instruction in one or more of the general areas of two-year college parallel, technical, vocational, and adult education programs, to serve as a legislative charter for such institutions, and to authorize the levying of local taxes and the issuing of local bonds for the support thereof. The major purpose of each and every institution operating under the provisions of this Chapter shall be and shall continue to be the offering of vocational and technical education and training, and of basic, high school level, academic education needed in order to profit from vocational and technical education, for students who are high school graduates or who are beyond the compulsory age limit of the public school system and who have left the public schools, provided, juveniles of any age committed to the Division of Juvenile Justice of the Department of Public Safety by a court of competent jurisdiction may, if approved by the director of the youth development center to which they are assigned, take courses offered by institutions of the system if they are otherwise qualified for admission.

The Community Colleges System Office is designated as the primary lead agency for delivering workforce development training, adult literacy training, and adult education programs in the State. (1963, c. 448, s. 23; 1969, c. 562, s. 1; 1979, c. 462, s. 2; 1985, c. 479, s. 68; 1997-443, s. 11A.118(a); 1998-202, s. 4(p); 2000-137, s. 4(s); 2001-95, s. 5; 2005-77, s. 1; 2011-145, s. 19.1(l).)

§ 115D-1.1: Repealed by Session Laws 2011-145, s. 7.1A(f), effective January 1, 2012.

§ 115D-1.2: Repealed by Session Laws 2011-145, s. 7.1A(f), effective January 1, 2012.

§ 115D-1.3. Accreditation of secondary school located in North Carolina shall not be a factor in admissions, loans, scholarships, or other educational policies.

(a)   For purposes of this section, the term "accreditation" shall include certification or any other similar approval process.

(b)   The State Board of Community Colleges shall adopt a policy that prohibits any community college from soliciting or using information regarding the accreditation of a secondary school located in North Carolina that a person attended as a factor affecting admissions, loans, scholarships, or other educational activity at the community college, unless the accreditation was conducted by a State agency. (2011-306, s. 2.)

§ 115D-2. Definitions.

As used in this Chapter:

(1)   The "administrative area" of an institution comprises the county or counties directly responsible for the local financial support and local administration of such institution as provided in this Chapter.

(2)   The term "community college" is defined as an educational institution operating under the provisions of this Chapter and dedicated primarily to the educational needs of the service area which it serves, and may offer

a.   The freshmen and sophomore courses of a college of arts and sciences, authorized by G.S. 115D-4.1;

b.   Organized credit curricula for the training of technicians; curricular courses may carry transfer credit to a senior college or university where the course is comparable in content and quality and is appropriate to a chosen course of study;

c.   Vocational, trade, and technical specialty courses and programs, and

d.   Courses in general adult education.

(3)   The term "institution" refers to any institution established pursuant to this Chapter.

(4)   The term "regional institution" means an institution whose service area as assigned by the State Board of Community Colleges includes three or more counties; provided, however, any institution receiving funds as a regional institution on May 1, 1987, shall continue to receive funds on that basis.

(5)   The term "State Board" refers to the State Board of Community Colleges.

(6)   The "tax-levying authority" of an institution is the board of commissioners of the county or all of the boards of commissioners of the counties, jointly, which constitute the administrative area of the institution.

(7)   Repealed by Session Laws 1987, c. 564, s. 1.

(8) "Vending facilities" has the same meaning as it does in G.S. 111-42(d), but also means any mechanical or electronic device dispensing items or something of value or entertainment or services for a fee, regardless of the method of activation, and regardless of the means of payment, whether by coin, currency, tokens, or other means. (1963, c. 448, s. 23; 1969, c. 562, s. 2; 1973, c. 590, s. 1; 1979, c. 462, s. 2; c. 553; c. 896, s. 1; 1979, 2nd Sess., c. 1130, s. 1; 1983, c. 761, s. 104; 1983 (Reg. Sess., 1984), c. 1034, s. 169; 1987, c. 564, s. 1; 1999-84, s. 1; 2005-103, s. 4; 2006-203, s. 35.)

§ 115D-2.1. State Board of Community Colleges.

(a) The State Board of Community Colleges is established.

(b) The State Board of Community Colleges shall consist of 21 members, as follows:

(1) The Lieutenant Governor or the Lieutenant Governor's designee shall be a member ex officio.
(2) The Treasurer of North Carolina or the Treasurer's designee shall be a member ex officio.

(3) The Governor shall appoint to the State Board four members from the State at large and one member from each of the six Trustee Association Regions defined in G.S. 115D-62. The initial appointments by the Governor shall be made effective July 1, 1980, or as soon as feasible thereafter. In order to establish regularly overlapping terms, the initial appointments by the Governor shall be made so that three expire June 30, 1981, three expire June 30, 1983, and four expire June 30, 1985. Each subsequent regular appointment by the Governor shall be for a term of six years and until a successor is appointed and qualifies. Any vacancy occurring among his appointees before the expiration of term shall be filled by appointment of the Governor; the member so appointed shall meet the same residential qualification, if any, as the member whom he succeeds and shall serve for the remainder of the unexpired term of that member.

(4) The General Assembly shall elect eight members of the State Board from the State at large in the following manner:

a. In 1980, the Senate shall elect three members, one of whom shall serve a term expiring June 30, 1981, one of whom shall serve a term expiring June 30, 1983, and one of whom shall serve a term expiring June 30, 1985. In 1985, the Senate shall elect two members to serve terms expiring June 30, 1991. Each subsequent regular election by the Senate shall be for a term of six years and until a successor is elected and qualifies.

b. In 1980, the House of Representatives shall elect four members, one of whom shall serve a term expiring June 30, 1981, one of whom shall serve a term expiring June 30, 1983, and two of whom shall serve a term expiring June 30, 1985. In 1985, the House of Representatives shall elect two members, to serve terms expiring June 30, 1991. Each subsequent regular election by the House of Representatives shall be for a term of six years and until a successor is elected and qualifies.

c. Repealed by Session Laws 1985, c. 227, s. 5.

d. The initial elections by the two houses of the General Assembly shall be held on or before July 1, 1980.

e. Any vacancy occurring among the members elected by the two houses of the General Assembly before the expiration of term shall be filled when the General Assembly next convenes. The member then elected shall be elected by the same house that elected the member whom he succeeds, and shall serve for the remainder of the unexpired term of that member.

f. At each session of the General Assembly held in an odd-numbered year, the Speaker of the House of Representatives and the President Pro Tempore of the Senate shall assign to either a standing or a special committee of that house the duty of receiving from the members of that house nominations of persons to be considered by that house for election to the State Board. The chairmen of the two committees shall jointly determine a common final date for receiving nominations from members of that house, and a common date for reporting to their respective houses their nominations for the State Board. Each committee shall screen the proposed candidates for nomination as to their qualifications, background, lack of statutory disabilities, and willingness and ability to serve if elected. Each Senator and each Representative may nominate only one candidate. When the nominating process is closed, each committee shall list all candidates and shall separately vote "aye" or "no" on each candidate to determine whether that person shall be listed as a nominee of the committee. The verbal vote of a majority of those members of the committee present and voting shall constitute one nominee of the committee. An individual cannot be a candidate for nomination to more than one place. If a sufficient number of candidates is submitted to each committee, then each committee shall nominate at least two persons for each place to be filled by that chamber, otherwise each committee shall nominate at least one person for each place to be filled by each of the House of Representatives and the Senate. No person may simultaneously be a candidate for election by both houses, and if one is nominated in both houses, he shall determine by which house he shall be nominated and so advise the chairman of both committees. The two houses shall, by joint resolution, fix a common date and time for the election of members of the State Board. At the election session in each house, the committee shall report its list of nominees with the term of office indicated for each nominee. The ballot in the House of Representatives shall also include the names of all other persons nominated by a member of that house who are determined by the committee to be qualified for the offices, with the committee's list of nominees being clearly set out on the ballot. No additional nominations shall be received from the floor. Each house shall then proceed to an election of the State Board. In order to be chosen, a nominee shall receive the votes of a majority of all members present and voting.

When each house has chosen one person for each place to be filled on the State Board, the chairman of the committee shall make a motion for the simultaneous election of those persons by that house to the indicated positions and for the indicated terms. The vote shall then be called electronically. If a majority of those voting shall vote "aye," persons named in the motion shall be declared to have been elected. Each house may adopt rules consistent with this section with respect to the election by that house of members of the State Board.

(5)   The person serving as president of the North Carolina Comprehensive Community College Student Government Association shall be an ex officio member of the State Board. If the president of the Association is unable for any reason to serve as the student member of the State Board, then pursuant to the constitution of the Association, the vice-president of the Association shall serve as the student member of the State Board. Any person serving as the student member of the State Board must be a student in good standing at a North Carolina community college. The student member of the State Board shall have all the rights and privileges of membership, except that the student member shall not have a vote.

(b1) Upon receipt of a referral from the State Ethics Commission in accordance with G.S. 138A-12(k) concerning a member of the State Board of Community Colleges, the principal clerk of the house of the General Assembly receiving the referral shall immediately refer the matter to the appropriate education committee of that house. That committee may recommend to that house a resolution providing for the removal of the Board member. If the committee's proposed resolution is adopted by a majority of the members present and voting of that house, the public servant shall be removed and the seat previously held by that Board member becomes vacant.

(c) No person may be appointed or elected to more than two consecutive terms of six years on the State Board.

(d) No member of the General Assembly, no officer or employee of the State, and no officer or employee of an institution under the jurisdiction of the State Board shall be eligible to serve on the State Board. No spouse of a member of the General Assembly or of an officer or employee of the Community College System or of an institution under the jurisdiction of the State Board shall be eligible to serve on the State Board. No person who within the prior five years has been an employee of the Community Colleges System Office shall be eligible to serve on the State Board.

(e) The Governor shall convene the membership of the State Board on July 1, 1980, or as soon as feasible thereafter. The State Board at that meeting shall elect from its appointed or elected membership a chairman and such other officers as it may deem necessary.

(f) At its first meeting after July 1, 1981, and every two years thereafter, the State Board shall elect from its membership a chairman and such other officers as it may deem necessary.

(g) The State Board of Community Colleges shall meet at stated times established by the State Board, but not less frequently than 10 times a year. The State Board of Community Colleges shall also meet with the State Board of Education and the Board of Governors of The University of North Carolina at least once a year to discuss educational matters of mutual interest and to recommend to the General Assembly such policies as are appropriate to encourage the improvement of public education at every level in this State; these joint meetings shall be hosted by the three Boards according to the schedule set out in G.S. 115C-11(b1). Special meetings of the State Board may be set at any regular meeting or may be called by the chairman. A majority of the qualified members of the State Board shall constitute a quorum for the transaction of business.

(h) Whenever any vacancy shall occur in the appointed membership of the State Board, the chairman shall inform the appropriate appointing authority of the vacancy.

(i) The State Board of Community Colleges may declare vacant the office of an appointed or elected member who does not attend three consecutive scheduled meetings without justifiable excuse. The chairman of the State Board shall notify the appropriate appointing or electing authority of any vacancy. (1979, c. 896, s. 2; 1979, 2nd Sess., c. 1130, s. 5; 1981, c. 47, s. 8; c. 474; 1983, c. 311; c. 479, ss. 1-3; 1985, c. 227, ss. 1-5; c. 428; 1987 (Reg. Sess., 1988), c. 1102, s. 2; 1991, c. 83, s. 1; 1993, c. 69, s. 2; 1995, c. 192, s. 1; c. 470, ss. 3, 4; 1997-456, ss. 18, 19; 1999-61, ss. 1, 2; 1999-84, s. 7; 2006-31, s. 1; 2006-201, s. 2(c); 2007-278, s. 3.)

§ 115D-3. Community Colleges System Office; staff.

The Community Colleges System Office shall be a principal administrative department of State government under the direction of the State Board of Community Colleges, and shall be separate from the free public school system of the State, the State Board of Education, and the Department of Public Instruction. The State Board has authority to adopt and administer all policies, regulations, and standards which it deems necessary for the operation of the System Office.

The State Board shall elect a President of the North Carolina System of Community Colleges who shall serve as chief administrative officer of the Community Colleges System Office. The compensation of this position shall be fixed by the State Board from funds provided by the General Assembly in the Current Operations Appropriations Act.

The President shall be assisted by such professional staff members as may be deemed necessary to carry out the provisions of this Chapter, who shall be elected by the State Board on nomination of the President. The compensation of the staff members elected by the Board shall be fixed by the State Board of Community Colleges, upon recommendation of the President of the Community College System, from funds provided in the Current Operations Appropriations Act. These staff members shall include such officers as may be deemed desirable by the President and State Board. Provision shall be made for persons of high competence and strong professional experience in such areas as academic affairs, public service programs, business and financial affairs, institutional studies and long-range planning, student affairs, research, legal affairs, health affairs and institutional development, and for State and federal programs administered by the State Board. In addition, the President shall be assisted by such other employees as may be needed to carry out the provisions of this Chapter, who shall be subject to the provisions of Chapter 126 of the General Statutes. The staff complement shall be established by the State Board on recommendation of the President to insure that there are persons on the staff who have the professional competence and experience to carry out the duties assigned and to insure that there are persons on the staff who are familiar with the problems and capabilities of all of the principal types of institutions represented in the system. The State Board of Community Colleges shall have all other powers, duties, and responsibilities delegated to the State Board of Education affecting the Community Colleges System Office not otherwise stated in this Chapter. (1963, c. 448, s. 23; 1971, c. 1244, s. 14; 1975, c. 699, s. 5; 1979, c. 462, s. 2; c. 896, s. 3; 1979, 2nd Sess., c. 1130, ss. 1, 2; 1981, c. 859, s. 35.2; 1983, c. 479, s. 4; c. 717, s. 26; 1983 (Reg. Sess., 1984), c. 1034, s. 164; 1985 (Reg. Sess., 1986), c. 955, ss. 19, 20; 1987, c. 564, s. 2; 1993, c. 522, s. 6; 1999-84, s. 8.)

§ 115D-4. Establishment of institutions.

The establishment of all community colleges shall be subject to the approval of the General Assembly upon recommendation of the State Board of Community Colleges. In no case, however, shall favorable recommendation be made by the State Board for the establishment of an institution until it has been demonstrated to the satisfaction of the State Board that a genuine educational need exists within a proposed administrative area, that existing public and private post-high school institutions in the area will not meet the need, that adequate local financial support for the institution will be provided, that public schools in the area will not be affected adversely by the local financial support required for the institution, and that funds sufficient to provide State financial support of the institution are available. (1963, c. 448, s. 23; 1965, c. 1028; 1971, c. 1244, s. 14; 1977, c. 154, s. 1; 1979, c. 462, s. 2; c. 896, s. 4; 1979, 2nd Sess., c. 1130, s. 1; 1983, c. 717, ss. 27-27.2; 1985 (Reg. Sess., 1986), c. 955, s. 21; 1987, c. 564, s. 3; 2006-203, s. 36; 2009-229, s. 1.)

§ 115D-4.1. College transfer program approval; standards for programs.

(a) Repealed by Session Laws 1995, c. 288, s. 1, effective September 1, 1995.

(b) The State Board of Community Colleges may approve the addition of the college transfer program to a community college. If addition of the college transfer program to an institution would require a substantial increase in funds, State Board approval shall be subject to appropriation of funds by the General Assembly for this purpose.

(c) Addition of the college transfer program shall not decrease an institution's ability to provide programs within its basic mission of vocational and technical training and basic academic education.

(d) The State Board of Community Colleges shall develop appropriate criteria and standards to regulate the addition of the college transfer program to institutions.

(e) The State Board of Community Colleges shall develop appropriate criteria and standards to regulate the operation of college transfer programs.

(f) The Board of Governors of The University of North Carolina shall report to each community college and to the State Board of Community Colleges in accordance with G.S. 116-11(10b) on the academic performance of that community college's transfer students. If the State Board of Community Colleges finds that college transfer students from a community college are not consistently performing adequately at a four-year college, the Board shall review the community college's program and determine what steps are necessary to remedy the problem. The Board shall report annually to the General Assembly on the reports it receives and on what steps it is taking to remedy problems that it finds. (1987, c. 564, s. 4; 1995, c. 288, s. 1; 1999-84, s. 2; 2011-145, s. 8.2(a).)

§ 115D-5. Administration of institutions by State Board of Community Colleges; personnel exempt from North Carolina Human Resources Act; extension courses; tuition waiver; in-plant training; contracting, etc., for establishment and operation of extension units of the community college system; use of existing public school facilities.

(a) The State Board of Community Colleges may adopt and execute such policies, regulations and standards concerning the establishment, administration, and operation of institutions as the State Board may deem necessary to insure the quality of educational programs, to promote the systematic meeting of educational needs of the State, and to provide for the equitable distribution of State and federal funds to the several institutions.

The State Board of Community Colleges shall establish standards and scales for salaries and allotments paid from funds administered by the State Board, and all employees of the institutions shall be exempt from the provisions of the North Carolina Human Resources Act. Any and all salary caps set by the State Board for community college presidents shall apply only to the State-paid portion of the salary. Except as otherwise provided by law, the employer contribution rate on the local-paid portion of the salary, to be paid from local funds, shall be set by the State Treasurer based on actuarial recommendations. The State Board shall have authority with respect to individual institutions: to approve sites, capital improvement projects, budgets; to approve the selection of the chief administrative officer; to establish and administer standards for professional personnel, curricula, admissions, and graduation; to regulate the awarding of degrees, diplomas, and certificates; to establish and regulate student tuition and fees within policies for tuition and fees established by the General Assembly; and to establish and regulate financial accounting procedures.

The State Board of Community Colleges shall require all community colleges to meet the faculty credential requirements of the Southern Association of Colleges and Schools for all community college programs.

(a1) Notwithstanding G.S. 66-58(c)(3) or any other provisions of law, the State Board of Community Colleges may adopt rules governing the expenditure of funds derived from bookstore sales by community colleges. These expenditures shall be consistent with the mission and purpose of the Community College System. Profits may be used in the support and enhancement of the bookstores, for student aid or scholarships, for expenditures of direct benefit to students, and for other similar expenditures authorized by the board of trustees, subject to rules adopted by the State Board. These funds shall not be used to supplement salaries of any personnel.

(a2) The State Board of Community Colleges shall comply with the provisions of G.S. 116-11(10a) to plan and implement an exchange of information between the public schools and the institutions of higher education in the State.

(a3)   The State Board of Community Colleges shall adopt the following rules to assist community colleges in their administration of procedures necessary to implement G.S. 20-11 and G.S. 20-13.2:

(1)   To establish the procedures a person who is or was enrolled in a community college must follow and the requirements that person must meet to obtain a driving eligibility certificate.

(2)   To require the person who is required under G.S. 20-11(n) to sign the driving eligibility certificate to provide the certificate if he or she determines that one of the following requirements is met:

a.   The person seeking the certificate is eligible for the certificate under G.S. 20-11(n)(1) and is not subject to G.S. 20-11(n1).

b.   The person seeking the certificate is eligible for the certificate under G.S. 20-11(n)(1) and G.S. 20-11(n1).

(3)   To provide for an appeal through the grievance procedures established by the board of trustees of each community college by a person who is denied a driving eligibility certificate.

(4)   To define exemplary student behavior and to define what constitutes the successful completion of a drug or alcohol treatment counseling program.

The State Board also shall develop policies as to when it is appropriate to notify the Division of Motor Vehicles that a person who is or was enrolled in a community college no longer meets the requirements for a driving eligibility certificate. The State Board also shall adopt guidelines to assist the presidents of community colleges in their designation of representatives to sign driving eligibility certificates.

The State Board shall develop a form for the appropriate individuals to provide their written, irrevocable consent for a community college to disclose to the Division of Motor Vehicles that the student no longer meets the conditions for a driving eligibility certificate under G.S. 20-11(n)(1) or G.S. 20-11(n1), if applicable, in the event that this disclosure is necessary to comply with G.S. 20-11 or G.S. 20-13.2. Other than identifying under which statutory subsection the student is no longer eligible, no other details or information concerning the student's school record shall be released pursuant to this consent.

(b) In order to make instruction as accessible as possible to all citizens, the teaching of curricular courses and of noncurricular extension courses at convenient locations away from institution campuses as well as on campuses is authorized and shall be encouraged. A pro rata portion of the established regular tuition rate charged a full-time student shall be charged a part-time student taking any curriculum course. In lieu of any tuition charge, the State Board of Community Colleges shall establish a uniform registration fee, or a schedule of uniform registration fees, to be charged students enrolling in extension courses for which instruction is financed primarily from State funds. The State Board of Community Colleges may provide by general and uniform regulations for waiver of tuition and registration fees for the following:

(1) Persons not enrolled in elementary or secondary schools taking courses leading to a high school diploma or equivalent certificate.

(2) Courses requested by the following entities that support the organizations' training needs and are on a specialized course list approved by the State Board of Community Colleges:
a. Volunteer fire departments.

b. Municipal, county, or State fire departments.

c. Volunteer EMS or rescue and lifesaving departments.

d. Municipal, county, or State EMS or rescue and lifesaving departments.

d1. Law enforcement, fire, EMS or rescue and lifesaving entities serving a lake authority that was created by a county board of commissioners prior to July 1, 2012.

e. Radio Emergency Associated Communications Teams (REACT) under contract to a county as an emergency response agency.

f. Municipal, county, or State law enforcement agencies.

g. The Division of Adult Correction of the Department of Public Safety for the training of full-time custodial employees and employees of the Division's Section of Community Corrections required to be certified under Chapter 17C of the General Statutes and the rules of the Criminal Justice and Training Standards Commission.

h. The Division of Juvenile Justice of the Department of Public Safety for the training of employees required to be certified under Chapter 17C of the General Statutes and the rules of the Criminal Justice and Training Standards Commission.

i. The Eastern Band of Cherokee Indians law enforcement, fire, EMS or rescue and lifesaving tribal government departments or programs.

(3) Repealed by Session Laws 2011-145, s. 8.12(a), effective July 1, 2011.

(4) Trainees enrolled in courses conducted under the Customized Training Program.

(5) through (9) Repealed by Session Laws 2011-145, s. 8.12(a), effective July 1, 2011.

(10) Elementary and secondary school employees enrolled in courses in first aid or cardiopulmonary resuscitation (CPR).
(11) Repealed by Session Laws 2013-360, s. 10.6, effective July 1, 2013.

(12) All curriculum courses taken by high school students at community colleges, in accordance with G.S. 115D-20(4) and this section.

(13) Human resources development courses for any individual who (i) is unemployed; (ii) has received notification of a pending layoff; (iii) is working and is eligible for the Federal Earned Income Tax Credit (FEITC); or (iv) is working and earning wages at or below two hundred percent (200%) of the federal poverty guidelines.

(14) Repealed by Session Laws 2011-145, s. 8.12(a), effective July 1, 2011.

The State Board of Community Colleges shall not waive tuition and registration fees for other individuals.

(b1) The State Board of Community Colleges shall not waive tuition and registration fees for community college faculty or staff members. Community colleges may, however, use State or local funds to pay tuition and registration fees for one course per semester for full-time community college faculty or staff members employed for a nine-, ten-, eleven-, or twelve-month term. Community colleges may also use State and local funds to pay tuition and registration fees for professional development courses and for other courses consistent with the academic assistance program authorized by the State Human Resources Commission.

(c)   No course of instruction shall be offered by any community college at State expense or partial State expense to any captive or co-opted group of students, as defined by the State Board of Community Colleges, without prior approval of the State Board of Community Colleges. All course offerings approved for State prison inmates must be tied to clearly identified job skills, transition needs, or both. Approval by the State Board of Community Colleges shall be presumed to constitute approval of both the course and the group served by that institution. The State Board of Community Colleges may delegate to the President the power to make an initial approval, with final approval to be made by the State Board of Community Colleges. A course taught without such approval will not yield any full-time equivalent students, as defined by the State Board of Community Colleges.

(c1)   Community colleges shall report full-time equivalent (FTE) student hours for correction education programs on the basis of contact hours rather than student membership hours. No community college shall operate a multi-entry/multi-exit class or program in a prison facility, except for a literacy class or program.

The State Board shall work with the Division of Adult Correction of the Department of Public Safety on offering classes and programs that match the average length of stay of an inmate in a prison facility.

(d)   Recodified as G.S. 115D-5.1(a) by Session Laws 2005-276, s. 8.4(a), effective July 1, 2005.

(e)   Repealed by Session Laws 1999-84, s. 3, effective May 21, 1999.

(f)   A community college may not offer a new program without the approval of the State Board of Community Colleges except that approval shall not be required if the tuition for the program will fully cover the cost of the program. If at any time tuition fails to fully cover the cost of a program that falls under the exception, the program shall be discontinued unless approved by the State Board of Community Colleges. If a proposed new program would serve more than one community college, the State Board of Community Colleges shall perform a feasibility study prior to acting on the proposal.

The State Board of Community Colleges shall report on an annual basis to the Governor, Lieutenant Governor, the Speaker of the House of Representatives, and the Joint Legislative Commission on Governmental Operations, on all new programs it approved during the year. The report shall include the specific reasons for which each program was approved.

(g) Funds appropriated to the Community Colleges System Office as operating expenses for allocation to the institutions comprising the North Carolina Community College System shall not be used to support recreation extension courses. The financing of these courses by any institution shall be on a self-supporting basis, and membership hours produced from these activities shall not be counted when computing full-time equivalent students (FTE) for use in budget-funding formulas at the State level.

(h) Whenever a community college offers real estate continuing education courses pursuant to G.S. 93A-4.1, the courses shall be offered on a self-supporting basis.

(i) Recodified as G.S. 115D-5.1(c) by Session Laws 2005-276, s. 8.4(a), effective July 1, 2005.

(j) The State Board of Community Colleges shall use its Board Reserve Fund for feasibility studies, pilot projects, start-up of new programs, and innovative ideas.

(k) Recodified as G.S. 115D-5.1(b) by Session Laws 2005-276, s. 8.4(a), effective July 1, 2005.

(l) The State Board shall review and approve lease purchase and installment purchase contracts as provided under G.S. 115D-58.15(b). The State Board shall adopt policies and procedures governing the review and approval process.

(m) (Repealed effective July 1, 2015) The State Board of Community Colleges shall maintain an education program auditing function that conducts an annual audit of each community college operating under the provisions of this Chapter. The purpose of the annual audit shall be to ensure that college programs and related fiscal operations comply with State law, State regulations,

State Board policies, and System Office guidance. The State Board of Community Colleges shall require auditors of community college programs to use a statistically valid sample size in performing program audits of community colleges. All education program audit findings shall be forwarded to the college president, local college board of trustees, the State Board of Community Colleges, and the State Auditor.

(n)   The North Carolina Community Colleges System Office shall provide the Department of Revenue with a list of all community colleges, including name, address, and other identifying information requested by the Department of Revenue. The North Carolina Community Colleges System Office shall update this list whenever there is a change.

(o)   All multicampus centers approved by the State Board of Community Colleges shall receive funding under the same formula. The State Board of Community Colleges shall not approve any additional multicampus centers without identified recurring sources of funding.

(p)   The North Carolina Community College System may offer courses, in accordance with the lateral entry program of study established under G.S. 115C-296(c1), to individuals who choose to enter the teaching profession by lateral entry.

(q)   Repealed by Session Laws 2009-451, s. 8.9, effective July 1, 2009.

(r)   The State Board of Community Colleges shall develop curriculum and continuing education standards for courses of instruction in American Sign Language and shall encourage community colleges to offer courses in American Sign Language as a modern foreign language.

(s)   The State Board of Community Colleges may establish, retain and budget fees charged to students taking the General Education Development (GED) test, including fees for retesting. Fees collected for this purpose shall be used only to (i) offset the costs of the GED test, including the cost of scoring the test, (ii) offset the costs of printing GED certificates, and (iii) meet federal and State reporting requirements related to the test.

(t)   The purpose of the first semester of the Gateway to College Program is to address additional support to successfully complete the program. Students may need to take developmental courses necessary for the transition to more challenging courses; therefore, the State Board of Community Colleges shall (i) permit high school students who are enrolled in Gateway to College Programs to enroll in developmental courses based on an assessment of their individual student needs by a high school and community college staff team and (ii) include this coursework in computing the budget FTE for the colleges.

(u) The State Board of Community Colleges shall direct each community college to adopt a policy that authorizes a minimum of two excused absences each academic year for religious observances required by the faith of a student. The policy may require that the student provide written notice of the request for an excused absence a reasonable time prior to the religious observance. The policy shall also provide that the student shall be given the opportunity to make up any tests or other work missed due to an excused absence for a religious observance.

(v) Community colleges may teach technical education, health care, developmental education, and STEM-related courses at any time during the year, including the summer term. Student membership hours from these courses shall be counted when computing full-time equivalent students (FTE) for use in budget funding formulas at the State level. (1963, c. 488, s. 23; 1967, c. 652; 1969, c. 1294; 1973, c. 768; 1975, c. 882; 1977, c. 1065; 1979, c. 462, s. 2; c. 896, ss. 5-7; 1979, 2nd Sess., c. 1130, s. 1; 1981, c. 609; c. 859, s. 35.1; c. 897; c. 1127, s. 43; 1983, c. 717, s. 28; 1983 (Reg. Sess., 1984), c. 1034, ss. 45, 46; 1985, c. 479, s. 67; 1985 (Reg. Sess., 1986), c. 955, s. 22; 1987, c. 282, s. 34; c. 564, ss. 8-10, 12, 33; c. 763, s. 1; 1989, c. 162; 1989 (Reg. Sess., 1990), c. 915, s. 1; c. 1066, s. 91; 1991, c. 689, ss. 44, 48; 1991 (Reg. Sess., 1992), c. 880, s. 4; 1993, c. 170, s. 2; c. 321, ss. 111, 117(e); c. 492, s. 2; 1993 (Reg. Sess., 1994), c. 769, s. 18.4; 1995, c. 288, s. 2; c. 324, s. 16.4; 1996, 2nd Ex. Sess., c. 18, ss. 17.4, 17.7(a); 1997-443, ss. 9.5, 9.6(a), 11A.118(a); 1997-507, s. 4; 1998-111, s. 3; 1998-202, s. 4(q); 1999-84, ss. 3, 9; 1999-243, s. 9; 2000-137, s. 4(t); 2001-111, s. 1; 2001-427, s. 9(b); 2001-487, s. 47(e); 2004-124, s. 8.4; 2005-193, s. 1; 2005-198, s. 3; 2005-247, s. 3; 2005-276, ss. 8.4(a), 8.6; 2005-395, s. 25; 2006-203, s. 37; 2007-154, s. 2(a); 2007-484, ss. 29(a), 35; 2008-107, ss. 8.11, 8.17, 8.18; 2009-208, s. 1; 2009-451, ss. 8.8, 8.9, 8.11(d), (e); 2009-570, s. 42; 2009-575, s. 5; 2010-31, ss. 8.3(d), 8.4(a), 8.11; 2010-112, s. 2; 2010-113, s. 1; 2011-145, ss. 8.2(b), 8.12(a), (b), 8.13, 19.1(h), (k), (l), 31.2; 2011-391, s. 18(a), (b); 2012-83, s. 41; 2012-142, ss. 8.3(a), 8.8; 2013-360, ss. 10.4(b), 10.6, 10.12, 10.15(a); 2013-382, s. 9.1(c).)

§ 115D-5.1. Workforce Development Programs.

(a) Community colleges shall assist in the preemployment and in-service training of employees in industry, business, agriculture, health occupation and governmental agencies. Such training shall include instruction on worker safety and health standards and practices applicable to the field of employment. The State Board of Community Colleges shall make appropriate regulations including the establishment of maximum hours of instruction which may be offered at State expense in each in-plant training program. No instructor or other employee of a community college shall engage in the normal management, supervisory and operational functions of the establishment in which the instruction is offered during the hours in which the instructor or other employee is employed for instructional or educational purposes.

(b) through (d) Repealed by Session Laws 2008-107, s. 8.7(a), effective July 1, 2008.

(e) There is created within the North Carolina Community College System the Customized Training Program. The Customized Training Program shall offer programs and training services to assist new and existing business and industry to remain productive, profitable, and within the State. Before a business or industry qualifies to receive assistance under the Customized Training Program, the President of the North Carolina Community College System shall determine that:

(1) The business is making an appreciable capital investment;

(2) The business is deploying new technology;

(2a) The business or individual is creating jobs, expanding an existing workforce, or enhancing the productivity and profitability of the operations within the State; and

(3) The skills of the workers will be enhanced by the assistance.

(f) The State Board shall report on an annual basis to the Joint Legislative Education Oversight Committee on:

(1) The total amount of funds received by a company under the Customized Training Program;

(1a) The types of services sought by the company, whether for new, expanding, or existing industry.

(2) The amount of funds per trainee received by that company;

(3) The amount of funds received per trainee by the community college delivering the training;

(4) The number of trainees trained by the company and community college; and

(5) The number of years that company has been funded.

(f1) Notwithstanding any other provision of law, the State Board of Community Colleges may adopt guidelines that allow the Customized Training Program to use funds appropriated for that program to support training projects for the various branches of the Armed Forces of the United States.

(f2) Funds available to the Customized Training Program shall not revert at the end of a fiscal year but shall remain available until expended. Up to ten percent (10%) of the college-delivered training expenditures and up to five percent (5%) of the contractor-delivered training expenditures for the prior fiscal year for Customized Training may be allotted to each college for capacity building at that college.

(f3) Of the funds appropriated in a fiscal year for the Customized Training Programs, the State Board of Community Colleges may approve the use of up to eight percent (8%) for the training and support of regional community college personnel to deliver Customized Training Program services to business and industry.

(g) The State Board shall adopt guidelines to implement this section. At least 20 days before the effective date of any criteria or nontechnical amendments to guidelines, the State Board must publish the proposed guidelines on the Community Colleges System Office's web site and provide notice to persons who have requested notice of proposed guidelines. In addition, the State Board must accept oral and written comments on the proposed guidelines during the 15 business days beginning on the first day that the State Board has completed these notifications. For the purpose of this subsection, a technical amendment is either of the following:

(1) An amendment that corrects a spelling or grammatical error.

(2) An amendment that makes a clarification based on public comment and could have been anticipated by the public notice that immediately preceded the public comment. (2005-276, s. 8.4(a), (b); 2005-445, s. 3; 2008-107, s. 8.7(a); 2009-451, s. 8.14(c); 2009-523, s. 2(b); 2009-570, s. 41; 2010-96, s. 14; 2011-183, s. 79.)

§ 115D-6. Withdrawal of State support.

The State Board of Community Colleges may withdraw or withhold State financial and administrative support of any institutions subject to the provisions of this Chapter in the event that:

(1) The required local financial support of an institution is not provided;

(2) Sufficient State funds are not available;

(3) The officials of an institution refuse or are unable to maintain prescribed standards of administration or instruction; or

(4) Local educational needs for such an institution cease to exist. (1963, c. 448, s. 23; 1979, c. 462, s. 2; c. 896, s. 8; 1979, 2nd Sess., c. 1130, s. 1.)

§ 115D-7. Establishment of private, nonprofit corporations.

The State Board of Community Colleges shall encourage the establishment of private, nonprofit corporations to support the community college system. The President of the Community Colleges System with the approval of the State Board of Community Colleges, may assign employees to assist with the establishment and operation of such nonprofit corporation and may make available to the corporation office space, equipment, supplies and other related resources; provided, the sole purpose of the corporation is to support the community college system.

The board of directors of each private, nonprofit corporation shall secure and pay for the services of the State Auditor's Office or employ a certified public accountant to conduct an audit of the financial accounts of the corporation. The board of directors shall transmit to the State Board of Community Colleges a copy of the annual financial audit report of the private nonprofit corporation. (1987, c. 383, s. 1; 1999-84, s. 10.)

§ 115D-8. Repealed by Session Laws 1999-84, s. 4.

§ 115D-9. Powers of State Board regarding certain fee negotiations, contracts, and capital improvements.

(a) The expenditures of any State funds for any capital improvements of existing institutions shall be subject to the prior approval of the State Board of Community Colleges and the Governor. The expenditure of State funds at any institution herein authorized to be approved by the State Board under G.S. 115D-4 shall be subject to the terms of the State Budget Act unless specifically otherwise provided in this Chapter.
(b) Notwithstanding G.S. 143-341(3), the State Board of Community Colleges may, with respect to design, construction, repair, or renovation of buildings, utilities, and other State-funded property developments of the North Carolina Community College System requiring the estimated expenditure of public money of four million dollars ($4,000,000) or less:

(1) Conduct the fee negotiations for all design contracts and supervise the letting of all construction and design contracts.

(2) Develop procedures governing the responsibilities of the North Carolina Community College System and its community colleges to perform the duties of the Department of Administration and the Director or Office of State Construction under G.S. 133-1.1(d) and G.S. 143-341(3).

(3) Use existing plans and specifications for construction projects, where feasible. Prior to designing a project, the State Board shall consult with the Department of Administration on the availability of existing plans and specifications and the feasibility of using them for a project.

(c) The State Board may delegate its authority under subsection (b) of this section to a community college if the community college is qualified under guidelines adopted by the State Board and approved by the State Building Commission and the Director of the Budget.

(d) The North Carolina Community College System shall use the standard contracts for design and construction currently in use for State capital improvement projects by the Office of State Construction of the Department of Administration.

(e) A contract may not be divided for the purpose of evading the monetary limit under this section.

(f) Notwithstanding any other provision of this Chapter, the Department of Administration shall not be the awarding authority for contracts awarded under subsections (b) or (c) of this section.

(g) The State Board shall annually report to the State Building Commission the following:

(1) A list of projects governed by this section.

(2) The estimated cost of each project along with the actual cost.

(3) The name of each person awarded a contract under this section.

(4) Whether the person or business awarded a contract under this section meets the definition of "minority business" or "minority person" as defined in G.S. 143-128.2(g).

(h) The provisions of G.S. 143-341(3) shall not apply to a capital improvement project funded with non-State funds if the State Board of Community Colleges determines that the college has the expertise necessary to manage the project unless the assistance of the Office of State Construction is requested. (2009-229, s. 2; 2011-145, s. 8.19(a).)

§ 115D-10. Reserved for future codification purposes.

§ 115D-11. Reserved for future codification purposes.

Article 2.

Local Administration.

§ 115D-12. Each institution to have board of trustees; selection of trustees.

(a) Each community college established or operated pursuant to this Chapter shall be governed by a board of trustees consisting of 13 members, or of additional members if selected according to the special procedure prescribed by the third paragraph of this subsection, who shall be selected by the following agencies. No member of the General Assembly may be appointed to a local board of trustees for a community college.

Group One - four trustees, elected by the board of education of the public school administrative unit located in the administrative area of the institution. If there are two or more public school administrative units, whether city or county units, or both, located within the administrative area, the trustees shall be elected jointly by all of the boards of education of those units, each board having one vote in the election of each trustee, except as provided in G.S. 115D-59. No board of education shall elect a member of the board of education or any person employed by the board of education to serve as a trustee, however, any such person currently serving on a board of trustees shall be permitted to fulfill the unexpired portion of the trustee's current term.

Group Two - four trustees, elected by the board of commissioners of the county in which the institution is located. Provided, however, if the administrative area of the institution is composed of two or more counties, the trustees shall be elected jointly by the boards of commissioners of all those counties, each board having one vote in the election of each trustee. Provided, also, the county commissioners of the county in which the community college has established a satellite campus may elect an additional two members if the board of trustees of the community college agrees. No more than one trustee from Group Two may be a member of a board of county commissioners. Should the boards of education or the boards of commissioners involved be unable to agree on one or more trustees the senior resident superior court judge in the superior court district or set of districts as defined in G.S. 7A-41.1 where the institution is located shall fill the position or positions by appointment.

Group Three - four trustees, appointed by the Governor.

Group Four - the president of the student government or the chairman of the executive board of the student body of each community college established pursuant to this Chapter shall be an ex officio nonvoting member of the board of trustees of each said institution.

(b)   All trustees shall be residents of the administrative area of the institution for which they are selected or of counties contiguous thereto with the exception of members provided for in subsection (a) of this section, Group Four.

(b1)   No person who has been employed full time by the community college within the prior 5 years and no spouse or child of a person currently employed full time by the community college shall serve on the board of trustees of that college.

(c)   Vacancies occurring in any group for whatever reason shall be filled for the remainder of the unexpired term by the agency or agencies authorized to select trustees of that group and in the manner in which regular selections are made. Should the selection of a trustee not be made by the agency or agencies having the authority to do so within 60 days after the date on which a vacancy occurs, whether by creation or expiration of a term or for any other reason, the Governor shall fill the vacancy by appointment for the remainder of the unexpired term. (1963, c. 448, s. 23; 1977, c. 823, s. 104; 1979, c. 462, s. 2; 1985, c. 757, s. 147; 1987, c. 564, ss. 10, 12; 1987 (Reg. Sess., 1988), c. 1037, s. 111; 1991, c. 283, s. 1; 1995, c. 470, s. 1; 2009-549, s. 19; 2013-410, s. 9.)

§ 115D-13. Terms of office of trustees.

(a)   The regular terms of trustees appointed in 1981 and trustees appointed in 1987 shall be extended for one year. The term of one or more trustees, as appropriate, elected pursuant to G.S. 115D-12 may be extended for one year so that these terms will be staggered, unless they are already staggered.

(b)   Except for the one year extensions of terms set forth in subsection (a) of this section, and for the ex officio member, as the terms of trustees currently in office expire, their successors shall be appointed for four-year terms.

All terms shall commence on July 1 of the year. (1963, c. 448, s. 23; 1977, c. 823, s. 5; 1979, c. 462, s. 2; 1985, c. 58; 1989, c. 521, s. 1.)

§ 115D-14. Board of trustees a body corporate; corporate name and powers; title to property.

The board of trustees of each institution shall be a body corporate with powers to enable it to acquire, hold, and transfer real and personal property, to enter into contracts, to institute and defend legal actions and suits, and to exercise such other rights and privileges as may be necessary for the management and administration of the institution in accordance with the provisions and purposes of this Chapter. The official title of each board shall be "The Trustees of _____" (filling in the name of the institution) and such title shall be the official corporate name of the institution.

The several boards of trustees shall hold title to all real and personal property donated to their respective institutions by private persons or purchased with funds provided by the tax-levying authorities of their respective institutions. Title to equipment furnished by the State shall remain in the State Board of Community Colleges. In the event that an institution shall cease to operate, title to all real and personal property donated to the institution or purchased with funds provided by the tax-levying authorities, except as provided for in G.S. 115D-14, shall vest in the county in which the institution is located, unless the terms of the deed of gift in the case of donated property provides otherwise, or unless in the case of two or more counties forming a joint institution the contract provided for in G.S. 115D-71 provides otherwise. (1963, c. 448, s. 23; 1979, c. 462, s. 2; c. 896, s. 13; 1979, 2nd Sess., c. 1130, s. 1.)

§ 115D-15. Sale, exchange or lease of property; use of proceeds from donated property.

(a)   The board of trustees of any institution organized under this Chapter may, with the prior approval of the North Carolina Community Colleges System Office, convey a right-of-way or easement for highway construction or for utility installations or modifications. When in the opinion of the board of trustees the use of any other real property owned or held by the board of trustees is unnecessary or undesirable for the purposes of the institution, the board of trustees, subject to prior approval of the State Board of Community Colleges, may sell, exchange, or lease the property. The board of trustees may dispose of any personal property owned or held by the board of trustees without approval of the State Board of Community Colleges. Personal property titled to the State Board of Community Colleges consistent with G.S. 115D-14 and G.S. 115D-58.5 may be transferred to another community college at no cost and without the approval of the Department of Administration, Division of Surplus Property.

Article 12 of Chapter 160A of the General Statutes shall apply to the disposal or sale of any real or personal property under this subsection. Personal property also may be disposed of under procedures adopted by the North Carolina Department of Administration. The proceeds of any sale or lease shall be used for capital outlay purposes, except as provided in subsection (b) of this section.

(b) Subject to rules adopted by the State Board, if real or personal property is donated to a community college to support a specific educational purpose, the board of trustees may use the proceeds from the sale or lease of the property according to the terms of the donation. The board of trustees shall use the procedures authorized under Article 12 of Chapter 160A of the General Statutes when selling or leasing property under this subsection. (1969, c. 338; 1979, c. 462, s. 2; c. 896, s. 13; 1979, 2nd Sess., c. 1130, s. 1; 1998-72, s. 1; 1998-217, s. 39; 2001-82, s. 1; 2011-145, s. 8.9.)

§ 115D-15.1. Disposition, acquisition, and construction of property by community college.

(a) Disposition. - Notwithstanding the provisions of G.S. 115D-14, 115D-15, and 160A-274, the board of trustees of a community college may, in connection with additions, improvements, renovations, or repairs to all or part of its property, lease, sell, or otherwise dispose of any of its property to the county in which the property is located for any price and on any terms negotiated between the board of trustees of the community college and the board of county commissioners.

(b) Transfer. - An agreement under subsection (a) of this section shall require the county to transfer the property back to the board of trustees of the community college when any financing agreement entered into by the county to finance the additions, improvements, renovations, and repairs has been satisfied.

Notwithstanding the transfer of property to the county, the provisions of subsection (d) of this section, G.S. 143-129, and G.S. 143-341 apply to the capital improvement project.

(c) Acquisition and Construction. - Notwithstanding the provisions of G.S. 115D-14 and G.S. 115D-20(3), the board of trustees of a community college may acquire, by any lawful method, any interest in real or personal property in the county in which the community college is located or in its service delivery area for use by the board of trustees. The board of trustees may contract for the construction, equipping, expansion, improvement, renovation, repair, or otherwise making available for use by the board of trustees of the community college of all or part of the property upon any terms negotiated between the board of trustees of the community college and the board of county commissioners.

(d) Approval. - The actions of a board of trustees of a community college taken pursuant to this section are subject to the approval of the State Board of Community Colleges.

(e) Contract Responsibility. - A county's obligations under a financing contract entered into by the county to finance improvements to real or personal property pursuant to this section shall be the responsibility of the county and not the responsibility of the board of trustees of the community college. (1999-115, s. 2; 2007-484, s. 29(b).)

§ 115D-16. Elective officials serving as trustees.

The office of trustee of any institution established or operated pursuant to this Chapter is hereby declared to be an office which may be held by the holder of any elective office, as defined in G.S. 128-1.1(d), in addition to and concurrently with those offices permitted by G.S. 128-1.1. Appointments made on or before July 1, 1985, by boards of county commissioners or local boards of education of their own members as trustees are hereby validated, ratified, and confirmed. (1979, c. 462, s. 2; 1985, c. 773.)

§ 115D-17. Compensation of trustees.

Trustees shall receive no compensation for their services but shall receive reimbursement, according to regulations adopted by the State Board of Community Colleges, for cost of travel, meals, and lodging while performing their official duties. The reimbursement of the trustees from State funds shall not exceed the amounts permitted in G.S. 138-5. (1963, c. 448, s. 23; 1979, c. 462, s. 2; c. 896, s. 13; 1979, 2nd Sess., c. 1130, s. 1.)

§ 115D-18. Organization of boards; meetings.

At the first meeting after its selection, each board of trustees shall elect from its membership a chairman, who shall preside at all board meetings, and a vice-chairman, who shall preside in the absence of the chairman. The trustees shall also elect a secretary, who may be a trustee, to keep the minutes of all board meetings. All three officers of the board shall be elected for a period of one year but shall be eligible for reelection by the board.

Each board of trustees shall meet as often as may be necessary for the conduct of the business of the institution but shall meet at least once every three months. Meetings may be called by the chairman of the board, a majority of the trustees, or the chief administrative officer of the institution. (1963, c. 448, s. 23; 1979, c. 462, s. 2; 2007-197, s. 1.)

§ 115D-19. Removal of trustees.

(a)   Should the State Board of Community Colleges have sufficient evidence that any member of the board of trustees of an institution is not capable of discharging, or is not discharging, the duties of his office as required by law or lawful regulation, or is guilty of immoral or disreputable conduct, the State Board shall notify the chairman of such board of trustees, unless the chairman is the offending member, in which case the other members of the board shall be notified. Upon receipt of such notice there shall be a meeting of the board of trustees for the purpose of investigating the charges, at that meeting a representative of the State Board of Community Colleges may appear to present evidence of the charges. The allegedly offending member shall be given proper and adequate notice of the meeting and the findings of the other members of the board shall be recorded, along with the action taken, in the minutes of the board of trustees. If the charges are, by an affirmative vote of two-thirds of the members of the board, found to be true, the board of trustees shall declare the office of the offending member to be vacant.

Nothing in this section shall be construed to limit the authority of a board of trustees to hold a hearing as provided herein upon evidence known or presented to it.

(b)   A board of trustees may declare vacant the office of a member who does not attend three consecutive, scheduled meetings without justifiable excuse. A board of trustees may also declare vacant the office of a member who, without justifiable excuse, does not participate within six months of appointment in a trustee orientation and education session sponsored by the North Carolina Association of Community College Trustees. The board of trustees shall notify the appropriate appointing authority of any vacancy. (1963, c. 448, s. 23; 1979, c. 462, s. 2; c. 896, s. 13; 1979, 2nd Sess., c. 1130, s. 1; 1989, c. 521, s. 2; 1995, c. 470, s. 2.)

§ 115D-20. Powers and duties of trustees.

The trustees of each institution shall constitute the local administrative board of such institution, with such powers and duties as are provided in this Chapter and as are delegated to it by the State Board of Community Colleges. The powers and duties of trustees shall include the following:

(1)   To elect a president or chief administrative officer of the institution for such term and under such conditions as the trustees may fix, such election to be subject to the approval of the State Board of Community Colleges.

(2)   To elect or employ all other personnel of the institution upon nomination by the president or chief administrative officer, subject to standards established by the State Board of Community Colleges. Trustees may delegate the authority of employing such other personnel to its president or chief administrative officer.

(3)   To purchase any land, easement, or right-of-way which shall be necessary for the proper operation of the institution, upon approval of the State Board of Community Colleges, and if necessary, to acquire land by condemnation in the same manner and under the same procedures as provided in General Statutes Chapter 40A. For the purpose of condemnation, the determination by the trustees as to the location and amount of land to be taken and the necessity therefor shall be conclusive.

(4)   To apply the standards and requirements for admission and graduation of students and other standards established by the State Board of Community Colleges. Notwithstanding any law or administrative rule to the contrary, local community colleges are permitted to offer the following programs:

a. Subject to the approval of the State Board of Community Colleges, local community colleges may collaborate with local school administrative units to offer courses through the following programs:

1. Cooperative innovative high school programs as provided by Part 9 of Article 16 of Chapter 115C of the General Statutes.

2. Academic transition pathways for qualified junior and senior high school students that lead to a career technical education certificate or diploma and academic transition pathways for qualified freshmen and sophomore high school students that lead to a career technical education certificate or diploma in industrial and engineering technologies.

3. College transfer certificates requiring the successful completion of thirty semester credit hours of transfer courses, including English and mathematics, for qualified junior and senior high school students.

b. During the summer quarter, persons less than 16 years old may be permitted to take noncredit courses on a self-supporting basis, subject to rules of the State Board of Community Colleges.

c. High school students may be permitted to take noncredit courses in safe driving on a self-supporting basis during the academic year or the summer.

d. High school students 16 years and older may be permitted to take noncredit courses, except adult basic skills, subject to rules promulgated by the State Board of Community Colleges.

(5) To receive and accept donations, gifts, devises, and the like from private donors and to apply them or invest any of them and apply the proceeds for purposes and upon the terms which the donor may prescribe and which are consistent with the provisions of this Chapter and the regulations of the State Board of Community Colleges.

(6) To provide all or part of the instructional services for the institution by contracting with other public or private organizations or institutions in accordance with regulations and standards adopted by the State Board of Community Colleges.

(7) To perform such other acts and do such other things as may be necessary or proper for the exercise of the foregoing specific powers, including

the adoption and enforcement of all reasonable rules, regulations, and bylaws for the government and operation of the institution under this Chapter and for the discipline of students.

(8) If a board of trustees of an institution provides access to its buildings and campus and the student information directory to persons or groups which make students aware of occupational or educational options, the board of trustees shall provide access on the same basis to official recruiting representatives of the military forces of the State and of the United States for the purpose of informing students of educational and career opportunities available in the military.

(9) To encourage the establishment of private, nonprofit corporations to support the institution. The president, with approval of the board of trustees, may assign employees to assist with the establishment and operation of such corporation and may make available to the corporation office space, equipment, supplies and other related resources; provided, the sole purpose of the corporation is to support the institution. The board of directors of each private, nonprofit corporation shall secure and pay for the services of the State Auditor's Office or employ a certified public accountant to conduct an annual audit of the financial accounts of the corporation. The board of directors shall transmit to the board of trustees a copy of the annual financial audit report of the private nonprofit corporation.

(10) To enter into guaranteed energy savings contracts pursuant to Part 2 of Article 3B of Chapter 143 of the General Statutes.

(10a) To enter into loan agreements under the Energy Improvement Loan Program pursuant to Part 3 of Article 36 of Chapter 143 of the General Statutes.

(11) To enter into lease purchase and installment purchase contracts for equipment and real property under G.S. 115D-58.15.

(12) Notwithstanding the provisions of this Chapter, a community college may permit the use of its personnel or facilities, in support of or by a private business enterprise located on a community college campus or in the service area of a community college for the specific purposes set out in G.S. 66-58(c)(3a) and G.S. 66-58(c)(3d). The board of trustees of a community college must specifically approve any use of facilities or personnel under this subdivision. The State Board shall adopt rules to implement this subdivision, G.S. 66-58(c)(3a), and G.S. 66-58(c)(3d).

(13) To enter into a public/private partnership in which all of the following conditions are met:

a. The agreement is approved in advance by the State Board of Community Colleges.

b. The board of trustees agrees to lease community college land to a private entity on condition that the entity construct a facility on the leased land.

c. The facility will be jointly owned and used by the private entity and the community college.

d. The board of trustees is not authorized to lease the facility as lessee under a long-term lease or capital lease from the private entity as lessor.

e. The board of trustees is not authorized to finance its portion of the facility by entering into an installment contract or other financing contract with the private entity.

f. State bond funds shall not be used to pay for construction of that part of the facility to be owned and used by the private entity.

g. The provisions of G.S. 143-341(3)a. apply to the construction of a facility under this subsection.

(14) To comply with the design and construction requirements regarding energy efficiency and water use in the Sustainable Energy-Efficient Buildings Program under Article 8C of Chapter 143 of the General Statutes. (1963, c. 448, s. 23; 1979, c. 462, s. 2; c. 896, s. 13; 1979, 2nd Sess., c. 1130, s. 1; 1981, c. 901, s. 2; 1983, c. 378, s. 1; c. 596, s. 1; 1985, c. 191; 1987, c. 383, s. 2; 1993 (Reg. Sess., 1994), c. 775, s. 7; 1998-111, s. 1; 2001-368, s. 2; 2003-286, s. 1; 2005-247, s. 2; 2006-259, s. 21; 2007-476, s. 1; 2008-203, s. 2; 2009-119, s. 1; 2011-145, s. 7.1A(h); 2011-284, s. 82; 2011-391, s. 13(c); 2011-419, s. 2; 2013-310, s. 2; 2013-360, s. 10.9(a).)

§ 115D-20.1. Policy prohibiting tobacco use in community college buildings, grounds, and at community college-sponsored events.

(a) As used in this section:

(1) "Tobacco product" includes cigarettes, cigars, blunts, bidis, pipes, chewing tobacco, snus, snuff, and any other items containing or reasonably resembling tobacco or tobacco products.

(2) "Tobacco use" includes smoking, chewing, dipping, or any other use of tobacco products.

(b) Local community college boards of trustees may adopt, implement, and enforce a written policy prohibiting at all times the use of any tobacco product by any person in community college buildings, in community college facilities, on community college campuses, in vehicles owned, leased, or operated by the local community college, and in or on any other community college property owned, leased, or operated by the local community college. The policy may also prohibit the use of all tobacco products by persons attending a community college-sponsored event.

(c) The policy adopted by a local community college board of trustees may include the following elements:

(1) Adequate notice of the policy to students, parents, the public, and school personnel.

(2) Posting of signs prohibiting at all times the use of tobacco products by any person in and on community college property.

(3) Requirements that community college personnel develop plans for successful implementation of and compliance with the policy.

(4) Permission for tobacco products to be included in instructional or research activities in community college buildings if the activity is conducted or supervised by the faculty member overseeing the instruction or research and the activity does not include smoking, chewing, or otherwise ingesting the tobacco product.

(d) Nothing in G.S. 130A-498, G.S. 143-595 through G.S. 143-601, or any other section prohibits a local community college board of trustees from adopting and enforcing a more restrictive policy on the use of tobacco in community college buildings, in community college facilities, on community college campuses, or at community college-related or community college-sponsored events, and in or on other community college property.

(e) The North Carolina Tobacco Prevention and Control Branch and the Health and Wellness Trust Fund Commission shall work with local community college boards of trustees to provide assistance with the development and implementation of the policy including providing information regarding smoking cessation and prevention resources. (2008-95, ss. 2, 3.)

§ 115D-21. Traffic regulations; fines and penalties.

(a) All of the provisions of Chapter 20 of the General Statutes relating to the use of highways of the State of North Carolina and the operation of motor vehicles thereon shall apply to the streets, roads, alleys and driveways on the campuses of all institutions in the North Carolina Community College System. Any person violating any of the provisions of Chapter 20 of the General Statutes in or on the streets, roads, alleys and driveways on the campuses of institutions in the North Carolina Community College System shall, upon conviction thereof, be punished as prescribed in this section and as provided by Chapter 20 of the General Statutes relating to motor vehicles. Nothing contained in this section shall be construed as in any way interfering with the ownership and control of the streets, roads, alleys and driveways on the campuses of institutions in the system as is now vested by law in the trustees of each individual institution in the North Carolina Community College System.

(b) The trustees are authorized and empowered to make additional rules and regulations and to adopt additional ordinances with respect to the use of the streets, roads, alleys and driveways and to establish parking areas on or off the campuses not inconsistent with the provisions of Chapter 20 of the General Statutes of North Carolina. Upon investigation, the trustees may determine and fix speed limits on streets, roads, alleys, and driveways subject to such rules, regulations, and ordinances, lower than those provided in G.S. 20-141. The trustees may make reasonable provisions for the towing or removal of unattended vehicles found to be in violation of rules, regulations and ordinances. All rules, regulations and ordinances adopted pursuant to the authority of this section shall be recorded in the proceedings of the trustees; shall be printed; and copies of such rules, regulations and ordinances shall be filed in the office of the Secretary of State of North Carolina. Violation of any such rules, regulations, or ordinances, is an infraction punishable by a penalty of not more than one hundred dollars ($100.00).

Regardless of whether an institution does its own removal and disposal of motor vehicles or contracts with another person to do so, the institution shall provide a hearing procedure for the owner. For purposes of this subsection, the definitions in G.S. 20-219.9 apply:

(1) If the institution operates in such a way that the person who tows the vehicle is responsible for collecting towing fees, all provisions of Article 7A, Chapter 20, apply.

(2) If the institution operates in such a way that it is responsible for collecting towing fees, it shall:

a. Provide by contract or ordinance for a schedule of reasonable towing fees,

b. Provide a procedure for a prompt fair hearing to contest the towing,

c. Provide for an appeal to district court from that hearing,

d. Authorize release of the vehicle at any time after towing by the posting of a bond or paying of the fees due, and

e. If the institution chooses to enforce its authority by sale of the vehicle, provide a sale procedure similar to that provided in G.S. 44A-4, 44A-5, and 44A-6, except that no hearing in addition to the probable cause hearing is required. If no one purchases the vehicle at the sale and if the value of the vehicle is less than the amount of the lien, the institution may destroy it.

(c) The trustees may by rules, regulations, or ordinances provide for a system of registration of all motor vehicles where the owner or operator does park on the campus or keeps said vehicle on the campus. The trustees shall cause to be posted at appropriate places on campus notice to the public of applicable parking and traffic rules, regulations, and ordinances governing the campus over which it has jurisdiction. The trustees may by rules, regulations, or ordinances establish or cause to have established a system of citations that may be issued to owners or operators of motor vehicles who violate established rules, regulations, or ordinances. The trustees shall provide for the administration of said system of citations; establish or cause to be established a system of fines to be levied for the violation of established rules, regulations and ordinances; and enforce or cause to be enforced the collection of said fines. The fine for each offense shall not exceed twenty-five dollars ($25.00). The trustees shall be empowered to exercise the right to prohibit repeated violators of such rules, regulations, or ordinances from parking on the campus.

(d) The clear proceeds of all civil penalties collected pursuant to this section shall be remitted to the Civil Penalty and Forfeiture Fund in accordance with G.S. 115C-457.2. (1971, c. 795, ss. 1-3; 1979, c. 462, s. 2; 1983, c. 420, s. 4; 1985, c. 764, s. 38; 2012-142, s. 8.9.)

§ 115D-21.1. Campus law enforcement agencies.

(a) The board of trustees of any community college may establish a campus law enforcement agency and employ campus police officers. These officers shall meet the requirements of Chapter 17C of the General Statutes, shall take the oath of office prescribed by Article VI, Section 7 of the Constitution, and shall have all the powers of law enforcement officers generally. The territorial jurisdiction of a campus police officer shall include all property owned or leased to the community college employing the officer and that portion of any public road or highway passing through the property and immediately adjoining it, wherever located.

(b) The board of trustees of any community college that establishes a campus law enforcement agency under subsection (a) of this section may enter into joint agreements with the governing board of any municipality to extend the law enforcement authority of campus police officers into the municipality's jurisdiction and to determine the circumstances under which this extension of authority may be granted.

(c) The board of trustees of any community college that establishes a campus law enforcement agency under subsection (a) of this section may enter into joint agreements with the governing board of any county, with the consent of the sheriff, to extend the law enforcement authority of campus police officers into the county's jurisdiction and to determine the circumstances under which this extension of authority may be granted. (1999-68, s. 1.)

§ 115D-22. State Retirement System for Teachers and State Employees; social security.

Solely for the purpose of applying the provisions of Chapter 135 of the General Statutes of North Carolina, "Retirement System for Teachers and State Employees, Social Security," the institutions of this Chapter are included within the definition of the term "public school," and the institutional employees are included within the definition of the term "teacher," as these terms are defined in G.S. 135-1. (1963, c. 448, s. 23; 1979, c. 462, s. 2.)

§ 115D-23. Workers' Compensation Act applicable to institutional employees.

The provisions of Chapter 97 of the General Statutes of North Carolina, the Workers' Compensation Act, shall apply to all institutional employees. The State Board of Community Colleges shall make the necessary arrangements to carry out those provisions of Chapter 97 which are applicable to employees whose wages are paid in whole or in part from State funds. The State shall be liable for compensation, based upon the average weekly wage as defined in the act, of an employee regardless of the portion of his wage paid from other than State funds.

The board of trustees of each institution shall be liable for workers' compensation for employees whose salaries or wages are paid by the board entirely from local public or special funds. Each board of trustees is authorized to purchase insurance to cover workers' compensation liability and to include the cost of insurance in the annual budget of the institution.

The provisions of this section shall not apply to any person, firm or corporation making voluntary contributions to institutions for any purpose, and such a person, firm, or corporation shall not be liable for the payment of any sum of money under the provisions of this section. (1963, c. 448, s. 23; 1979, c. 462, s. 2; c. 714, s. 2; c. 896, s. 13; 1979, 2nd Sess., c. 1130, s. 1.)

§ 115D-24. Waiver of governmental immunity from liability for negligence of agents and employees of institutions; liability insurance.

The board of trustees of any institution, by obtaining liability insurance as provided in G.S. 115D-53, is authorized to waive its governmental immunity from liability for the death or injury of person or for property damage caused by the negligence or tort of any agent or employee of the board of trustees when the agent or employee is acting within the scope of his authority or the course of his employment. All automobiles, buses, trucks, or other motor vehicles intended primarily for use on the public roads and highways which are the property of a board of trustees shall be insured at all times with liability insurance as provided in G.S. 115D-53. Governmental immunity shall be deemed to have been waived by the act of obtaining liability insurance, but only to the extent that the board is indemnified for the negligence or torts of its agents and employees and only as to claims arising after the procurement of liability insurance and while such insurance is in force. (1963, c. 448, s. 23; 1979, c. 462, s. 2.)

§ 115D-25. Purchase of annuity or retirement income contracts for employees.

Notwithstanding any provision of law relating to salaries or salary schedules for the pay of faculty members, administrative officers, or any other employees of community colleges, the board of trustees of any of the above institutions may authorize the finance officer or agent of same to enter into annual contracts with any of the above officers, agents and employees which provide for reductions in salaries below the total established compensation or salary schedule for a term of one year. The financial officer or agent shall use the funds derived from the reduction in the salary of the officer, agent or employee to purchase a nonforfeitable annuity or retirement income contract for the benefit of said officer, agent or employee. An officer, agent or employee who has agreed to a salary reduction for this purpose shall not have the right to receive the amount of the salary reduction in cash or in any other way except the annuity or retirement income contract. Funds used for the purchase of an annuity or retirement income contract shall not be in lieu of any amount earned by the officer, agent or employee before his election for a salary reduction has become effective. The agreement for salary reductions referred to in this section shall be effected under any necessary regulations and procedures adopted by the State Board of Community Colleges and on forms prepared by the State Board of Community Colleges. Notwithstanding any other provisions of this section or law, the amount by which the salary of an officer, agent or employee is reduced pursuant to this section shall not be excluded, but shall be included, in computing and making payroll deductions for social security and retirement system purposes, and in computing and providing matching funds for retirement system purposes.

In lieu of the annuity and related contracts provided for under this section, interests in custodial accounts pursuant to Section 401(f), Section 403(b)(7), and related sections of the Internal Revenue Code of 1986 as amended may be purchased for the benefit of qualified employees under this section with the funds derived from the reduction in the salaries of such employees. (1965, c. 366; 1979, c. 462, s. 2; c. 896, s. 13; 1979, 2nd Sess., c. 1130, s. 1; 1987, c. 564, s. 11; 1989, c. 526, s. 2.)

§ 115D-25.1. Dependent care assistance program.

The State Board of Community Colleges is authorized to provide eligible employees of constituent institutions a program of dependent care assistance as available under Section 129 and related sections of the Internal Revenue Code of 1986, as amended. The State Board may authorize constituent institutions to enter into annual agreements with employees who elect to participate in the program to provide for a reduction in salary. With the approval of the Director of the Budget, savings in the employer's share of contributions under the Federal Insurance Contributions Act on account of the reduction in salary may be used to pay some or all of the administrative expenses of the program. Should the State Board decide to contract with a third party to administer the terms and conditions of a program of dependent care assistance, it may select a contractor only upon a thorough and completely competitive procurement process. (1989, c. 458, s. 2; 1991 (Reg. Sess., 1992), c. 1044, s. 14(c); 1993, c. 561, s. 42; 1993 (Reg. Sess., 1994), c. 769, s. 7.28A; 1997-443, s. 33.20(a); 1999-237, s. 28.27(a).)

§ 115D-25.2. Flexible Compensation Plan.

Notwithstanding any other provisions of law relating to the salaries of employees of community college boards of trustees, the State Board of Community Colleges is authorized to provide a plan of flexible compensation to eligible employees of constituent institutions for benefits available under Section 125 and related sections of the Internal Revenue Code of 1986 as amended. This plan shall not include those benefits provided to employees under Articles 1, 3B, and 6 of Chapter 135 of the General Statutes nor any vacation leave, sick leave, or any other leave that may be carried forward from year to year by employees as a form of deferred compensation. If a plan of flexible compensation is offered, then a TRICARE supplement shall be offered. In providing a plan of flexible compensation, the State Board may authorize constituent institutions to enter into agreements with their employees for reductions in the salaries of employees electing to participate in the plan of flexible compensation provided by this section. With the approval of the Director of the Budget, savings in the employer's share of contributions under the Federal Insurance Contributions Act on account of the reduction in salary may be used to pay some or all of the administrative expenses of the program. Should the State Board decide to contract with a third party to administer the terms and conditions of a plan of flexible compensation as provided by this section, it may select such a contractor only upon a thorough and completely advertised competitive procurement process. (1989 (Reg. Sess., 1990), c. 1059, s. 2; 1991 (Reg. Sess., 1992), c. 1044, s. 14(g); 1993, c. 561, s. 42; 1993 (Reg. Sess., 1994), c. 769, s. 7.28A; 1997-443, s. 33.20(a); 1999-237, s. 28.27(a); 2013-292, s. 2.)

§ 115D-25.3. Voluntary shared leave.

The State Board of Community Colleges, in cooperation with the State Board of Education and the State Human Resources Commission, shall adopt rules and policies to allow any employee at a community college to share leave voluntarily with an immediate family member who is an employee of a community college, public school, or State agency; and with a coworker's immediate family member who is an employee of a community college, public school, or State agency. For the purposes of this section, the term "immediate family member" means a spouse, parent, child, brother, sister, grandparent, or grandchild. The term includes the step, half, and in-law relationships. The term "coworker" means that the employee donating the leave is employed by the same agency, department, institution, university, local school administrative unit, or community college as the employee whose immediate family member is receiving the leave. (2003-9, s. 3; 2003-284, s. 30.14A(c); 2013-382, s. 9.1(c).)

§ 115D-26. Conflict of interest.

All local trustees and employees of community colleges covered under this Chapter are subject to the conflict of interest provisions found in G.S. 14-234. (1981, c. 157, s. 5; 1987, c. 564, s. 9; 2001-409, s. 5.)

Article 2A.

Privacy of Employee Personnel Records.

§ 115D-27. Personnel files not subject to inspection.

Personnel files of employees of boards of trustees, former employees of boards of trustees, or applicants for employment with boards of trustees shall not be subject to inspection and examination as authorized by G.S. 132-6. For purposes of this Article, a personnel file consists of any information gathered by the board of trustees which employs an individual, previously employed an individual, or considered an individual's application for employment, and which information relates to the individual's application, selection or nonselection, promotion, demotion, transfer, leave, salary, suspension, performance evaluation, disciplinary action, or termination of employment wherever located or in whatever form. (1991, c. 84. s. 3.)

§ 115D-28. Certain records open to inspection.

(a) Each board of trustees shall maintain a record of each of its employees, showing the following information with respect to each employee:

(1) Name.

(2) Age.

(3) Date of original employment or appointment.

(4) The terms of any contract by which the employee is employed whether written or oral, past and current, to the extent that the board has the written contract or a record of the oral contract in its possession.

(5) Current position.

(6) Title.

(7) Current salary.

(8) Date and amount of each increase or decrease in salary with that community college.

(9) Date and type of each promotion, demotion, transfer, suspension, separation, or other change in position classification with that community college.

(10) Date and general description of the reasons for each promotion with that community college.

(11) Date and type of each dismissal, suspension, or demotion for disciplinary reasons taken by the community college. If the disciplinary action was a dismissal, a copy of the written notice of the final decision of the board of trustees setting forth the specific acts or omissions that are the basis of the dismissal.

(12) The office or station to which the employee is currently assigned.

(b) For the purposes of this section, the term "salary" includes pay, benefits, incentives, bonuses, and deferred and all other forms of compensation paid by the employing entity.

(c) Subject only to rules and regulations for the safekeeping of records adopted by the board of trustees, every person having custody of the records shall permit them to be inspected and examined and copies made by any person during regular business hours. Any person who is denied access to any record for the purpose of inspecting, examining or copying the record shall have a right to compel compliance with the provisions of this section by application to a court of competent jurisdiction for a writ of mandamus or other appropriate relief. (1991, c. 84, s. 3; 2007-508, s. 2; 2010-169, s. 18(c).)

§ 115D-29. Confidential information in personnel files; access to information.

(a) All information contained in a personnel file, except as otherwise provided in this Article, is confidential and shall not be open for inspection and examination except to the following persons:

(1) The employee, applicant for employment, former employee, or his properly authorized agent, who may examine his own personnel file at all

reasonable times in its entirety except for letters of reference solicited prior to employment;

(2)   The president and other supervisory personnel;

(3)   Members of the board of trustees and the board's attorney;

(4)   A party by authority of a subpoena or proper court order may inspect and examine a particular confidential portion of an employee's personnel file; and

(5)   An official of an agency of the federal government, State government or any political subdivision thereof. Such an official may inspect any personnel records when such [an] inspection is deemed by the college of the employee, applicant, or former employee whose record is to be inspected as necessary and essential to the pursuance of a proper function of said agency; provided, however, that such information shall not be divulged for purposes of assisting in a criminal prosecution, nor for purposes of assisting in a tax investigation.

(b)   Notwithstanding any other provision of this Article, any president may, in his discretion, or shall at the direction of the board of trustees, inform any person or corporation of any promotion, demotion, suspension, reinstatement, transfer, separation, dismissal, employment or nonemployment of any applicant, employee or former employee employed by or assigned to the board of trustees or whose personnel file is maintained by the board and the reasons therefor and may allow the personnel file of the person or any portion to be inspected and examined by any person or corporation provided that the board has determined that the release of the information or the inspection and examination of the file or any portion is essential to maintaining the integrity of the board or to maintaining the level or quality of services provided by the board; provided, that prior to releasing the information or making the file or any portion available as provided herein, the president shall prepare a memorandum setting forth the circumstances which he and the board deem to require the disclosure and the information to be disclosed. The memorandum shall be retained in the files of the president and shall be a public record.

(c)   Notwithstanding any provision of this section to the contrary, the Retirement Systems Division of the Department of State Treasurer may disclose the name and mailing address of former community college employees to domiciled, nonprofit organizations representing 2,000 or more active or retired

State government, local government, or public school employees. (1991, c. 84, s. 3; 2008-194, s. 11(c).)

§ 115D-30. Remedy of employee objecting to material in file.

An employee, former employee or applicant for employment who objects to material in his file may place in his file a statement relating to the materials he considers to be inaccurate or misleading. An employee, former employee or applicant for employment who objects to material in his file because he considers it inaccurate or misleading, and the material has not been placed there in connection with a grievance procedure established by the board of trustees, may seek the removal of such material from the file through grievance procedures to be established by each board of trustees. (1991, c. 84. s. 3.)

Article 3.

Financial Support.

§ 115D-31. State financial support of institutions.

(a)   The State Board of Community Colleges shall be responsible for providing, from sources available to the State Board, funds to meet the financial needs of institutions, as determined by policies and regulations of the State Board, for the following budget items:

(1)   Plant Fund. - Furniture and equipment for administrative and instructional purposes, library books, and other items of capital outlay approved by the State Board. Provided, the State Board may, on an equal matching-fund basis from appropriations made by the State for the purpose, grant funds to individual institutions for the purchase of land, construction and remodeling of institutional buildings determined by the State Board to be necessary for the instructional programs or administration of such institutions. For the purpose of determining amount of matching State funds, local funds shall include expenditures made prior to the enactment of this Chapter or prior to an institution becoming a community college pursuant to the provisions of this Chapter, when such expenditures were made for the purchase of land, construction, and remodeling of institutional buildings subsequently determined

by the State Board to be necessary as herein specified, and provided such local expenditures have not previously been used as the basis for obtaining matching State funds under the provisions of this Chapter or any other laws of the State. Notwithstanding the provisions of this subdivision, G.S. 116-53(b), or G.S. 143C-4-5, appropriations by the State of North Carolina for capital or permanent improvements for community colleges may be matched with any prior expenditure of non-State funds for capital construction or land acquisition not already used for matching purposes.

(2)   Current Operating Expenses:

a.   General administration. - Salaries and other costs as determined by the State Board necessary to carry out the functions of general administration.

b.   Instructional services. - Salaries and other costs as determined by the State Board necessary to carry out the functions of instructional services.

c.   Support services. - Salaries and other costs as determined by the State Board necessary to carry out the functions of support services.

(3)   Additional Support for Regional Institutions as Defined in G.S. 115D-2(4). - Matching funds to be used with local funds to meet the financial needs of the regional institutions for the items set out in G.S. 115D-32(a)(2)a. Amount of matching funds to be provided by the State under this section shall be determined as follows: The population of the administrative area in which the regional institution is located shall be called the "local factor," the combined populations of all other counties served by the institution shall be called the "State factor." When the budget for the items listed in G.S. 115D-32(a)(2)a has been approved under the procedures set out in G.S. 115D-45, the administrative area in which the regional institution is located shall provide a percentage to be determined by dividing the local factor by the sum of the local factor and the State factor. The State shall provide a percentage of the necessary funds to meet this budget, the percentage to be determined by dividing the State factor by the sum of the local factor and the State factor. If the local administrative area provides less than its proportionate share, the amount of State funds provided shall be reduced by the same proportion as were the administrative area funds.

Wherever the word "population" is used in this subdivision, it shall mean the population of the particular area in accordance with the latest United States census.

(b) The State Board is authorized to accept, receive, use, or reallocate to the institutions any federal funds or aids that have been or may be appropriated by the government of the United States for the encouragement and improvement of any phase of the programs of the institutions.

(b1) A local community college may use all State funds allocated to it, except for Literacy funds and Customized Training funds, for any authorized purpose that is consistent with the college's Institutional Effectiveness Plan. Each local community college shall include in its Institutional Effectiveness Plan a section on how funding flexibility allows the college to meet the demands of the local community and to maintain a presence in all previously funded categorical programs.

(c) State funds appropriated to the State Board of Community Colleges for equipment and library books, except for funds appropriated to the Equipment Reserve Fund, shall revert to the General Fund 12 months after the close of the fiscal year for which they were appropriated. Encumbered balances outstanding at the end of each period shall be handled in accordance with existing State budget policies. The System Office shall identify to the Office of State Budget and Management the funds that revert at the end of the 12 months after the close of the fiscal year.

(d) State funds appropriated to the State Board of Community Colleges for the Equipment Reserve Fund shall be allocated to institutions in accordance with the equipment allocation formula for the fiscal period. An institution to which these funds are allocated shall spend the funds only in accordance with an equipment acquisition plan developed by the institution and approved by the State Board.

These funds shall not revert and shall remain available until expended in accordance with an approved plan.

(e) If receipts for community college tuition and fees exceed the amount certified in General Fund Codes at the end of a fiscal year, the State Board of Community Colleges shall transfer the amount of receipts and fees above those budgeted to the Enrollment Growth Reserve. Funds in the Enrollment Growth Reserve shall not revert to the General Fund and shall remain available to the State Board until expended. The State Board may allocate funds in this reserve to colleges experiencing an enrollment increase greater than five percent (5%) of budgeted enrollment levels. (1963, c. 448, s. 23; 1973, c. 590, ss. 2, 3; c. 637, s. 1; 1979, c. 462, s. 2; c. 896, s. 13; c. 946, s. 1; 1979, 2nd Sess., c. 1130,

s. 1; 1981, c. 157, s. 2; 1985, c. 757, s. 146; 1987, c. 564, ss. 9, 12; 1995, c. 324, s. 16; 1998-212, s. 10.2(a); 1999-84, s. 11; 1999-237, s. 9.3(a); 2000-140, s. 93.1(a); 2001-424, s. 12.2(b); 2006-203, s. 38; 2010-31, s. 8.2; 2011-145, s. 8.4.)

§ 115D-31.1. Liability insurance.

Notwithstanding the provisions of G.S. 115D-32(a)(2)b2 and any other provision of the law to the contrary, boards of trustees of all institutions in this Chapter may use State funds to pay the lawful premiums of liability insurance as provided in this section. (1983, c. 761, s. 105.)

§ 115D-31.2. Maintenance of plant.

Notwithstanding any provisions of law to the contrary, any community college that has an out-of-county student head count served on the main campus of the college in excess of fifty percent (50%) of the total student head count as defined by the State Board of Community Colleges, shall be provided funds for the purpose of "operations of plant". Each college that qualifies for these funds shall receive a pro rata amount of the funds that are appropriated for this purpose. (1993, c. 321, s. 110; 2001-424, s. 30.13.)

§ 115D-31.3. Institutional performance accountability.

(a)   Implementation of Accountability Measures and Performance Standards. - The State Board of Community Colleges shall adopt and implement a system of accountability measures and performance standards for the Community College System. At least once every three years, the State Board of Community Colleges shall review, and revise if necessary, the accountability measures and performance standards to ensure that they are appropriate for use in recognition of successful institutional performance. If the State Board determines that accountability measures and performance standards must be revised following a review required by this subsection, the State Board shall report to the Joint Legislative Education Oversight Committee prior to the implementation of any proposed revisions.

(b) through (d) Repealed by Session Laws 2000-67, s. 9.7, effective July 1, 2000.

(e) Mandatory Performance Measures. - The State Board of Community Colleges shall evaluate each college on the following eight performance measures:

(1) Progress of basic skills students.

(2) Attainment of General Educational Development (GED) diplomas by students.

(3) Performance of students who transfer to a four-year institution.

(4) Success of developmental students in subsequent college-level English courses.

(5) Success of developmental students in subsequent college-level math courses.

(5a) Progress of first-year curriculum students.

(6) Repealed by Session Laws 2012-142, s. 8.5, effective July 1, 2012.

(7) Curriculum student retention and graduation.

(8) Repealed by Session Laws 2012-142, s. 8.5, effective July 1, 2012.

(9) Attainment of licensure and certifications by students.

The State Board may also evaluate each college on additional performance measures.

(f) Publication of Performance Ratings. - Each college shall publish its performance on the eight measures set out in subsection (e) of this section (i) annually in its electronic catalog or on the Internet and (ii) in its printed catalog each time the catalog is reprinted.

The Community Colleges System Office shall publish the performance of all colleges on all eight measures.

(g) Recognition of Successful Institutional Performance. - For the purpose of recognition of successful institutional performance, the State Board of Community Colleges shall evaluate each college on the eight performance measures set out in subsection (e) of this section. Subject to the availability of funds, the State Board may allocate funds among colleges based on the evaluation of each institution's performance, including at least the following components:

(1) Program quality evaluated by determining a college's rate of student success on each measure as compared to a systemwide performance baseline and goal.

(2) Program impact on student outcomes evaluated by the number of students succeeding on each measure.

(g1) Carryforward of Funds Allocated Based on Performance. - A college that receives funds under subsection (g) of this section may retain and carry forward an amount up to or equal to its performance-based funding allocation for that year into the next fiscal year.

(h) through (j) Repealed by Session Laws 2013-360, s. 10.5(a), effective July 1, 2013. (1999-237, s. 9.2(a); 2000-67, s. 9.7; 2001-186, s. 1; 2006-66, s. 8.9(a); 2007-230, s. 1; 2007-484, s. 29.5(a); 2007-527, s. 19; 2012-142, s. 8.5; 2013-360, s. 10.5(a).)

§ 115D-32. Local financial support of institutions.

(a) The tax-levying authority of each institution shall be responsible for providing, in accordance with the provisions of G.S. 115D-33 or 115D-34, as appropriate, adequate funds to meet the financial needs of the institutions for the following budget items:

(1) Plant Fund: Acquisition of land; erection of all buildings; alterations and additions to buildings; purchase of automobiles, buses, trucks, and other motor vehicles; purchase or rental of all equipment necessary for the maintenance of buildings and grounds and operation of plants; and purchase of all furniture and equipment not provided for administrative and instructional purposes.

(2) Current expenses:

a. Plant operation and maintenance:

1. Salaries of janitors, maids, watchmen, maintenance and repair employees.

2. Cost of fuel, water, power, and telephone services.

3. Cost of janitorial supplies and materials.

4. Cost of operation of motor vehicles.

5. Cost of maintenance and repairs of buildings and grounds.

6. Maintenance and replacement of furniture and equipment provided from local funds.

7. Maintenance of plant heating, electrical, and plumbing equipment.

8. Maintenance of all other equipment, including motor vehicles, provided by local funds.

9. Rental of land and buildings.

10. Any other expenses necessary for plant operation and maintenance.

b. Support services:

1. Cost of insurance for buildings, contents, motor vehicles, workers' compensation for institutional employees paid from local funds, and other necessary insurance.

2. Any tort claims awarded against the institution due to the negligence of the institutional employees.

3. Cost of bonding institutional employees for the protection of local funds and property.

4. Cost of elections held in accordance with G.S. 115D-33 and 115D-35.

5. Legal fees incurred in connection with local administration and operation of the institution.

(b)   The board of trustees of each institution may apply local public funds provided in accordance with G.S. 115D-33(a), as appropriate, or private funds, or both, to the supplementation of items of the current expense budget financed from State funds, provided a budget is submitted in accordance with G.S. 115D-54.

(c)   The board of trustees of each institution may apply institutional funds provided in accordance with G.S. 115D-54(b)(3) for such purposes as may be determined by the board of trustees of the institution.

(d)   The counties that agree to have satellite campuses of community colleges located in them accept the maintenance and utility costs of these satellite campuses. (1963, c. 448, s. 23; 1979, c. 462, s. 2; 1981, c. 157, s. 3; 1985, c. 757, s. 148(a); 1987, c. 564, s. 11; 1995, c. 509, s. 64; 1999-84, s. 5.)

§ 115D-33. Providing local public funds for institutions established under this Chapter; elections.

(a)   Except as provided in G.S. 115D-34, the tax-levying authority of an institution may provide for local financial support of the institution as follows:

(1)   By appropriations from nontax revenues in a manner consistent with the Local Government Budget and Fiscal Control Act, provided the continuing authority to make such appropriations shall have been approved by a majority of the qualified voters of the administrative area who shall vote on the question in an election held for such purpose, or

(2)   By a special annual levy of taxes within a maximum annual rate which maximum rate shall have been approved by a majority of the qualified voters of the administrative area who shall vote on the question of establishing or increasing the maximum annual rate in an election held for such purpose or both, and

(3)   By issuance of bonds, in the case of capital outlay funds, provided that each issuance of bonds shall be approved by a majority of the qualified voters of each county of the administrative area who shall vote on the question in an election held for that purpose. All bonds shall be subject to the Local Government Finance Act (Chapter 159) and shall be issued pursuant to

Subchapter IV, Long-Term Financing, (§ 159-43 et seq.) of Chapter 159 of the General Statutes.

(b)   At the election on the question of approving authority of the board of commissioners of each county in an administrative area (the tax-levying authority) to appropriate funds from nontax revenues or a special annual levy of taxes or both, the ballot furnished the qualified voters in each county may be worded substantially as follows: "For the authority of the board of commissioners to appropriate funds either from nontax revenues or from a special annual levy of taxes not to exceed an annual rate of _____ cents per one hundred dollars ($100.00) of assessed property valuation, or both, for the financial support of ____ (name of the institution)" plus any other pertinent information and "Against the authority of the board of commissioners, etc.," with a square before each proposition, in which the voter may make a cross mark (X), but any other form of ballot containing adequate information and properly stating the question to be voted upon shall be construed as being in compliance with this section.

(c)   The question of approving authority to appropriate funds, to levy special taxes and the question of approving an issue of bonds, when approval of each or both shall be necessary for the establishment or conversion of an institution, shall be submitted at the same election.

(d)   All elections shall be held in the same manner as elections held under Article 4, Chapter 159, of the General Statutes, the Local Government Bond Act, and shall be held on a date permitted by G.S. 163-287.

(e)   The State Board of Community Colleges shall ascertain that authority to provide adequate funds for the establishment and operation of an institution has been approved by the voters of a proposed administrative area before favorably recommending approval of the establishment of an institution.

(f)   Notwithstanding any present provisions of this Chapter, the tax-levying authority of each institution may at its discretion and upon its own motion provide by appropriations of nontax revenue, tax revenue, or both, funds for the support of institutional purposes as set forth in G.S. 115D-32; but nothing herein shall be construed to authorize the issuance of bonds without a vote of the people. (1963, c. 448, s. 23; 1971, c. 402; 1979, c. 462, s. 2; c. 896, s. 13; 1979, 2nd Sess., c. 1130, s. 1; 1983, c. 717, s. 27.3; 2013-381, s. 10.18.)

§ 115D-34. Providing local public funds for institutions previously established.

(a) For counties in which, immediately prior to the enactment of this Chapter, there was in operation or authorized a public community college or industrial education center which hereafter shall be operated pursuant to the provisions of this Chapter, the following provisions shall apply in providing local financial support for each such institution:

(1) Community colleges: The board of commissioners of a county in which is located a public community college heretofore operated or authorized to operate pursuant to Article 3, Chapter 116, of the General Statutes of North Carolina, may continue to levy special taxes annually for the local financial support of the institution as a community college as provided in G.S. 115D-32, to the maximum rate last approved by the voters of the county in accordance with the above Article. The board of commissioners may also provide all or part of such funds by appropriations, in a manner consistent with the Local Government Budget and Fiscal Control Act, from nontax revenues. The question of increasing the maximum annual rate of a special tax may be submitted at an election held in accordance with the provisions of G.S. 115D-33(d) and the appropriate provisions of G.S. 115D-35.

(2) Industrial education centers: The board of commissioners of a county in which is located an industrial education center heretofore operated or authorized to operate as part of the public school system and which hereafter shall be operated as a community college as defined in this Chapter may levy special taxes annually at a rate sufficient to provide funds for the financial support of the institute or college as required by G.S. 115D-32(a). The board of commissioners may also provide all or part of such funds by appropriations, in a manner consistent with the Local Government Budget and Fiscal Control Act, from nontax revenues. The board of commissioners is authorized to provide additional funds, either by special tax levies or by appropriations from nontax revenues, or both, to an amount equal to that required to be provided above, for the purpose of supplementing the current expense budget of the institute or college financed from State funds.

(b) The board of commissioners of a county in which is located one of the above public community colleges or industrial education centers may provide funds for capital outlay for such institution by the issuance of bonds. All bonds shall be issued in accordance with the appropriate provisions of G.S. 115D-33 and 115D-35.

(c) Public funds provided a community college or industrial education center prior to its becoming subject to the provisions of this Chapter and which remain to the credit of the institution upon its becoming subject to these provisions shall be expended only for the purposes prescribed by law when such funds were provided the institution. (1963, c. 448, s. 23; 1965, c. 842, s. 1; 1979, c. 462, s. 2; 1987, c. 564, ss. 20, 34.)

§ 115D-35. Requests for elections to provide funds for institutions.

(a) Formal requests for elections on the question of authority to appropriate nontax revenues or levy special taxes, or both, and to issue bonds, when such elections are to be held for the purpose of establishing an institution, shall be originated and submitted only in the following manner:

(1) Proposed multiple-county administrative areas: Formal requests for elections may be submitted jointly by all county boards of education in the proposed administrative area, or by petition of fifteen percent (15%) of the number of qualified voters of the proposed area who voted in the last preceding election for Governor, to the boards of commissioners of all counties in the proposed area, who shall fix the time for such election by joint resolution on a date permitted by G.S. 163-287, which shall be entered in the minutes of each board.

(2) Proposed single-county administrative area: Formal requests shall be submitted by the board of education of any public school administrative unit within the county of the proposed administrative area or by petition of fifteen percent (15%) of the number of qualified voters of the county who voted in the last preceding election for Governor, to the board of commissioners of the county of the proposed administrative area, who shall fix the time for such election by resolution on a date permitted by G.S. 163-287, which shall be entered in the minutes of the board.

(b) Formal requests for elections on any of the questions specified in (a) above, or on the question of increasing the maximum annual rate of special taxes for the financial support of an institution with a properly established board of trustees, may be submitted to the tax-levying authority only by such board of trustees.

(c) All formal requests for elections regarding the levy of special taxes shall state the maximum annual rate for which approval is to be sought in an election.

(d) Nothing in this section shall be construed to deny or limit the power of the tax-levying authority of an institution to hold elections, of its own motion, on any or all the questions provided in this section, subject to the provisions of this Article. (1963, c. 448, s. 23; 1979, c. 462, s. 2; 2013-381, s. 10.19.)

§ 115D-36. Elections on question of the addition of a college transfer program at an institution and issuance of bonds therefor.

Whenever the board of trustees of an institution requests the State Board of Community Colleges to authorize the addition of a college transfer program, the Board shall require, as a prerequisite to such addition:

(1) The authorization by the voters of the administrative area of an annual levy of taxes within a specified maximum annual rate sufficient to provide the required local financial support for the institution after the addition of the college transfer program, in an election held in accordance with the appropriate provisions of G.S. 115D-33 and 115D-35.

(2) The approval by the voters of the administrative area of the issuance of bonds for capital outlay necessary for the institution after the addition of the college transfer program, in an election held in accordance with the appropriate provisions of G.S. 115D-33 and 115D-35. (1968, c. 443, s. 23; 1979, c. 462, s. 2; c. 896, s. 13; 1979, 2nd Sess., c. 1130, s. 1; 1987, c. 564, s. 5.)

§ 115D-37. Payment of expenses of special elections under Chapter.

The cost of special elections held under the authority of this Chapter in connection with the establishment of an institution shall be paid out of the general fund of the county or counties which shall conduct such elections. All special elections held on behalf of a duly established institution shall be paid by such institution and the expenses may be included in the annual institutional budgets. (1963, c. 448, s. 23; 1979, c. 462, s. 2.)

§ 115D-38. Authority to issue bonds and notes, to levy taxes and to appropriate nontax revenues.

Counties are authorized to issue bonds and notes and to levy special taxes to meet payments of principal and interest on such bonds or notes and to levy special taxes for the special purpose of providing local financial support of an institution and otherwise to appropriate nontax revenues for the financial support of an institution, in the manner and for the purposes provided in this Chapter.

Taxes authorized by this section are declared to be for a special purpose and may be levied notwithstanding any constitutional limitation or limitations imposed by any general or special law. (1963, c. 448, s. 23; 1979, c. 462, s. 2.)

§ 115D-39. Student tuition and fees.

(a) The State Board of Community Colleges shall fix and regulate all tuition and fees charged to students for applying to or attending any institution pursuant to this Chapter.

The receipts from all student tuition and fees, other than student activity fees, shall be State funds and shall be deposited as provided by regulations of the State Board of Community Colleges.

The legal resident limitation with respect to tuition, set forth in G.S. 116-143.1 and G.S. 116-143.3, shall apply to students attending institutions operating pursuant to this Chapter; provided, however, that when an employer other than the Armed Forces, as that term is defined in G.S. 116-143.3, pays tuition for an employee to attend an institution operating pursuant to this Chapter and when the employee works at a North Carolina business location, the employer shall be charged the in-State tuition rate; provided further, however, a community college may charge in-State tuition to up to one percent (1%) of its out-of-state students, rounded up to the next whole number, to accommodate the families transferred by business, the families transferred by industry, or the civilian families transferred by the Armed Forces, consistent with the provisions of G.S. 116-143.3, into the State. Notwithstanding these requirements, a refugee who lawfully entered the United States and who is living in this State shall be deemed to qualify as a domiciliary of this State under G.S. 116-143.1(a)(1) and as a State resident for community college tuition purposes as defined in G.S. 116-143.1(a)(2). Also, a nonresident of the United States who has resided in

North Carolina for a 12-month qualifying period and has filed an immigrant petition with the United States Immigration and Naturalization Service shall be considered a State resident for community college tuition purposes.

(a1)   In addition, federal law enforcement officers, firefighters, EMS personnel, and rescue and lifesaving personnel whose permanent duty station is within North Carolina shall also be eligible for the State resident community college tuition rate for courses that support their organizations' training needs and are approved for this purpose by the State Board of Community Colleges.

(b)   In addition, any person lawfully admitted to the United States who satisfied the qualifications for assignment to a public school set out under G.S. 115C-366 and graduated from the public school to which the student was assigned shall also be eligible for the State resident community college tuition rate. This subsection does not make a person a resident of North Carolina for any other purpose.

(c)   In addition, a person sponsored under this subsection who is lawfully admitted to the United States is eligible for the State resident community college tuition rate. For purposes of this subsection, a North Carolina nonprofit entity is a charitable or religious corporation as defined in G.S. 55A-1-40 that is incorporated in North Carolina and that is exempt from taxation under section 501(c)(3) of the Internal Revenue Code, or a civic league incorporated in North Carolina under Chapter 55A of the General Statutes that is exempt from taxation under section 501(c)(4) of the Internal Revenue Code. A nonresident of the United States is sponsored by a North Carolina nonprofit entity if the student resides in North Carolina while attending the community college and the North Carolina nonprofit entity provides a signed affidavit to the community college verifying that the entity accepts financial responsibility for the student's tuition and any other required educational fees. Any North Carolina nonprofit entity that sponsors a nonresident of the United States under this subsection may sponsor no more than five nonresident students annually under this subsection. This subsection does not make a person a resident of North Carolina for any other purpose.

(d)   A community college may add the cost of textbooks purchased at the college's bookstore to the tuition rates established pursuant to subsection (a) of this section for all purposes associated with billing the armed services for the enrollment of members of the armed services, as defined in G.S. 116-143.3, if the student's branch of the armed services permits the addition of textbooks to tuition costs in its tuition assistance program. The college may retain the funds attributable to the cost of the textbooks. (1963, c. 448, s. 23; 1979, c. 462, s. 2; c. 896, s. 13; 1979, 2nd Sess., c. 1130, s. 1; 1981, c. 157, s. 4; 1983 (Reg. Sess., 1984), c. 1034, s. 58; 1989, c. 752, s. 85; 1991 (Reg. Sess., 1992), c. 1044, s. 25(a); 1993, c. 561, s. 50(a); 1996, 2nd Ex. Sess., c. 18, s. 17.1(a); 2000-67, s. 9.8; 2003-284, ss. 8.16(b), 8.16A(a); 2010-31, s. 8.4(b); 2011-145, s. 8.12(d); 2011-183, s. 80; 2011-184, s. 1.)

§ 115D-39.1. Tuition surcharge.

(a) Notwithstanding the provisions of G.S. 115D-39.1(a), a community college may, with the approval of the State Board of Community Colleges:

(1) Implement a tuition surcharge of up to thirty-three and one-third percent (33 1/3%) of the statewide tuition rate to fund a new instructional program that is necessary to attract industry to the area, and

(2) Use the proceeds of an endowed scholarship, consistent with the terms of the endowment, to offset the cost of the tuition charge.

(b) All students enrolled in the new program, except for students for whom tuition and registration are waived by law or regulation, shall be charged the tuition surcharge. The funds collected from the endowment shall be deposited into an unrestricted institutional fund account at the community college.

(c) This section applies only to an endowed scholarship in excess of five million dollars ($5,000,000).

(d) The State Board shall adopt rules to implement this section. (2007-367, s. 1.)

§ 115D-40. Repealed by Session Laws 1999-237, s.9.4(c).

§ 115D-40.1. Financial Assistance for Community College Students.

(a) Need-Based Assistance Program. - It is the intent of the General Assembly that the Community College System make these financial aid funds available to the neediest students who are not eligible for other financial aid programs that fully cover the required educational expenses of these students. The State Board may use some of these funds as short-term loans to students who anticipate receiving the federal HOPE or Lifetime Learning Tax Credits.

(b) Targeted Assistance. - Notwithstanding subsection (a) of this section, the State Board may allocate up to ten percent (10%) of the funds appropriated for Financial Assistance for Community College Students to the following students:

(1) Students who enroll in low-enrollment programs that prepare students for high-demand occupations.

(2) Students with disabilities who have been referred by the Department of Health and Human Services, Division of Vocational Rehabilitation, and are enrolled in a community college.

(c) Administration of Program. - The State Board shall adopt rules and policies for the disbursement of the financial assistance provided in subsections (a) and (b) of this section. Degree, diploma, and certificate students must complete a Free Application for Federal Student Aid (FAFSA) to be eligible for financial assistance. The State Board may contract with the State Education Assistance Authority for administration of these financial assistance funds. These funds shall not revert at the end of each fiscal year but shall remain available until expended for need-based financial assistance. The interest earned on the funds provided in subsections (a) and (b) of this section may be used to support the costs of administering the Community College Grant Program. If the interest earnings are not adequate to support the administrative costs, up to one percent (1%) of funds provided in subsection (a) of this section may be used to support the costs of administering the Community College Grant Program.

(d) Participation in Federal Loan Programs. - All community colleges shall participate in the William D. Ford Federal Direct Loan Program, unless the board of trustees of an institution adopts a resolution declining to participate in the Program. The State Board shall ensure that at least one counselor is available at each college to inform students about federal programs and funds available to assist community college students, including, but not limited to, Pell Grants, HOPE and Lifetime Learning Tax Credits, and, for participating colleges, the William D. Ford Federal Direct Loan Program, and to actively encourage students to utilize these federal programs and funds. The board of trustees of any institution that has declined to participate in the William D. Ford Federal

Direct Loan Program through the adoption of a resolution may rescind the resolution and participate in the Program but shall not have the authority to again decline participation in the Program. (1999-237, s. 9.4(a), (b); 2001-229, ss. 1, 2; 2003-52, s. 1; 2003-385, s. 1; 2009-451, s. 8.4; 2010-31, s. 8.5(b); 2011-148, ss. 1, 2; 2011-154, ss. 1, 2; 2011-155, ss. 1, 2; 2011-178, ss. 1, 2; 2012-31, s. 1; 2012-142, s. 8.11(c); 2013-360, s. 10.13; 2013-410, s. 43.)

§ 115D-40.2. Semester limitation on eligibility for North Carolina Community College grants.

(a) Except as otherwise provided by this section, a student shall not receive a need-based grant from the North Carolina Community College Grant Program for more than six full-time academic semesters, or the equivalent if enrolled part-time.

(b) Upon application by a student, the community college may grant a waiver to the student who may then receive a grant from the North Carolina Community College Grant Program for the equivalent of one additional full-time academic semester if the student demonstrates that any of the following have substantially disrupted or interrupted the student's pursuit of a degree, diploma, or certificate: (i) a military service obligation, (ii) serious medical debilitation, (iii) a short-term or long-term disability, or (iv) other extraordinary hardship. The State Board shall establish policies and procedures to implement the waiver provided by this subsection. (2013-360, s. 11.15(c).)

§ 115D-41. Restrictions on contracts with local school administrative units; use of community college facilities by public school students pursuant to cooperative programs.

(a) Community college contracts with local school administrative units shall not be used by these agencies to supplant funding for a public school high school teacher providing courses offered pursuant to G.S. 115D-20(4) who is already employed by the local school administrative unit. In no event shall a community college contract with a local school administrative unit to provide high school level courses.

(b) Existing community college facilities that comply with the North Carolina State Building Code and applicable local ordinances for community college facilities may be used without modification for public school students in joint or cooperative programs such as middle or early college programs and dual enrollment programs. Designs for new community college facilities that comply with the North Carolina State Building Code and applicable local ordinances for community college facilities also may be used without modification for these students.

For the purpose of establishing Use and Occupancy Classifications, these programs shall be considered "Business - Group B" in the same manner as other community college uses. (1991 (Reg. Sess., 1992), c. 900, s. 82(a); 2006-66, s. 8.11(a); 2006-221, s. 5; 2009-206, s. 1; 2011-145, s. 7.1A(g).)

§ 115D-42. North Carolina Community Colleges Instructional Trust Fund.

(a) There is established the North Carolina Community Colleges Instructional Trust Fund. The purpose of this Trust Fund is to supplement the funds raised by community college foundations to enhance the academic missions of community colleges.

(b) The State Board of Community Colleges is authorized to allocate funds from the Instructional Trust Fund to the community colleges and to adopt rules to implement the provisions of this section.

(c) State funds from the Trust Fund and matching funds raised by foundations shall be used by the board of trustees of a community college only to enhance the academic mission of the college. State funds shall be used only for scholarships or financial aid for needy students.

Expenditures of the matching funds raised by foundations shall directly relate to education and shall be used only for:

(1) Resource center materials;

(2) Professional development of instructional faculty and staff in cases in which (i) professional development will improve the quality of performance provided by the employee and (ii) the employee makes a commitment to remain at the college for a prescribed period of time;

(3) Professional development of instructional faculty and staff in cases in which professional development is necessary to enhance the employee's ability to meet newly mandated instructional or performance requirements; and

(4) Other purposes authorized by the State Board of Community Colleges that are consistent with the college's mission.

(d) Every two dollars ($2.00) raised by the community college foundations for the Trust Fund during the 2003-2004 fiscal year shall be matched with one dollar ($1.00) of State funds. The maximum matching contribution from the State shall not exceed twenty-five thousand dollars ($25,000) for each of the 58 community colleges. These funds shall be reserved for each community college and held in escrow in the Trust Fund. A community college foundation may apply for matching funds after it raises twenty-five thousand dollars ($25,000). The chairperson of each community college foundation shall certify to the North Carolina Community College System Office that (i) new funds have been raised by the community college foundation to match the amount of funds held in escrow in the Trust Fund, (ii) the amount raised by the community college foundation has not been used previously for matching purposes, (iii) the amount raised by the college shall be used only as provided in subsection (c) of this section, and (iv) matching State funds shall be used only for scholarships or financial aid for needy students.

(e) The State Board of Community Colleges may request an audit of the State funds expended under this section from any community college foundation. (2003-284, s. 8.14(a).)

§ 115D-43. Funds for an intercollegiate athletics program.

No State funds, student tuition receipts, or student aid funds shall be used to create, support, maintain, or operate an intercollegiate athletics program at a community college. (2011-145, s. 8.10.)

§ 115D-44 Reserved for future codification purposes.

Article 4.

Budgeting, Accounting, and Fiscal Management.

§§ 115D-45 through 115D-53. Recodified as §§ 115D-54 to 115D-58.12.

Article 4A.

Budgeting, Accounting, and Fiscal Management.

§ 115D-54. Preparation and submission of institutional budget.

(a) By a date determined by the State Board, trustees of each institution shall prepare for submission a budget request as provided in G.S. 115D-54(b) on forms provided by the State Board of Community Colleges. The budget shall be based on estimates of available funds if provided by the funding authorities or as estimated by the institution. The State Current Fund shall be based on available funds. All other funds shall be based on needs as determined by the board of trustees and shall include the following:

(1)   State Current Fund.

(2)   County Current Fund.

(3)   Institutional Fund.

(4)   Plant Fund.

(b) The budget shall be prepared and submitted for approval according to the following procedures:

(1)   State Current Fund Budget. - The budget request shall contain the items of current operating expenses as provided in G.S. 115D-31 for which State funds are requested. The approving authority for the State current fund budget request shall be the board of trustees and the State Board of Community Colleges.

(2)   County Current Fund Budget. - The budget request shall contain the items of current operating expenses, as provided in G.S. 115D-32, for which

county funds are requested. The approving authority for the county current fund budget request shall be the board of trustees and the local tax-levying authority. The State Board of Community Colleges shall have approving authority pursuant to G.S. 115D-33 with respect to required local funding.

(3)   Institutional Fund Budget. - The budget request shall contain the items of current operating expenses, loan funds, scholarship funds, auxiliary enterprises, State, private, and federal grants and contracts and endowment funds for which institutional funds are requested. The approving authority for the institutional fund budget request shall be the board of trustees of the institution.

(4)   Plant Fund Budget. - The budget request shall contain the items of capital outlay, as provided in G.S. 115D-31 and 115D-32, for which funds are requested, from whatever source. The board of trustees shall submit the budget to the local tax-levying authority. The local tax-levying authority shall approve or disapprove, in whole or in part, that portion of the budget requesting local public funds. After approval by the local tax-levying authority, the board of trustees shall submit the budget to the State Board of Community Colleges on a date designated by the State Board. The State Board may approve or disapprove, in whole or in part, that portion of the budget requesting State or federal funds. Plant funds provided for construction and major renovations shall be permanent appropriations until the conclusion of the project for which appropriated.

(c)   No public funds shall be provided an institution, either by the tax-levying authority or by the State Board of Community Colleges, except in accordance with the budget provisions of this Article.

(d)   The preparation of a budget for and the payment of interest and principal on indebtedness incurred on behalf of an institution shall be the responsibility of the county finance officer or county finance officers of the administrative areas, and the board of trustees of the institution shall have no duty or responsibility in this connection.

(e)   "Trust and Agency Fund" means funds held by an institution as custodian or fiscal agent for others such as student organizations, individual students, or faculty members. Trust and agency funds need not be budgeted. (1963, c. 448, s. 23; 1979, c. 462, s. 2; c. 896, s. 13; 1979, 2nd Sess., c. 1130, s. 1; 1981, c. 157, s. 1; 2001-112, s. 1; 2007-484, s. 29(c).)

§ 115D-55. Budget management.

(a)   Approval of Budget by Local Tax-Levying Authority. - By a date fixed by the local tax-levying authority, the budget shall be submitted to the local tax-levying authority for approval of that portion within its authority as stated in G.S. 115D-54(b). On or before July 1, or such later date as may be agreeable to the board of trustees, but in no instance later than September 1, the local tax-levying authority shall determine the amount of county revenue to be appropriated to an institution for the budget year. The local tax-levying authority may allocate part or all of an appropriation by purpose, function, or project as defined in the budget manual as adopted by the State Board of Community Colleges.

The local tax-levying authority shall have full authority to call for all books, records, audit reports, and other information bearing on the financial operation of the institution except records dealing with specific persons for which the persons' rights of privacy are protected by either federal or State law.

Nothing in this Article shall be construed to place a duty on the local tax-levying authority to fund a deficit incurred by an institution through failure of the institution to comply with the provisions of this Article or rules and regulations issued pursuant hereto.

(b)   Approval of Budget by State Board of Community Colleges. - After notification by the local tax-levying authority of the amount appropriated, the budget shall be submitted to the State Board of Community Colleges on a date designated by the State Board of Community Colleges for approval of that portion within its authority as stated in G.S. 115D-54(b). The State Board of Community Colleges shall approve the budget for each institution in such amount as the State Board decides is available and necessary for the operation of the institution.

The State Board of Community Colleges shall have authority to call for all books, records, audit reports and other information bearing on the financial operation of the institution except records dealing with specific persons for which the persons' rights of privacy are protected by either federal or State law.

Nothing in this Article shall be construed to place a duty on the State Board of Community Colleges to fund a deficit incurred by an institution through failure of the institution to comply with the provisions of this Article or rules and regulations issued pursuant hereto. (1981, c. 157, s. 1; 2001-112, s. 2; 2007-484, s. 29(d).)

§ 115D-56. Final adoption of budget.

Upon notification of approval by the State Board of Community Colleges, the board of trustees shall adopt a budget resolution as defined in the budget manual as adopted by the State Board of Community Colleges, which shall comply with the resolution of the State Board and the appropriations of the tax-levying authorities and all other funding agencies. (1981, c. 157, s. 1.)

§ 115D-57. Interim budget.

In case the adoption of the budget resolution is delayed until after July 1, the board of trustees shall authorize the president, through interim provisions, to pay salaries and the other ordinary expenses of the institution for the interval between the beginning of the fiscal year and the adoption of the budget resolution. Interim provisions so made shall be charged to the proper allocations in the budget resolution. (1981, c. 157, s. 1.)

§ 115D-58. Amendments to the budget; budget transfers.

(a) The State Board of Community Colleges shall adopt rules and regulations governing the amendment of the budget for an institution. The board of trustees may amend the budget at any time after its adoption pursuant to the rules and regulations of the State Board.

(b) If the local tax-levying authority allocates part or all of an appropriation pursuant to G.S. 115D-55, the board of trustees must obtain approval of the local tax-levying authority for an amendment to the budget which increases or decreases the amount of that appropriation allocated to a purpose, function, or project by twenty-five percent (25%) or more from the amount contained in the budget ordinance adopted by the local tax-levying authority or such lesser percentage as specified by the local tax-levying authority in the original budget ordinance, so long as such percentage is not less than ten percent (10%).

(c) The board of trustees may, by appropriate resolution, authorize the president to transfer moneys from one appropriation to another within the same fund, subject to any limitations established by regulations adopted pursuant to this section, and subject to any limitations and procedures prescribed by the board of trustees or State for federal laws or regulations. Any such transfer shall be reported to the board of trustees at its next regular meeting and entered into its minutes. (1981, c. 157, s. 1.)

§ 115D-58.1. Federal contracts and grants.

The board of trustees of any institution may apply for and accept grants from the federal government or any agency thereof, in order to carry out the institution's mission. In exercising this authority, the board of trustees may enter into and carry out contracts with the federal government or any agency thereof, may agree to and comply with any lawful and reasonable condition attached to such a grant including, in the case of a grant from the Economic Development Administration, the granting of a security interest to the Economic Development Administration in any real property or equipment purchased with the grant, limiting the sale or use of the real property or equipment as prescribed by regulations of the Economic Development Administration, and may make expenditures from any funds so granted. The State Board of Community Colleges shall adopt rules and regulations governing the application for and the acceptance of grants under this section. (1981, c. 157, s. 1; 2001-211, s. 1.)

§ 115D-58.2. Allocation of revenue to the institution by the local tax-levying authority.

(a) The local tax-levying authority of each institution shall provide, as needed, funds to meet the monthly expenditures, including salaries and other necessary operating expenses, as set forth in a statement prepared by the board of trustees and in accordance with the approved budget. Upon the basis of the approved budget, the county finance officer shall make available to the institution the moneys requested by the board of trustees no later than the fifteenth day of the month for which funds are requested.

(b) Funds received by the trustees of an institution from insurance payments for loss or damage to buildings shall be used for the repair or replacement of such buildings, or, if the buildings are not repaired or replaced, to reduce proportionally the institutional indebtedness borne by the counties of the administrative area of the institution receiving the insurance payments. If such payments, which are not used to repair or replace institutional buildings, exceed the total institutional indebtedness borne by all counties of the administrative area, such excess funds shall remain to the credit of the institution and shall be applied to the next succeeding plant fund budget until the excess funds shall be expended. Funds received by the trustees of an institution for loss or damage to the contents of buildings shall be divided between the board of trustees and the State Board of Community Colleges in proportion to the value of the lost contents owned by the board of trustees and the State, respectively. Until these funds shall have been expended, they shall either be used for repair or replacement of lost contents or be credited to the institution for succeeding plant and current expense budgets as appropriate. (1963, c. 448, s. 23; 1979, c. 462, s. 2; c. 896, s. 13; 1979, 2nd Sess., c. 1130, s. 1; 1981, c. 157, s. 1.)

§ 115D-58.3. Provision for disbursement of State money.

The deposit of money in the State treasury to the credit of the institution shall be made in monthly installments, and additionally as necessary, at such time and in such manner as may be convenient for the operation of the community college system. Before an installment is credited, the institution shall certify to the Community Colleges System Office, the expenditures to be made by the institution from the State Current Fund during the month.

The Community Colleges System Office shall determine whether the moneys requisitioned are due the institution, and upon determining the amount due, shall cause the requisite amount to be credited to the institution. Upon receiving notice from the Community Colleges System Office that the amount has been placed to the credit of the institution, the institution may issue State warrants up to the amount so certified. Money in the State Current Fund and other moneys made available by the State Board of Community Colleges shall be released only on warrants drawn on the State Treasurer, signed by two officials of the institution designated for this purpose by the board of trustees. (1963, c. 448, s. 23; 1965, c. 448, s. 2; 1979, c. 462, s. 2; c. 896, s. 13; 1979, 2nd Sess., c. 1130, s. 1; 1981, c. 157, s. 1; 1999-84, s. 13.)

§ 115D-58.4. Provisions for disbursement of local money.

All local public funds received by or credited to an institution shall be disbursed on checks signed by the two officials of the institution who shall have been designated by the board of trustees. The officials so designated shall countersign a check only if the funds required by such check are within the amount of funds remaining to the credit of the institution and are within the unencumbered balance of the appropriation for the item of expenditure according to the approved budgets of the institution. Each check shall be accompanied by an invoice, statement, voucher, or other basic document which indicates, to the satisfaction of the signing officials, that the issuance of such check is proper. (1963, c. 448, s. 23; 1965, c. 488, s. 2; 1979, c. 462, s. 2; c. 896, s. 13; 1979, 2nd Sess., c. 1130, s. 1; 1981, c. 157, s. 1.)

§ 115D-58.5. Accounting system.

(a) Each institution shall establish and maintain an accounting system consistent with procedures as prescribed by the Community Colleges System Office and the State Controller, which shows its assets, liabilities, equities, revenues, and expenditures.

(b) Each institution shall be governed in its purchasing of all supplies, equipment, and materials by contracts made by or with the approval of the Purchase and Contract Division of the Department of Administration except as provided in G.S. 115D-58.14. No contract shall be made by any board of trustees for purchases unless provision has been made in the budget of the institution to provide payment thereof. In order to protect the State purchase contracts, it is the duty of the board of trustees and administrative officers of each institution to pay for such purchases promptly in accordance with the contract of purchase. Equipment shall be titled to the State Board of Community Colleges if derived from State or federal funds.

(c) The operations of each institution shall be subject to oversight of the State Auditor pursuant to Article 5A of Chapter 147 of the General Statutes.

(d) Repealed by Session Laws 1983, c. 913, s. 18. (1963, c. 448, s. 23; 1979, c. 462, s. 2; c. 896, s. 13; 1979, 2nd Sess., c. 1130, s. 1; 1981, c. 157, s. 1; 1983, c. 913, s. 18; 1998-68, s. 1; 1999-84, s. 14; 2000-67, s. 7(c).)

§ 115D-58.6. Investment of idle cash.

(a) Definitions. - As used in this section, the following definitions apply:

(1) Cash balance. - The amount equal to all moneys received into institutional fund accounts minus all expenses and withdrawals from those accounts in an official depository of the institution as designated by the local board of trustees consistent with G.S. 115D-58.7.

(2) Official depository. - One or more banks, savings and loan associations, or trust companies in North Carolina that a community college board of trustees has designated consistent with G.S. 115D-58.7.

(a1) Deposits. - The institution may deposit at interest all or part of the cash balance of any fund in an official depository of the institution. Moneys may be deposited at interest in any official depository of the institution in the form of such deposit accounts as may be approved for county governments. In addition, moneys may be deposited in the form of such deposit accounts as provided for a local government or public authority in G.S. 159-30(b1). Investment deposits shall be secured as provided in G.S. 159-31(b).

(b) through (d) Repealed by Session Laws 2011-145, s. 8.20(a), effective July 1, 2011.

(d1) Investments. - The institution may invest all or part of the cash balance of any fund in an official depository of the institution. The institution shall manage investments subject to whatever restrictions and directions the board of trustees may impose. The institution shall have the power to purchase, sell, and exchange securities on behalf of the board of trustees. The investment program shall be so managed that investments and deposits can be converted into cash when needed.

(1) Moneys shall be invested only in the form of investments pursuant to G.S. 159-30(c) to county governments or in any form of investment established or managed by an investment advisor who is registered and in good standing with either the Securities and Exchange Commission or the North Carolina Secretary of State, Securities Division, and is a member of the Securities Investor Protection Corporation. Money in endowment funds may be invested pursuant to G.S. 147-69.2. Provided, however, the institution may elect to deposit at interest any local funds with the State Treasurer for investment as

special trust funds pursuant to the provisions of G.S. 147-69.3, and the interest thereon shall accrue to the institution as local funds.

(2)   The investment securities listed in G.S. 159-30(c) may be bought, sold, and traded by private negotiation, and the institutions may pay all incidental costs thereof and all reasonable costs of administering the investment and deposit program from local funds. The institution shall be responsible for their safekeeping and for keeping accurate investment accounts and records.

(e)   Interest earned on deposits and investments shall be credited to the fund whose cash is deposited or invested. Cash of several funds may be combined for deposit or investment if not otherwise prohibited by law; and when such joint deposits or investments are made, interest earned shall be prorated and credited to the various funds on the basis of the amounts thereof invested, figured according to an average periodic balance or some other sound accounting principle. Interest earned on the deposit or investment of bond funds shall be deemed a part of the bond proceeds.

(f)   Registered securities acquired for investment may be released from registration and transferred by signature of the official designated by the board of trustees.

(g)   The board of trustees shall appoint an Investment Committee which shall consist of a minimum of three people who have sufficient financial background to review and evaluate investment options. These individuals should have experience in institutional or retail investment management with knowledge of fixed income and public equities. This committee shall make recommendations to the Board on those investment options, as well as monitor the performance of investments once made.

(h)   The board of trustees shall discharge their duties with respect to the management and investment of college funds as follows:

(1)   Investment decisions shall be solely in the interest of the college and the students, faculty, and staff of the college.

(2)   The investments shall be for the exclusive purpose of providing an adequate return to the college.

(3)   Investments shall be made with the care, skill, and caution under the circumstances then prevailing which a prudent person acting in a like capacity

and familiar with those matters would use in the conduct of an activity of like character and purpose.

(4)   Investment decisions shall be made impartially, taking into account the best interest of the college, with special attention to conflicts of interest or potential conflicts of interest.

(5)   Investments shall incur only costs that are appropriate and reasonable. (1981, c. 157, s. 1; c. 612, s. 1; 2005-394, s. 3; 2011-145, s. 8.20(a); 2013-305, s. 2.)

§ 115D-58.7. Selection of depository; deposits to be secured.

(a)   Each board of trustees shall designate as the official depositories of the institution one or more banks, savings and loan associations or trust companies in this State. It shall be unlawful for any money belonging to an institution, other than moneys required to be deposited with the State Treasurer, to be deposited in any place, bank, savings and loan associations, or trust company other than an official depository except as permitted in G.S. 115D-58.6(a1). However, public moneys may be deposited in official depositories in Negotiable Order of Withdrawal (NOW) accounts where permitted by applicable federal or State regulations.

(b)   Money deposited in an official depository or deposited at interest pursuant to G.S. 115D-58.6(a1) shall be secured in the manner prescribed in G.S. 159-31(b). When deposits are secured in accordance with this subsection, no public officer or employee may be held liable for any losses sustained by an institution because of the default or insolvency of the depository. (1981, c. 157, s. 1; c. 612, s. 1; 2011-145, s. 8.20(b).)

§ 115D-58.8. Facsimile signatures.

The board of trustees may provide by appropriate resolution for the use of facsimile signature machines, signature stamps, or similar devices in signing checks and drafts. The board shall charge some bonded officer or employee with the custody of the necessary machines, stamps, plates, or other devices, and that person and the sureties on his official bond are liable for any illegal, improper, or unauthorized use of them. Rules and regulations governing the use and control of the facsimile signature shall be adopted by the State Board of Community Colleges. (1981, c. 157, s. 1.)

§ 115D-58.9. Daily deposits.

All moneys regardless of source or purpose collected or received by an officer, employee, or agent of an institution shall be deposited intact in accordance with this section. Each officer, employee and agent of an institution whose duty it is to collect or receive any moneys shall deposit his collections and receipts daily. If the board of trustees gives its approval, deposits may be required only when the moneys on hand amount to as much as two hundred fifty dollars ($250.00), but in any event, a deposit shall be made on the last business day of the month. All deposits shall be made in an official depository. Tuition and all revenues declared by law to be State moneys or otherwise required to be deposited with the State Treasurer shall be deposited pursuant to the rules of the State Treasurer pursuant to G.S. 147-77. (1981, c. 157, s. 1.)

§ 115D-58.10. Surety bonds.

The State Board of Community Colleges shall determine what State employees and employees of institutions shall give bonds for the protection of State funds and property and the State Board is authorized to place the bonds and pay the premiums thereon from State funds.

The board of trustees of each institution shall require all institutional employees authorized to draw or approve checks or vouchers drawn on local funds, and all persons authorized or permitted to receive institutional funds from whatever source, and all persons responsible for or authorized to handle institutional property, to be bonded by a surety company authorized to do business with the State in such amount as the board of trustees deems sufficient for the protection of such property and funds. The tax-levying authority of each institution shall provide the funds necessary for the payment of the premiums of such bonds. (1963, c. 448, s. 23; 1979, c. 462, s. 2; c. 896, s. 13; 1979, 2nd Sess., c. 1130, s. 1; 1981, c. 157, s. 1.)

§ 115D-58.11. Fire and casualty insurance on institutional buildings and contents.

(a)   The board of trustees of each institution, in order to safeguard the investment in institutional buildings and their contents, shall:

(1)   Insure and keep insured each building owned by the institution to the extent of the current insurable value, as determined by the insured and insurer, against loss by fire, lightning, and the other perils embraced in extended coverage.

(2)   Insure and keep insured equipment and other contents of all institutional buildings that are the property of the institution or the State or which are used in the operation of the institution.

(b)   The tax-levying authority of each institution shall provide the funds necessary for the purchase of the insurance required in G.S. 115D-58.11(a).

(c)   Boards of trustees may purchase insurance from companies duly licensed and authorized to sell insurance in this State or may obtain insurance in accordance with the provisions of Article 16, Chapter 115, of the General Statutes, "State Insurance of Public School Property." (1963, c. 448, s. 23; 1979, c. 462, s. 2; 1981, c. 157, s. 1.)

§ 115D-58.12. Liability insurance; tort actions against boards of trustees.

(a)   Boards of trustees may purchase liability insurance only from companies duly licensed and authorized to sell insurance in this State or from other qualified companies as determined by the Department of Insurance. Each contract of insurance must, by its terms, adequately insure the board of trustees against any and all liability for any damages by reason of death or injury to person or property proximately caused by the negligence or torts of the agents and employees of such board of trustees or institution when acting within the scope of their authority or the course of their employment. Any company which enters into such a contract of insurance with a board of trustees by such act waives any defense based upon the governmental immunity of such board.

(b)   Any person sustaining damages, or in case of death, his personal representative, may sue a board of trustees insured under this section for the recovery of such damages in any court of competent jurisdiction in this State, but only in a county of the administrative area of the institution against which the suit is brought; and it shall be no defense to any such action that the negligence or tort complained of was in pursuance of a governmental, municipal, or discretionary function of such board of trustees, to the extent that such board is insured as provided by this section.

(c) Nothing in this section shall be construed to deprive any board of trustees of any defense whatsoever to any action for damages, or to restrict, limit, or otherwise affect any such defense; and nothing in this section shall be construed to relieve any person sustaining damages or any personal representative of any decedent from any duty to give notice of such claim to the board of trustees or commence any civil action for the recovery of damages within the applicable period of time prescribed or limited by law.

(d) No part of the pleadings which relate to or allege facts as to a defendant's insurance against liability shall be read or mentioned in the presence of the trial jury in any action brought pursuant to this section. Liability shall not attach unless the plaintiff shall waive the right to have all issues of law and fact relating to insurance in such action determined by a jury, and such issues shall be heard and determined by the judge without resort to a jury, and the jury shall be absent during any motions, arguments, testimony, or announcements of findings of fact or conclusions of law with respect thereto, unless the defendant shall request jury trial thereon.

(e) The board of trustees of all institutions in this Chapter is authorized to pay as a necessary expense the lawful premiums of liability insurance provided in this section. (1963, c. 448, s. 23; 1979, c. 462, s. 2; 1981, c. 157, s. 1; 1985, c. 489.)

§ 115D-58.13. Vending facilities.

Moneys received by an institution on account of operation of vending facilities shall be deposited, budgeted, appropriated, and expended in accordance with the provisions of this Article. (1983 (Reg. Sess., 1984), c. 1034, s. 170.)

§ 115D-58.14. Purchasing flexibility.

(a) Community colleges may purchase supplies, equipment, and materials from noncertified sources that are available under State term contracts, subject to the following conditions:

(1) The purchase price, including the cost of delivery, is less than the cost under the State term contract;

(2) The cost of the purchase shall not exceed the bid value benchmark established under G.S. 143-53.1; and

(3) The items are the same or substantially similar in quality, service, and performance as items available under State term contracts.

(a1) Notwithstanding the provisions of this section, a community college may purchase, in any lawful manner, an item that is neither available under State term contracts nor substantially similar to an item available under State term contracts.

(b) The State Board of Community Colleges and the Department of Administration shall jointly adopt policies and procedures for monitoring the implementation of this section, including without limitation (i) definitions of substantial similarity, (ii) the content and frequency of reports and audits of such purchases, and (iii) a process for identifying any term contract existing as of October 1, 2009, with respect to which the exercise of purchasing flexibility could constitute a breach of that contract.

In the formation of each new term contract entered into after October 1, 2009, the Department of Administration shall, in its discretion, either provide in the contract for the purchasing flexibility set out in this section or make the term contract inapplicable to community colleges.

(c) The State Board of Community Colleges, in consultation with the Department of Administration, shall review the purchasing process for community colleges and may increase or decrease the purchasing/delegation benchmark for each community college based on the college's overall capabilities, including staff resources, purchasing compliance reviews, and audit reports. The State Board may, in its discretion, reduce a community college's purchasing/delegation benchmark at anytime. The State Board shall not increase a community college's purchasing/delegation benchmark by more than fifteen percent (15%) in any calendar year without the concurrence of the Department of Administration within 60 days of submission. The maximum purchasing/delegation benchmark for a community college shall be one hundred thousand dollars ($100,000). (1998-68, s. 2; 2005-103, s. 5; 2009-132, s. 1.)

§ 115D-58.15. Lease purchase and installment purchase contracts for equipment and real property.

(a) Authority. - Notwithstanding any other provision of law to the contrary, the board of trustees of a community college may use lease purchase or installment purchase contracts to purchase or finance the purchase of equipment or real property as provided in this section. A college shall not have more than five State-funded contracts in effect at any one time.

(b) Contract Approval. - Contracts for more than one hundred thousand dollars ($100,000) or for a term of more than three years shall be subject to review and approval as provided in this subsection. If the source of funds for payment of the obligation by the community college is intended to be local funds, the contract must be approved by resolution of the tax-levying authority, and the authority must acknowledge in writing its understanding that the community college may require appropriations from the tax-levying authority in order to meet the college's obligations under the contract. The tax-levying authority may in each fiscal year appropriate sufficient funds to meet the amounts to be paid during the fiscal year under the contract. The source of funds for lease purchase or installment purchase contracts for real property shall be local funds. If the source of funds for payment of the obligation by the community college is intended to be State funds, the contract must be approved by resolution of the State Board of Community Colleges. The State Board may in each fiscal year allocate sufficient funds to meet the amounts to be paid during the fiscal year under the contract.

(c) Local Government Commission. - A contract that is subject to approval by the tax-levying authority also shall be subject to approval by the Local Government Commission as provided in Article 8 of Chapter 159 of the General Statutes if the contract:

(1) Extends for five or more years from the date of the contract;

(2) Obligates the board of trustees to pay sums of money to another, regardless of whether the payee is a party to the contract; and

(3) Obligates the board of trustees to pay five hundred thousand dollars ($500,000) or more over the full term of the contract.

(d) Application of Section. - When determining whether a contract is subject to approval under this section the total cost of exercising an option to upgrade property shall be taken into consideration. The term of a contract shall include periods that may be added to the original term through the exercise of an option to renew or extend.

(e) Nonsubstitution Clause. - No contract entered into under this section may contain a nonsubstitution clause that restricts the right of a board of trustees to:

(1) Continue to provide a service or activity; or

(2) Replace or provide a substitute for any property financed or purchased by the contract.

(f) Nonappropriations Clause. - No deficiency judgment may be rendered against any board of trustees, any tax-levying authority, the State Board of Community Colleges, or the State of North Carolina in any action for breach of a contractual obligation authorized by this section. The taxing power of a tax-levying authority and the State is not and may not be pledged directly or indirectly to secure any moneys due under a contract authorized by this section. (1998-111, s. 2; 2007-484, s. 29(e); 2013-310, s. 1.)

§ 115D-58.16. Audits.

(a) Each community college shall be subject to a financial audit a minimum of once every two years. Community colleges may use State funds to contract with the State Auditor or with a certified public accountant to perform the audits. The colleges shall submit the results of the audits to the State Board of Community Colleges.

The State Board of Community Colleges shall ensure that all colleges are audited in accordance with this section.

(b) Notwithstanding the provisions of Chapter 143D of the General Statutes, a community college shall not be subject to the EAGLE program administered by the Office of the State Controller unless (i) there is a finding of internal control problems in the most recent financial audit of the college or (ii) the State Board of Community Colleges determines that a college should be subject to the program. (2011-145, s. 8.15; 2013-360, s. 10.15(b).)

Article 5.

Special Provisions.

§ 115D-59. Multiple-county administrative areas.

Should two or more counties determine to form an administrative area for the purpose of establishing and supporting an institution, the boards of commissioners of all such counties shall jointly propose a contract to be submitted to the State Board of Community Colleges as part of the request for establishment of an institution. The contract shall provide, in terms consistent with this Chapter, for financial support of the institution, selection of trustees, termination of the contract and the administrative area, and any other necessary provisions. The State Board of Community Colleges shall have authority to approve the terms of the contract as a prerequisite for granting approval of the establishment of the institution and the administrative area. (1963, c. 448, s. 23; 1979, c. 462, s. 2; c. 896, s. 13; 1979, 2nd Sess., c. 1130, s. 1.)

§ 115D-60. Special provisions for Central Piedmont Community College.

(a) The board of commissioners of Mecklenburg County is authorized to provide the local financial support for the Central Piedmont Community College as provided in G.S. 115D-32 by levying a special tax to a maximum annual rate equal to the maximum rate last approved by the voters of the county for the support of the Central Piedmont Community College as operated pursuant to Article 3, Chapter 116, of the General Statutes of North Carolina, or by appropriations from nontax revenues, or by both. The question of increasing the maximum annual rate may be submitted at an election held in accordance with the provisions of G.S. 115D-33(d) and the appropriate provisions of G.S. 115D-35.

(b) When, in the opinion of the board of trustees of said institution, the use of any building, building site, or other real property owned or held by said board is unnecessary or undesirable for the purposes of said institution the board of trustees may sell, exchange, or lease such property in the same manner as is provided by law for the sale, exchange, or lease of school property by county or city boards of education. The proceeds of any such sale or lease shall be used for capital outlay purposes. (1963, c. 448, s. 23; 1965, c. 402; 1979, c. 462, s. 2.)

§ 115D-61. Special provisions for Coastal Carolina Community College.

All local taxes heretofore authorized by the voters of Onslow County to be levied annually for the local financial support of the Onslow County Industrial Education Center may continue to be levied by the board of commissioners of Onslow County for the purpose of providing local financial support of the institution under its present name. (1967, c. 279; 1979, c. 462, s. 2.)

§ 115D-62. Trustee Association Regions.

The State is divided into six Trustee Association Regions as follows:

Region 1: The counties of Buncombe, Cherokee, Clay, Cleveland, Gaston, Graham, Haywood, Henderson, Jackson, Lincoln, Macon, Madison, McDowell, Polk, Rutherford, Swain, and Transylvania.

Region 2: The counties of Alexander, Alleghany, Ashe, Avery, Burke, Cabarrus, Caldwell, Catawba, Iredell, Mitchell, Rowan, Surry, Watauga, Wilkes, Yadkin, and Yancey.

Region 3: The counties of Alamance, Davidson, Caswell, Davie, Durham, Forsyth, Franklin, Granville, Guilford, Orange, Person, Randolph, Rockingham, Stokes, Vance, Warren, and Wake.

Region 4: The counties of Anson, Chatham, Cumberland, Harnett, Hoke, Johnston, Lee, Mecklenburg, Montgomery, Moore, Richmond, Robeson, Scotland, Stanly, and Union.

Region 5: The counties of Bladen, Brunswick, Carteret, Craven, Columbus, Duplin, Greene, Jones, Lenoir, New Hanover, Onslow, Pamlico, Pender, Sampson, and Wayne.

Region 6: The counties of Beaufort, Bertie, Camden, Chowan, Currituck, Dare, Edgecombe, Gates, Halifax, Hertford, Hyde, Martin, Nash, Northampton, Pasquotank, Perquimans, Pitt, Tyrrell, Washington, and Wilson. (1979, c. 896, s. 9; 1993, c. 69, s. 1.)

§§ 115D-63 through 115D-67. Reserved for future codification purposes.

Article 5A.

North Carolina Center for Applied Textile Technology at Gaston College.

§ 115D-67.1. Purpose of the Center.

The purpose of the North Carolina Center for Applied Textile Technology is to develop a world-class workforce for the textile industry in North Carolina; support the textile industry by identifying problems confronting the industry and assisting the industry in solving them; garner support from the textile industry for the work of the Center; and serve as a statewide center of excellence that serves all components of the textile industry. (2005-103, s. 3.)

§ 115D-67.2. Advisory Board.

(a)   The Advisory Board to the North Carolina Center for Applied Textile Technology is hereby established. The purpose of the Advisory Board is to assist in the advancement and administration of the Applied Textile Technology Center.

(b)   The Advisory Board shall consist of 14 members as follows:

(1)   The President of Gaston College, who shall serve ex officio.

(2)	Two members who are residents of North Carolina appointed by the National Council of Textile Organizations.

(2a)	Two members appointed by the Southern Textile Association, Inc.

(3)	Two members appointed by the board of the North Carolina Center for Applied Textile Technology Foundation.

(4)	Two members appointed by the board of trustees of Gaston College.

(5)	Three members appointed by the State Board of Community Colleges.

(6)	One member appointed by the dean of the College of Textiles at North Carolina State University.

(7)	The Director of the Manufacturing Solutions Center at Catawba Valley Community College who shall serve ex officio as a nonvoting member.

The appointing entities shall attempt to appoint members who are distributed geographically throughout the State; members representing large and small companies; and members from each segment of the diverse textile industry including spun yarn manufacturing, filament yarn manufacturing, knitting, weaving, dyeing and finishing, apparel, nonwoven, technical/medical textiles, and fiber producers.

(c)	In order for the terms of members to be staggered, one initial member appointed by the North Carolina Manufacturers Association, Inc., one member appointed by the North Carolina Center for Applied Textile Technology Foundation, one member appointed by the board of trustees of Gaston College, and two members appointed by the State Board of Community Colleges shall serve for two-year terms. The remainder of the initial appointees shall serve for four-year terms. Subsequent terms shall be for four years. Initial terms shall begin July 1, 2005.

Members may serve for no more than two consecutive four-year terms. Members appointed to an initial term of two years and members appointed to fill a vacancy may serve two consecutive four-year terms after the expiration of their term of less than four years.

All vacancies occurring on the board shall be filled for the remainder of the unexpired term by the appointing authority making the original appointment.

Members shall receive per diem, travel, and subsistence allowances in accordance with G.S. 138-5 and G.S. 138-6, as appropriate.

(d)   The Advisory Board is a public body as defined in G.S. 143-318.10(b) and is subject to all provisions of G.S. 143-318.9 through G.S. 143-318.18. (2005-103, s. 3; 2010-31, s. 8.8(a); 2013-410, s. 36(a).)

§ 115D-67.3. Director and other Center personnel.

The President of Gaston College shall appoint an individual to serve as the director of the Center from a list of two or more candidates recommended by the Advisory Board. If the President rejects the recommended candidates, the Advisory Board shall submit two or more additional candidates. The director, after consultation with the Advisory Board and subject to the approval of the President of Gaston College, shall select other staff members of the Center. The director and other staff members of the Center are employees of Gaston College and are subject to the personnel policies of Gaston College. (2005-103, s. 3.)

§ 115D-67.4. Fees collected by the Center; purchases using Center funds.

Notwithstanding any other provision of law, all fees collected by the Applied Textile Technology Center for services to the textile industry, except for regular curriculum and continuing education tuition receipts, shall be retained by the Center and used for the operations of the Center. Purchases made by the Center using these funds are not subject to the provisions of Article 3 of Chapter 143 of the General Statutes. However, the Center shall: (i) submit all proposed agreements or contracts for supplies, materials, printing, equipment, and contractual services that exceed one million dollars ($1,000,000) authorized by this section to the Attorney General or the Attorney General's designee for review as provided in G.S. 114-8.3; and (ii) include in all agreements or contracts to be awarded by the Center under this section a standard clause which provides that the State Auditor and internal auditors of the Center may audit the records of the contractor during and after the term of the contract to verify accounts and data affecting fees and performance. The Center shall not award a cost plus percentage of cost agreement or contract for any purpose. (2005-103, s. 3; 2010-194, s. 17; 2011-326, s. 15(q).)

Article 6.

Textile Training School.

§§ 115D-68 through 115D-71: Repealed by Session Laws 2005-103, s. 2, effective July 1, 2005.

Article 6A.

Motorcycle Safety Instruction.

§ 115D-72. Motorcycle Safety Instruction Program.

(a)   There is created a Motorcycle Safety Instruction Program for the purpose of establishing statewide motorcycle safety instruction to be delivered through the Community Colleges System Office. The Program may be administered by a motorcycle safety coordinator who shall be responsible for the planning, curriculum, and completion requirements of the Program. The State Board of Community Colleges may elect a motorcycle safety coordinator upon nomination of the President of the Community College System, and the compensation of the motorcycle safety coordinator shall be fixed by the State Board upon recommendation of the President of the Community College System pursuant to G.S. 115D-3. The State Board of Community Colleges may contract with an appropriate public or private agency or person to carry out the duties of the motorcycle safety coordinator.

(b)   The Motorcycle Safety Instruction Program shall be implemented through the Community Colleges System Office at institutions which choose to provide the Program. The motorcycle safety coordinator shall select and facilitate the training and certification of instructors who will implement the Program. (1989, c. 755, s. 1; 1993, c. 320, s. 5; 1999-84, s. 15.)

§§ 115D-73 through 115D-76. Reserved for future codification purposes.

Article 7.

Miscellaneous Provisions.

§ 115D-77. Nondiscrimination policy.

It is the policy of the State Board of Community Colleges and of local boards of trustees of the State of North Carolina not to discriminate among students on the basis of race, gender, national origin, religion, age, or disability.

The State Board and each board of trustees shall give equal opportunity for employment and compensation of personnel at community colleges, without regard to race, religion, color, creed, national origin, sex, age, or disability, except where specific age, sex or physical or mental requirements constitute bona fide occupational qualifications. (1979, c. 462, s. 2; c. 896, s. 13; 1979, 2nd Sess., c. 1130, s. 1; 1991, c. 84, s. 4; 1999-84, s. 6.)

§ 115D-78. Access to information and public records; small business counseling information.

(a) In accordance with Chapter 132 of the General Statutes, all rules, regulations and public records of the State Board of Community Colleges, the Community Colleges System Office, and local boards of trustees shall be available for examination and reproduction on payment of fees by any person.

(b) Notwithstanding subsection (a) of this section, documents submitted to the North Carolina Community College System's Small Business Center Network by an individual seeking business counseling or technical assistance and documents created by the Network to provide the individual with counseling and technical assistance are not public records as defined by G.S. 132-1. (1979, c. 462, s. 2; c. 896, s. 13; 1979, 2nd Sess., c. 1130, s. 1; 1999-84, s. 16; 2011-297, s. 1.)

§ 115D-79. Open meetings.

All official meetings of the State Board of Community Colleges and of local boards of trustees shall be open to the public in accordance with the provisions of G.S. 143-318.1 through 143-318.7. (1979, c. 462, s. 2; c. 896, s. 13; 1979, 2nd Sess., c. 1130, s. 1.)

§ 115D-80: Repealed by Session Laws 2011-145, s. 8.18(b1), as amended by Session Laws 2011-391, s. 19, effective July 1, 2011.

§ 115D-81. Saving clauses.

(a) Continuation of Existing Law. - The provisions of this Chapter, insofar as they are the same as those of existing laws, are intended as a continuation of such laws and not as new enactments. The repeal by the act enacting this Chapter of any statute or part thereof shall not revive any statute or part thereof previously repealed or suspended. The provisions of this section shall not affect title to, or ownership of, any real or personal property vested before April 26, 1979. This Chapter shall not in any way affect or repeal any local acts in conflict with the terms of this Chapter.

(b) Existing Rights and Liabilities. - The provisions of this Chapter shall not affect any act done, liability incurred or right accrued or vested, or affect any suit or prosecution pending or to be instituted to enforce any right or penalty or punish any offense under the authority of statutes repealed by the act enacting this Chapter. (1979, c. 462, s. 2.)

§§ 115D-82 through 115D-86. Reserved for future codification purposes.

Article 8.

Proprietary Schools.

§ 115D-87. Definitions.

The following definitions apply in this Article:

(1) Person. - Any individual, association, partnership or corporation, and includes any director, receiver, referee, trustee, executor, or administrator as well as a natural person.

(2) Proprietary school. - An educational institution having a physical presence within North Carolina that meets all of the following conditions:

a. It is privately owned by a sole proprietorship, partnership, limited liability company, or corporation.

b. It is established as a business entity or as a nonprofit charitable organization.

c. It offers instruction to individuals who (i) have completed their elementary and secondary education or (ii) are beyond the age of compulsory secondary school attendance and have demonstrated an ability to benefit from that instruction for the attainment of educational objectives, vocational objectives, or both.

d. It charges tuition or receives any consideration from a student for any portion of the instruction in any form, including written or audiovisual material.

e. It educates, trains, or claims or offers to educate or train students in a program leading toward (i) examinations for licensing in a profession or vocation, (ii) employment at a beginning or advanced level, or (iii) a postsecondary educational credential below the associate degree level.

The term includes a branch or extension of a private postsecondary educational institution of another state that is located in this State or that offers educational services or education at a physical location within this State. Delivery systems employed may include, but are not limited to, (i) correspondence, (ii) classrooms, (iii) hotels or other temporary dwelling units or areas, or (iv) electronic communications such as those used in distance education. Distance education is education, training courses, or programs delivered to a student who is geographically separate from the instructor. It does not include institutions licensed by G.S. 116-15.

If a school has physical locations and offers classes in more than one county, the school's operation in each county shall constitute a separate proprietary school, as defined in this section. (1955, c. 1372, art. 30, ss. 1, 2; 1957, c. 1000; 1961, c. 1175, s. 1; 1981, c. 423, s. 1; 1987, c. 442, s. 2; 1989 (Reg. Sess., 1990), c. 877, s. 1; 1993, c. 553, s. 32.2; 2011-21, s. 1; 2011-326, s. 16(a).)

§ 115D-88. Exemptions.

It is the purpose of this Article to include all private schools operated for profit: Provided, that the following schools shall be exempt from the provisions of this Article:

(1) Nonprofit schools conducted by (i) charities that are exempt from taxation under section 501(c)(3) of the Internal Revenue Code where no fee or tuition is charged to the student or (ii) religious institutions.

(2) Schools maintained or classes conducted by employers for their own employees where no fee or tuition is charged to the student.

(3) Courses of instruction given by any fraternal society, civic club, or benevolent order, which courses are not operated for profit.

(4) Any school for which there is another legally existing licensing or approving board or agency in this State.

(4a) Classes or schools that are equipment-specific to purchasers, users, classes, or schools offering training or instruction to acquaint purchasers or users with equipment capabilities.

(4b) Repealed by Session Laws 2011-21, s. 2, effective July 1, 2011.

(4c) Classes or schools that the State Board, acting by and through the State Board of Proprietary Schools determines are avocational, recreational, self-improvement, or continuing education for already trained and occupationally qualified individuals.

(5) Any established university, professional, or liberal arts college, public or private school regulated or recognized pursuant to Chapter 115C of the General Statutes or by any other State Agency, or any State institution which has heretofore offered, or which may hereinafter offer one or more courses covered in this Article: Provided, that the tuition fees and charges, if any, made by such university, college, high school, or State institution shall be collected by their regular officers in accordance with the rules prescribed by the board of trustees or governing body of such university, college, high school, or State institution; but provisions of the Article shall apply to all proprietary schools as defined in this Article, and operated within the State of North Carolina as such institutions, except schools for which there are other legally existing licensing boards or agencies.

(6) Any institution that is exempt from licensure pursuant to G.S. 116-15(c). (1955, c. 1372, art. 30, ss. 1, 2; 1957, c. 1000; 1961, c. 1175, s. 2; 1981, c. 423, s. 1; 1983, c. 768, s. 10; 1987, c. 442, s. 2; 1989 (Reg. Sess., 1990), c. 877, s. 2; 2011-21, s. 2; 2011-308, s. 2.)

§ 115D-89. State Board of Community Colleges to administer Article; issuance of diplomas by schools; investigation and inspection; rules.

(a) The State Board of Community Colleges, acting by and through the State Board of Proprietary Schools, shall have authority to administer and enforce this Article and to grant and issue licenses to proprietary schools whose sustained curriculum is of a grade equal to that prescribed for similar public schools and educational institutions of the State and which have met the standards set forth by the Board, including but not limited to course offerings, adequate facilities, financial stability, competent personnel and legitimate operating practices.

(b) Any such proprietary school may by and with the approval of the State Board of Community Colleges issue certificates and diplomas.

(c) The State Board, acting by and through the State Board of Proprietary Schools, shall formulate the criteria and the standards evolved thereunder for the approval of such schools or educational institutions, provide for adequate investigations of all schools applying for a license and issue licenses to those applicants meeting the standards fixed by the State Board, maintain a list of schools approved under the provisions of this Article which list shall be available for the information of the public, and provide for periodic inspection of all schools licensed under the provisions of this Article. Through periodic reports required of licensed schools and by inspections made by authorized representatives, the State Board of Community Colleges, acting by and through the State Board of Proprietary Schools, shall have general supervision over proprietary schools in the State, the object of said supervision being to protect the health, safety and welfare of the public by having the proprietary schools maintain adequate, safe and sanitary school quarters, sufficient and proper facilities and equipment, sufficient and qualified teaching and administrative staff, and satisfactory programs of operation and instruction, and to have the school carry out its advertised promises and contracts made with its students and patrons. To this end, the State Board of Community Colleges, acting by and through the State Board of Proprietary Schools, is authorized to issue such rules not inconsistent with the provisions of this Article as are necessary to administer the provisions of this Article.

The State Board, acting by and through the State Board of Proprietary Schools, may request any occupational licensing or approving board or agency in this State to adopt rules requiring the approval of that board or agency for a course of study. Under these rules, the board or agency shall pass on the adequacy of equipment, curricula, and instructional personnel. The State Board of Community Colleges may deny approval to a course of study that is not approved by such board or agency. (1955, c. 1372, art. 30, s. 4; 1957, c. 1000; 1961, c. 1175, s. 3; 1981, c. 423, s. 1; 1987, c. 442, ss. 1, 2; 1989 (Reg. Sess., 1990), c. 877, s. 3; 2011-21, s. 3; 2011-308, s. 3.)

§ 115D-89.1. State Board of Proprietary Schools.

(a)   The State Board of Proprietary Schools is established in the North Carolina Community Colleges System Office.

(b)   The State Board of Proprietary Schools shall consist of seven members as follows:

(1)   The President of the North Carolina Community College System or the President's designee.

(2)   Two members appointed by the Governor.

(3)   Two members appointed by the General Assembly upon the recommendation of the President Pro Tempore of the Senate, one of whom shall be the owner or director of a proprietary school licensed in the State with less than 100 total annual enrollment of students and one the owner or director of a proprietary school or group of proprietary schools licensed in the State with more than 750 total annual enrollment of students.

(4)   Two members appointed by the General Assembly upon the recommendation of the Speaker of the House of Representatives, one of whom shall be the owner or director of a proprietary school licensed in the State with between 100 and 750 total annual enrollment of students and one the owner or director of a proprietary school licensed in the State.

The appointing authorities shall appoint members who have a demonstrated history of experience in proprietary or public postsecondary education, an understanding of standards of quality in postsecondary education, and leadership beyond a particular institution.

(c) No member of the General Assembly, spouse of a member of the General Assembly, or officer or employee of the State shall be eligible to serve on the State Board of Proprietary Schools as appointed members.

(d) One initial member appointed by each appointing authority shall be appointed for a term ending December 30, 2014; the other member shall be appointed for a term ending December 30, 2017. Subsequent appointments shall be for six-year terms beginning on January 1. No person shall be appointed or elected to more than two consecutive six-year terms.

Vacancies in appointments made by the Governor shall be filled by the Governor. Vacancies in the appointments made by the General Assembly shall be filled in accordance with G.S. 120-122.

(e) The State Board of Proprietary Schools may declare vacant the office of a member who does not attend three consecutive scheduled meetings without justifiable excuse. The Chair of the State Board of Proprietary Schools shall notify the appropriate appointing authority of any such vacancy.

(f) The State Board of Proprietary Schools shall elect from its membership a chair and such other officers as it may deem necessary. Officers shall serve for a term of two years.

(g) The State Board of Proprietary Schools shall meet at stated times established by the State Board of Proprietary Schools but not less frequently than four times a year. Special meetings of the State Board of Proprietary Schools may be set at any regular meeting or may be called by the chair. A majority of the qualified members of the State Board of Proprietary Schools shall constitute a quorum for the transaction of business. (2011-308, s. 1.)

§ 115D-89.2. Office of Proprietary Schools; staff.

The Office of Proprietary Schools shall be the principal administrative unit under the direction of the State Board of Proprietary Schools. Unless otherwise specified in G.S. 115D-89.3, the State Board of Proprietary Schools has authority to recommend for adoption and to administer all policies, regulations, and standards which it deems necessary for the operation of the Office of Proprietary Schools.

The State Board of Proprietary Schools shall hire an executive director of the Office of Proprietary Schools, who shall serve as chief administrative officer of the Office of Proprietary Schools, or contract with an outside consultant to serve as the executive director. The compensation of this position shall be fixed by the State Board of Proprietary Schools from funds provided by fees deposited in the Commercial Education Fund.

The State Board of Proprietary Schools may hire other employees as it deems necessary to carry out the provisions of this Article. The compensation of the staff members hired by the State Board of Proprietary Schools shall be fixed by the State Board of Proprietary Schools upon recommendation of the Executive Director of the Office of Proprietary Schools. The Executive Director shall provide an annual projected operating budget to the State Board of Proprietary Schools at a time each year designated by the State Board of Proprietary Schools. The budget will be approved by the State Board of Proprietary Schools from funds provided by fees deposited in the Commercial Education Fund. (2011-308, s. 1; 2012-142, s. 8.9A(b).)

§ 115D-89.3. State Board of Proprietary Schools and State Board of Community Colleges; licensing authority and coordination of responsibilities to administer Article.

The State Board of Community Colleges, having the authority under G.S. 115D-89 to grant and issue licenses to proprietary schools by and through the State Board of Proprietary Schools, shall receive written recommendation from the State Board of Proprietary Schools concerning applicants for licenses and annual renewal applications for licenses. The State Board of Proprietary Schools shall prepare and have approved by the State Board of Community Colleges a certificate of license that reflects the recommendation of the State Board of Proprietary Schools and approval by the State Board of Community Colleges. The State Board of Community Colleges shall also receive from the State Board of Proprietary Schools and have authority concerning proposed changes to the General Statutes and rules affecting proprietary schools. The State Board of Community Colleges shall receive a written report annually from the State Board of Proprietary Schools to include the number of schools receiving initial licenses during the previous year, a list of currently licensed proprietary schools, school closures during the previous year, including a complete report of actions concerning any catastrophic closures, complaints received and resulting decisions or actions, total fees received, and balances of the Commercial Education Fund and the Student Protection Fund. The State Board of Proprietary Schools shall provide the State Board of Community Colleges with any information requested. (2011-308, s. 1.)

§ 115D-89.4. Powers of the State Board of Proprietary Schools.

(a) In order to carry out the purposes of this Article, the State Board of Proprietary Schools, subject to other provisions of this Article, shall:

(1) Have the powers of a body corporate, including the power to make contracts and to alter the same as may be deemed expedient;

(2) Be authorized and empowered to rent and lease such property, real or personal, as the State Board of Proprietary Schools may deem proper to carry out the purposes and provisions of this Article, all or any of them;

(3) Establish an office for the transaction of its business at such place or places as, in the opinion of the State Board of Proprietary Schools, shall be advisable or necessary in carrying out the purposes of this Article;

(4) Be authorized and empowered to pay from the Commercial Education Fund all necessary costs and expenses involved in and incident to the formation, organization, and administration of the State Board of Proprietary Schools and all other costs and expenses reasonably necessary or expedient in carrying out and accomplishing the purposes of this Article; and

(5) Be authorized and empowered to do any and all other acts and things in this Article authorized or required to be done, whether or not included in the general powers listed in this section.

(b) The purchase of goods and services by the State Board of Proprietary Schools shall be exempt from the requirements of Article 3 of Chapter 143 of the General Statutes. (2012-142, s. 8.9A(a).)

§ 115D-90. License required; application for license; school bulletins; requirements for issuance of license; license restricted to courses indicated; supplementary applications.

(a) No person shall operate, conduct or maintain or offer to operate in this State a proprietary school unless a license is first secured from the State Board of Community Colleges granted in accordance with the provisions of this Article and the rules adopted by the Board under the authority of G.S. 115D-89. The license, when issued, shall constitute the formal acceptance by the Board of the educational programs and facilities of each school approved.

(b) Application for a license shall be filed in the manner and upon the forms prescribed and furnished by the State Board of Proprietary Schools for that purpose. Such application shall be signed by the applicant and properly verified and shall contain such of the following information as may apply to the particular school for which a license is sought:

(1) The title or name of the school or classes, together with the name and address of the owners and of the controlling officers thereof.

(2) The general field of instruction.

(3) The place or places where such instruction will be given.

(4) A specific listing of the equipment available for instruction in each field.

(5) The qualifications of instructors and supervisors.

(6) Financial resources available to equip and to maintain the school or classes.

(7) Such additional information as the State Board, acting by and through the State Board of Proprietary Schools, may deem necessary to enable it to determine the adequacy of the program of instruction and matters pertaining thereto. Each application shall be accompanied by a copy of the current bulletin or catalog of the school which shall be in published form and certified by an authorized official of the school as being current, true, and correct in content and policy. The school bulletin shall contain the following information:

a. Identifying data, such as volume number and date of publication.

b. Names of the institution and its governing body, officials and faculty.

c. A calendar of the institution showing legal holidays, beginning and ending date of each quarter, term or semester, and other important dates.

d. Institution's policy and regulations relative to leave, absences, class cuts, make-up work, tardiness and interruptions for unsatisfactory attendance.

e. Institution's policy and regulations on enrollment with respect to enrollment dates and specific entrance requirements for each course.

f. Institution's policy and regulations relative to standards of progress required of the student by the institution. This policy will define the grading system of the institution; the minimum grades considered satisfactory; conditions for interruption for unsatisfactory grades or progress and description of the probationary period, if any, allowed by the institution; and conditions of reentrance for those students dismissed for unsatisfactory progress. A statement will be made regarding progress records kept by the institution and furnished the student.

g. Institution's policy and regulations relating to student conduct and conditions for dismissal for unsatisfactory conduct.

h. Detailed schedule for fees, charges for tuition, books, supplies, tools, student activities, laboratory fees, service charges, rentals, deposits, and all other charges.

i. Policy and regulations of the institution relative to the refund of the unused portion of tuition, fees and other charges in the event the student does not enter the course or withdraws or is discontinued therefrom. The policy and regulations shall provide for, at a minimum, a full refund if a student withdraws before the first day of class or the school cancels the class and a seventy-five percent (75%) refund if the student withdraws within the first twenty-five percent (25%) of the period of enrollment for which the student was charged.

j. A description of the available space, facilities and equipment.

k. A course outline for each course for which approval is requested, showing:

1. Subjects or units in the course,

2. Type of skill to be learned, and

3. Approximate (i) time; (ii) clock hours, and (iii) credit hours or credit hours equivalent, as appropriate, to be spent on each subject or unit.

I. Policy and regulations of the institution relative to granting credit for previous educational training.

(c) After due investigation and consideration on the part of the State Board, acting by and through the State Board of Proprietary Schools, as provided herein, a license shall be granted to the applicant when it is shown to the satisfaction of the State Board that said applicant, school, programs of study or courses are found to have met the following criteria:

(1) The courses, curriculum and instruction are consistent in quality, content and length with similar courses in public schools and other private schools in the State, with recognized accepted standards.

(2) There is in the institution adequate space, equipment, instructional material and instructor personnel to provide training of good quality.

(3) Education and experience qualifications of director, administrators and instructors are adequate.

(4) The institution maintains a written record of the previous education and training of the student.

(5) A copy of the course outline, schedule of tuition, fees and other charges, regulations pertaining to absences, grading policy and rules of operation and conduct will be furnished the student upon enrollment.

(6) Upon completion of training, the student is given a certificate or diploma by the institution indicating the approved course or subjects and indicating that training was satisfactorily completed.

(7) Adequate records as prescribed by the State Board of Community Colleges, acting by and through the State Board of Proprietary Schools, are kept to show attendance and progress or grades and satisfactory standards relating to attendance, progress and conduct are enforced.

(8) The school complies with all local, city, county, municipal, State and federal regulations, such as fire codes, building and sanitation codes. The State Board of Community Colleges may require such evidence of compliance as is deemed necessary.

(9) The school is financially sound and capable of fulfilling its commitments for training.

(10) The school does not exceed its enrollment limitation as established by the State Board of Community Colleges.

(11) The school does not utilize advertising of any type which is erroneous or misleading, either by actual statement, omission or intimation.

(12) The school's administrators, directors, owners and instructors are of good reputation and character.

(13) Such additional criteria as may be deemed necessary by the State Board of Community Colleges.

(d) Any license issued shall be restricted to the programs of instruction or courses or subjects specifically indicated in the application for a license. The holder of a license shall present a supplementary application as may be directed by the State Board of Proprietary Schools for approval of additional programs of instruction, courses, or subjects, in which it is desired to offer instruction during the effective period of the license. (1955, c. 1372, art. 30, ss. 3, 4; 1957, c. 1000; 1961, c. 1175, s. 4; 1981, c. 423, s. 1; 1987, c. 442, ss. 1, 2; 1989 (Reg. Sess., 1990), c. 877, s. 4; 1991, c. 636, s. 11; 2011-21, ss. 4, 5; 2011-308, s. 4.)

§ 115D-91. Duration and renewal of licenses; notice of change of ownership, administration, etc.; license not transferable.

(a) All licenses issued shall expire on June 30.

(b) Unless a duration is otherwise prescribed by the State Board of Community Colleges, licenses shall be renewable annually on July 1 if all of the following conditions are met:

(1) An application for the renewal of the license has been filed in the form and manner prescribed by the State Board, acting by and through the State Board of Proprietary Schools.

(2) The renewal fee has been paid.

(3) The school and its courses, facilities, faculty and all other operations are found to meet the criteria set forth in the requirements for a school to secure an original license.

(c) After a license is granted to any school by the State Board of Community Colleges on the basis of its application, it shall be the responsibility of said school to notify immediately the State Board of any changes in the ownership, administration, location, faculty, the instructional program or other changes as may affect significantly the course of instruction offered.

(d) In the event of the sale of such school, the license already granted to the original owner or operators thereof shall not be transferable to the new ownership or operators. Provided, however, the State Board of Proprietary Schools may issue a 90-day, temporary operating license to a school upon its sale if the school held a valid, current license prior to the sale, and if the State Board of Proprietary Schools finds that the school is likely to qualify after the sale for a license under this Article. (1955, c. 1372, art. 30, s. 4; 1957, c. 1000; 1961, c. 1175, s. 5; 1981, c. 423, s. 1; 1987, c. 442, ss. 1, 2; 1989 (Reg. Sess., 1990), c. 877, s. 5; 2011-21, s. 6; 2011-308, s. 5.)

§ 115D-92. Authority to establish fees; Commercial Education Fund established; refund of fees.

The State Board of Proprietary Schools, as provided in G.S. 115D-89.3, shall establish reasonable fees for licenses, renewals, and approvals granted, and for inspections performed pursuant to this Article in accordance with Article 2A of Chapter 150B of the General Statutes.

The fees and licenses collected under this section shall be placed in a special fund to be designated the "Commercial Education Fund" and shall be used under the supervision and direction of the State Board of Proprietary Schools for the administration of this Article. No license fee shall be refunded in the event the application is rejected or the license suspended or revoked. (1961, c. 1175,

s. 6; 1981, c. 423, s. 1; 1987, c. 442, ss. 1, 2; 1989 (Reg. Sess., 1990), c. 877, s. 6; 2011-308, s. 6.)

§ 115D-93. Suspension, revocation or refusal of license; notice and hearing; judicial review; grounds.

(a) A refusal to issue, refusal to renew, suspension of, or revocation of a license under this section shall be made in accordance with Chapter 150B of the General Statutes.

(b) A decision under this section to refuse to grant, refuse to renew, suspend, or revoke a license is subject to judicial review in accordance with Article 4 of Chapter 150B of the General Statutes.

(c) The State Board, acting by and through the State Board of Proprietary Schools, shall have the power to refuse to issue or renew any such license and to suspend or revoke any such license theretofore issued in case it finds one or more of the following:

(1) That the applicant for or holder of such a license has violated any of the provisions of this Article or any of the rules promulgated thereunder.

(2) That the applicant for or holder of such a license has knowingly presented to the State Board of Community Colleges false or misleading information relating to approval or license.

(3) That the applicant for or holder of such a license has failed or refused to permit authorized representatives of the State Board of Community Colleges to inspect the school, or has refused to make available to them at any time upon request full information pertaining to matters within the purview of the State Board of Community Colleges under the provisions of this Article.

(4) That the applicant for or holder of such a license has perpetrated or committed fraud or deceit in advertising the school or in presenting to the prospective students written or oral information relating to the school, to employment opportunities, or to opportunities for enrollment in other institutions upon completion of the instruction offered in the school.

(5)   That the applicant or licensee has pleaded guilty, entered a plea of nolo contendere or has been found guilty of a crime involving moral turpitude by a judge or jury in any state or federal court.

(6)   That the applicant or licensee has failed to provide or maintain premises, equipment or conditions which are adequate, safe and sanitary, in accordance with such standards of the State of North Carolina or any of its political subdivisions, as are applicable to such premises and equipment.

(7)   That the licensee is employing teachers, supervisors or administrators who have not been approved by the State Board, acting by and through the State Board of Proprietary Schools.

(8)   That the licensee has failed to provide and maintain adequate premises, equipment, materials or supplies, or has exceeded the maximum enrollment for which the school or class was licensed.

(9)   That the licensee has failed to provide and maintain adequate standards of instruction or an adequate and qualified administrative, supervisory or teaching staff.

(10)   That the applicant for or a holder of a license has failed to provide a required bond or bond alternative.

(11)   That the applicant for or holder of a license has failed to pay assessments into the Student Protection Fund. (1961, c. 1175, s. 7; 1973, c. 1331, s. 3; 1981, c. 423, s. 1; 1987, c. 442, ss. 1, 2; c. 827, s. 53; 1989 (Reg. Sess., 1990), c. 877, s. 7; 2009-562, s. 1; 2011-308, s. 7.)

§ 115D-94: Repealed by Session Laws 1983 (Regular Session, 1984), c. 995, s. 17.

§ 115D-95. Bonds required.

(a)   Requirement. - An applicant for a license must comply with the bond requirements in this section. The bond covers the potential loss by students of the school of prepaid tuition and other payments made by them to a school licensed under this Article by reason of the school ceasing to operate for any reason, including the suspension, revocation, or nonrenewal of a school's license, bankruptcy, or foreclosure.

(b) Amount. - An applicant for a license must file a bond with the North Carolina State Board of Community Colleges executed by the applicant as a principal and by a bonding company authorized to do business in this State. The bond must be payable to the State Board of Community Colleges, must be conditioned on fulfillment of the school's obligations, and must remain in effect until cancelled by the bonding company. The bonding company may cancel the bond upon 30 days' notice to the State Board of Community Colleges.

The application must set out calculations made by the applicant to determine the amount of bond required with the application. The required amount is determined as follows:

(1) Initial licensure. - For an applicant for initial licensure of a school, the bond amount is the amount determined by the State Board that is adequate to provide indemnification to any student, or the student's parent or guardian who has suffered a loss of tuition, fees, or any other instructional-related expenses paid to the school. A bond amount shall be at least twenty-five thousand dollars ($25,000).

(2) First four renewals. - For a school that has been licensed for one year but less than six years, the bond shall be in an amount equal to the greatest amount of unearned paid tuition in the school's possession at anytime during the prior fiscal year. The bond amount shall be evaluated by the school quarterly and reported to the State Board or its representative. A quarterly evaluation requiring an increase of five percent (5%) or more in the amount of the bond held by the school shall require an immediate increase in the bond amount. Bond amounts also shall be evaluated pursuant to this subdivision and the rules of the State Board of Community Colleges and State Board of Proprietary Schools at the time of the school's annual license renewal and increased if necessary regardless of the amount of the change.

(3) Schools in operation more than five years. - A guaranty bond shall be required for license renewal for a school that has been continuously licensed to operate for more than five years in the State, as follows:

a. If the balance of the Student Protection Fund in G.S. 115D-95.1 is below the catastrophic loss amount, the school shall file a guaranty bond in an amount equal to the maximum amount of prepaid tuition held by the school during the prior fiscal year multiplied by the percentage amount the fund is deficient.

b. If the school held prepaid tuition in excess of the Student Protection Fund catastrophic loss amount during the prior fiscal year, in addition to any bond amount required by sub-subdivision a. of this subdivision, the school shall file a guaranty bond for the difference between the prepaid tuition amount held in the previous fiscal year and the Fund catastrophic loss amount.

(c) An applicant that is unable to secure a bond may seek a waiver of the guaranty bond from the State Board of Community Colleges and approval of one of the guaranty bond alternatives set forth in this subsection. With the approval of the State Board, an applicant may obtain in lieu of a bond:

(1) An assignment of a savings account in an amount equal to the bond required (i) which is in a form acceptable to the State Board of Community Colleges; (ii) which is executed by the applicant; and (iii) which is executed by a state or federal savings and loan association, state bank, or national bank, that is doing business in North Carolina and whose accounts are insured by a federal depositors corporation; and (iv) for which access to the account in favor of the State of North Carolina is subject to the same conditions as for a bond in subsection (b) of this section.

(2) A certificate of deposit (i) which is executed by a state or federal savings and loan association, state bank, or national bank, which is doing business in North Carolina and whose accounts are insured by a federal depositors corporation; and (ii) which is either payable to the State of North Carolina, unrestrictively endorsed to the State Board of Community Colleges; in the case of a negotiable certificate of deposit, is unrestrictively endorsed to the State Board of Community Colleges; or in the case of a nonnegotiable certificate of deposit, is assigned to the State Board of Community Colleges in a form satisfactory to the State Board; and (iii) for which access to the certificate of deposit in favor of the State of North Carolina is subject to the same conditions as for a bond in subsection (b) of this section. (1955, c. 1372, art. 30, s. 5; 1957, c. 1000; 1961, c. 1175, s. 9; 1981, c. 423, s. 1; 1987, c. 442, ss. 1, 2; 1989 (Reg. Sess., 1990), c. 824, s. 1; 2009-562, s. 2; 2011-308, s. 8.)

§ 115D-95.1. Student Protection Fund.

(a) Definitions. - As used in this section:

(1) "Catastrophic loss amount" means the amount of funds required to protect prepaid student tuition in case of a large-scale event that would draw against the Student Protection Fund. The amount is one million dollars ($1,000,000).

(2) "Fund cap amount" means the catastrophic loss amount plus a reserve amount. The amount is one million five hundred thousand dollars ($1,500,000).

(b) Student Protection Fund. - The Student Protection Fund is established in the Department of State Treasurer as a statewide fee-supported fund. Interest accruing to the Fund is credited to the Fund. The State Board of Proprietary Schools administers the Fund. The purpose of the Fund is to compensate students enrolled in a proprietary school licensed under this Article who have suffered a loss of tuition, fees, or any other instructional-related expenses paid to the school by reason of the failure of the school to offer or complete student instruction, academic services, or other goods and services related to course enrollment if the school ceases to operate for any reason, including the suspension, revocation, or nonrenewal of a school's license, bankruptcy, or foreclosure.

(c) Student Protection Fund Advisory Committee. - The State Board of Proprietary Schools shall serve as the Student Protection Advisory Committee. The Committee shall advise the State Board of Community Colleges on matters related to the Fund, including, but not limited to, the adjustment of the catastrophic loss amount and Fund cap amount.

(d) Initial Payment. - Prior to its first year of operation in the State, each proprietary school shall pay an initial amount of one thousand two hundred fifty dollars ($1,250) into the Fund.

(e) Annual Revenue Payment. - Each proprietary school operating in the State shall pay annually into the Fund an amount based on its annual gross tuition revenue generated in the State as follows:

Annual Gross Tuition Revenue	Amount of Assessment
$1.00 - $25,000	$200.00
$25,001 - $50,000	$250.00
$50,001 - $100,000	$300.00

$100,001 - $200,000	$400.00
$200,001 - $300,000	$500.00
$300,001 - $400,000	$600.00
$400,001 - $500,000	$700.00
$500,001 - $750,000	$1,000
$750,001 - $1,000,000	$1,250
$1,000,001 - $1,500,000	$1,500
$1,500,001 - $2,000,000	$2,000
Greater than $2,000,000	$2,000 plus one-twentieth of one percent (.05%) of annual gross tuition revenue over $2,000,000.

(f) Suspension of Payments. - If the Student Protection Fund balance is equal to or exceeds the Fund cap amount, the State Board of Proprietary Schools shall suspend payments into the Fund for schools that have been continuously licensed in the State for more than eight years. The State Board of Proprietary Schools shall require schools to resume payments into the Fund if the balance of the Fund is less than the catastrophic loss amount.

(g) Catastrophic Assessments. - If claims against the Student Protection Fund exceed the catastrophic loss amount, the State Board of Proprietary Schools may assess additional fees to the extent necessary to compensate students qualified for repayment under the Fund. The amount of the catastrophic assessment shall not exceed one-half of the amount of the annual revenue payment required by subsection (e) of this section. If the amount of the catastrophic assessment will be insufficient to cover qualified claims, the State Board shall develop a method of allocating funds among claims.

(h) Payment Required for Proprietary School Licensure. - The full and timely payment into the Fund pursuant to this section is a condition of licensure.

(i) Payments Nonrefundable. - No payment to the Student Protection Fund shall be refunded in the event that a school's license application is rejected or a school's license is suspended or revoked.

(j) Student Repayment. - A student, or the student's parent or guardian, who has suffered a loss of tuition, fees, or any other instructional-related expenses paid to a proprietary school licensed under this Article by reason of the school ceasing to operate for any reason, including the suspension, revocation, or nonrenewal of a school's license, bankruptcy, or foreclosure, may qualify for repayments under the Student Protection Fund. The State Board of Community Colleges first must issue repayment from the bonds issued under G.S. 115D-95. If the Student Protection Fund is insufficient to cover the qualified claims, the State Board must develop a method of allocating funds among claims.

(k) Rules. - The State Board of Proprietary Schools shall adopt rules for the implementation of this section. (2009-562, s. 4; 2011-308, s. 9.)

§ 115D-96. Operating school without license or bond made misdemeanor.

Any person, or each member of any association of persons or each officer of any corporation who opens and conducts a proprietary school without first having obtained the license herein required, and without first having executed the bond, paid the assessments into the Student Protection Fund, or both, as required by law, shall be guilty of a Class 3 misdemeanor, and each day the school continues to be open and operated shall constitute a separate offense. (1955, c. 1372, art. 30, s. 7; 1957, c. 1000; 1961, c. 1175, s. 10; 1981, c. 423, s. 1; 1987, c. 442, s. 2; 1989 (Reg. Sess., 1990), c. 877, s. 8; 1993, c. 539, s. 894; 1994, Ex. Sess., c. 24, s. 14(c); 2009-562, s. 3; 2011-21, s. 7.)

§ 115D-97. Contracts with unlicensed schools and evidences of indebtedness made null and void.

All contracts entered into by proprietary schools with students or prospective students, and all promissory notes or other evidence of indebtedness taken in lieu of cash payments by such schools shall be null and void unless such schools are duly licensed as required by this Article. (1957, c. 1000; 1961, c. 1175, s. 11; 1981, c. 423, s. 1; 1987, c. 442, s. 2; 1989 (Reg. Sess., 1990), c. 877, s. 9; 2011-21, s. 8.)

Chapter 115E.

Private Educational Facilities Finance Act.

§§ 115E-1 through 115E-23: Recodified as §§ 159D-35 through 159D-57 by Session Laws 2000-179, s. 1, effective July 1, 2000.

Chapter 116.

Higher Education.

Article 1.

The University of North Carolina.

Part 1. General Provisions.

§ 116-1. Purpose.

(a) In order to foster the development of a well-planned and coordinated system of higher education, to improve the quality of education, to extend its benefits and to encourage an economical use of the State's resources, the University of North Carolina is hereby redefined in accordance with the provisions of this Article.

(b) The University of North Carolina is a public, multicampus university dedicated to the service of North Carolina and its people. It encompasses the 16 diverse constituent institutions and other educational, research, and public service organizations. Each shares in the overall mission of the university. That mission is to discover, create, transmit, and apply knowledge to address the needs of individuals and society. This mission is accomplished through instruction, which communicates the knowledge and values and imparts the skills necessary for individuals to lead responsible, productive, and personally satisfying lives; through research, scholarship, and creative activities, which advance knowledge and enhance the educational process; and through public service, which contributes to the solution of societal problems and enriches the quality of life in the State. In the fulfillment of this mission, the university shall seek an efficient use of available resources to ensure the highest quality in its service to the citizens of the State.

Teaching and learning constitute the primary service that the university renders to society. Teaching, or instruction, is the primary responsibility of each of the constituent institutions. The relative importance of research and public service, which enhance teaching and learning, varies among the constituent institutions, depending on their overall missions. (1971, c. 1244, s. 1; 1995, c. 507, s. 15.17.)

§ 116-2. Definitions.

As used in this Article, unless the context clearly indicates a contrary intent:

(1) "Board" means the Board of Governors of the University of North Carolina.

(2) "Board of trustees" means the board of trustees of a constituent institution.

(3) "Chancellor" means the chancellor of a constituent institution.

(4) "Constituent institution" or "institution" means one of the 16 public institutions of higher education, to wit, the University of North Carolina at Chapel Hill, North Carolina State University at Raleigh, the University of North Carolina at Greensboro, the University of North Carolina at Charlotte, the University of North Carolina at Asheville, the University of North Carolina at Wilmington, Appalachian State University, East Carolina University, Elizabeth City State University, Fayetteville State University, North Carolina Agricultural and Technical State University, North Carolina Central University, North Carolina School of the Arts, redesignated effective August 1, 2008, as the "University of North Carolina School of the Arts," Pembroke State University, redesignated effective July 1, 1996, as the "University of North Carolina at Pembroke", Western Carolina University, and Winston-Salem State University, and the constituent high school, the North Carolina School of Science and Mathematics.

(5) "President" means the President of the University of North Carolina.

(6) "Vending facilities" has the same meaning as it does in G.S. 111-42(d), but also means any mechanical or electronic device dispensing items or something of value or entertainment or services for a fee, regardless of the method of activation, and regardless of the means of payment, whether by coin, currency, tokens, or other means. (1971, c. 1244, s. 1; 1983 (Reg. Sess., 1984), c. 1034, s. 171; 1995 (Reg. Sess., 1996), c. 603, s. 1; 2006-66, s. 9.11(a); 2006-203, s. 39; 2008-192, s. 1.)

§ 116-2.1. Repealed by Session Laws 1971, c. 1244, s. 1.

Part 2. Organization, Governance and Property of the University.

§ 116-3. Incorporation and corporate powers.

The Board of Trustees of the University of North Carolina is hereby redesignated, effective July 1, 1972, as the "Board of Governors of the University of North Carolina." The Board of Governors of the University of North Carolina shall be known and distinguished by the name of "the University of North Carolina" and shall continue as a body politic and corporate and by that name shall have perpetual succession and a common seal. It shall be able and capable in law to take, demand, receive, and possess all moneys, goods, and chattels that shall be given for the use of the University, and to apply to same according to the will of the donors; and by gift, purchase, or devise to receive, possess, enjoy, and retain forever any and all real and personal estate and funds, of whatsoever kind, nature, or quality the same may be, in special trust and confidence that the same, or the profits thereof, shall be applied to and for the use and purpose of establishing and endowing the University, and shall have power to receive donations from any source whatever, to be exclusively devoted to the purposes of the maintenance of the University, or according to the terms of donation.

The corporation shall be able and capable in law to bargain, sell, grant, alien, or dispose of and convey and assure to the purchasers any and all such real and personal estate and funds as it may lawfully acquire when the condition of the grant to it or the will of the devisor does not forbid it; and shall be able and capable in law to sue and be sued in all courts whatsoever; and shall have power to open and receive subscriptions, and in general may do all such things as are usually done by bodies corporate and politic, or such as may be necessary for the promotion of learning and virtue. (1971, c. 1244, s. 1.)

§ 116-3.3. Mediation matters.

(a) Evidence of statements made and conduct occurring in a mediation of a personnel matter involving The University of North Carolina or a constituent institution shall not be subject to discovery and shall be inadmissible in any proceeding in any action on the same claim or any other claim, administrative or judicial, except in a proceeding to enforce a signed settlement agreement. Such evidence is not a public record under Chapter 132 of the General Statutes. Any evidence discoverable or admissible prior to the mediation shall remain discoverable and admissible, whether or not it is presented or discussed during mediation.

(b)   No mediator, person training to become a mediator, nor participant in a mediation of a personnel matter involving The University of North Carolina or a constituent institution shall be compelled to testify or produce evidence with respect to the mediation of the personnel matter in any civil proceeding, except to attest to the signing of any such agreement. (2004-154, s. 1.)

§ 116-4. Constituent institutions of the University of North Carolina.

The University of North Carolina shall be composed of the following institutions of higher education: the University of North Carolina at Chapel Hill, North Carolina State University at Raleigh, the University of North Carolina at Greensboro, the University of North Carolina at Charlotte, the University of North Carolina at Asheville, the University of North Carolina at Wilmington, Appalachian State University, East Carolina University, Elizabeth City State University, Fayetteville State University, North Carolina Agricultural and Technical State University, North Carolina Central University, North Carolina School of the Arts, redesignated effective August 1, 2008, as the "University of North Carolina School of the Arts," Pembroke State University, redesignated effective July 1, 1996, as the "University of North Carolina at Pembroke", Western Carolina University and Winston-Salem State University, and the constituent high school, the North Carolina School of Science and Mathematics. (1971, c. 1244, s. 1; 1995 (Reg. Sess., 1996), c. 603, s. 2; 2006-66, s. 9.11(b); 2008-192, s. 2.)

§ 116-4.1. Repealed by Session Laws 1971, c. 1244, s. 1.

§ 116-5. Initial membership of Board of Governors.

(a)   Commencing July 1, 1972, and continuing for the terms hereinafter stated and until their successors are chosen, the Board of Governors shall consist of the following members:

(1) Three persons elected prior to January 1, 1972, by and from the membership of the Board of Trustees of East Carolina University and two persons elected prior to January 1, 1972, by and from the membership of the board of trustees of each of the following institutions: Appalachian State University, North Carolina Agricultural and Technical State University, North Carolina Central University, and Western Carolina University.

(2) One person elected prior to January 1, 1972, by and from the membership of the board of trustees of each of the following institutions: Elizabeth City State University, Fayetteville State University, North Carolina School of the Arts, redesignated effective August 1, 2008, as the "University of North Carolina School of the Arts," Pembroke State University, redesignated effective July 1, 1996, as the "University of North Carolina at Pembroke", and Winston-Salem State University.

(3) Sixteen persons elected prior to January 1, 1972, by and from the membership of the Board of Trustees of the University of North Carolina.

(4) Two persons elected prior to January 1, 1972, by the Board of Higher Education from its eight members-at-large. These shall be nonvoting members whose terms shall expire on June 30, 1973.

(b) Of the 16 persons elected by the Board of Trustees of the University of North Carolina, four shall serve a term ending on June 30, 1973, four shall serve a term ending on June 30, 1975, four shall serve a term ending on June 30, 1977, and four shall serve a term ending on June 30, 1979. On January 1, 1972, or as soon as practicable thereafter, those 16 persons shall by lot or other means acceptable to them determine which of them shall be assigned the terms ending in 1973, 1975, 1977, and 1979 respectively. Of the 11 persons elected by the boards of trustees of the institutions listed in G.S. 116-5(a)(1), three shall serve a term ending in 1973, three shall serve a term ending on June 30, 1975, three shall serve a term ending on June 30, 1977, and two shall serve a term ending on June 30, 1979. On January 1, 1972, or as soon as practicable thereafter, those 11 persons shall by lot or other means acceptable to them determine which of them shall be assigned the terms ending in 1973, 1975, 1977, and 1979 respectively. Of the five persons elected by the boards of trustees of the institutions listed in G.S. 116-5(a)(2), the member elected from the Board of Trustees of the University of North Carolina School of the Arts shall serve a term ending on June 30, 1973, and of the remaining members, one shall serve a term ending on June 30, 1975, one shall serve a term ending on June 30, 1977, and two shall serve a term ending on June 30, 1979. On January 1,

1972, or as soon as practicable thereafter, those four persons, excluding the member from the University of North Carolina School of the Arts, shall by lot or other means acceptable to them determine which of them shall be assigned the terms ending in 1975, 1977, and 1979 respectively.

(c) Any vacancy occurring in the membership of the Board of Governors between July 1, 1972, and June 30, 1973, shall be filled by appointment of the Governor, and the person appointed shall serve for the remainder of the unexpired term.

(d) The Governor shall serve ex officio as a member and as chairman of the Board of Governors until December 31, 1972. (1971, c. 1244, s. 1; 1995 (Reg. Sess., 1996), c. 603, s. 3; 2008-192, ss. 3, 12.)

§ 116-6. Election and terms of members of Board of Governors.

(a) As the terms of members of the Board of Governors provided for in G.S. 116-5 expire, their successors shall be elected by the Senate and House of Representatives. Sixteen members shall be elected at the regular legislative session in 1993 and every two years thereafter. The Senate and the House of Representatives shall each elect one-half of the persons necessary to fill the vacancies on the Board of Governors.

(b) Repealed by Session Laws 2001-503, s. 1.

(c) In electing members to the Board of Governors, the Senate and the House of Representatives shall select from a slate of candidates made in each house. The slate shall be prepared as provided by resolution of each house. If a sufficient number of nominees who are legally qualified are submitted, then the slate of candidates shall list at least twice the number of candidates for the total seats open. All qualified candidates shall compete against all other qualified candidates. In 1993 and biennially thereafter, each house shall hold their elections within 30 legislative days after appointments to their education committees are complete.

(d) All terms shall commence on July 1 of odd-numbered years and all members shall serve for four-year overlapping terms.

(e) No person may be elected to:

(1) More than three full four-year terms in succession;

(2) A four-year term if preceded immediately by election to two full eight-year terms in succession; or

(3) A four-year term if preceded immediately by election to an eight-year term and a four-year term in succession.

Resignation from a term of office does not constitute a break in service for the purpose of this subsection. Service prior to the beginning of those terms in 1989 shall be included in the limitations.

(f) Any person who has served at least one full term as chairman of the Board of Governors shall be a member emeritus of the Board of Governors for one four-year term beginning at the expiration of that member's regular elected term. Any person already serving as an emeritus member may serve an additional four-year term beginning July 1, 1991. Members emeriti have all the rights and privileges of membership except they do not have a vote.

(g) Effective July 1, 1991, and thereafter, any person who has served at least one term as a member of the Board of Governors after having served as Governor of North Carolina shall be a member emeritus of the Board of Governors, with all the rights and privileges of membership as in G.S. 116-6(f). (1971, c. 1244, s. 1; 1987, c. 228; 1989, c. 274; 1991, c. 220, ss. 2, 3; c. 436, s. 1; 2001-503, s. 1.)

§ 116-6.1. Student member of the Board of Governors.

(a) Commencing July 1, 1991, and during his continuance as a student in good standing at a constituent institution of The University of North Carolina, the person serving as president of the University of North Carolina Association of Student Governments (UNCASG) or his designee shall serve ex officio as a member of the Board of Governors. This student member shall be in addition to the 32 members elected to the Board of Governors.

(b) The student member shall have all the rights and privileges of membership, except that he shall not have a vote. (1991, c. 220, s. 1.)

§ 116-7. General provisions concerning members of the Board of Governors.

(a)   All members of the Board of Governors shall be selected for their interest in, and their ability to contribute to the fulfillment of, the purposes of the Board of Governors, and all members shall be deemed members-at-large, charged with the responsibility of serving the best interests of the whole State. In electing members, the objective shall be to obtain the services of the citizens of the State who are qualified by training and experience to administer the affairs of The University of North Carolina. Members shall be selected based upon their ability to further the educational mission of The University through their knowledge and understanding of the educational needs and desires of all the State's citizens, and their economic, geographic, political, racial, gender, and ethnic diversity.

(b)   No member of the General Assembly or officer or employee of the State, The University of North Carolina, or any constituent institution may be a member of the Board of Governors. No spouse of a member of the General Assembly, or of an officer or employee of The University of North Carolina, or of any constituent institution may be a member of the Board of Governors. Any member of the Board of Governors who is elected or appointed to the General Assembly or who becomes an officer or employee of the State or of any constituent institution or whose spouse is elected or appointed to the General Assembly or becomes an officer or employee of The University of North Carolina or of any constituent institution shall be deemed thereupon to resign from his membership on the Board of Governors.

(b1)   Upon receipt of a referral from the State Ethics Commission in accordance with G.S. 138A-12(k) concerning a member of the Board of Governors, the principal clerk of the house of the General Assembly receiving the referral shall immediately refer the matter to the appropriate education committee of that house. That committee may recommend to that house a resolution providing for the removal of the Board member. If the committee's proposed resolution is adopted by a majority of the members present and voting of that house, the public servant shall be removed and the seat previously held by that Board member becomes vacant.

(c)   Whenever any vacancy shall occur in the elected membership of the Board of Governors, it shall be the duty of the Board to inform the Speaker of the House of Representatives and the President of the Senate of the vacancy. The chamber that originally elected the vacating member shall elect a person to fill the vacancy. The vacancy shall remain unfilled until the appropriate chamber of the General Assembly elects a person to fill the vacancy.

The vacancy shall be filled not later than the adjournment sine die of the next regular session of the General Assembly. The election shall be for the remainder of the unexpired term. Whenever a member shall fail, for any reason other than ill health or service in the interest of the State or nation, to be present for four successive regular meetings of the Board, his place as a member shall be deemed vacant. (1971, c. 1244, s. 1; 1977, c. 875; 1982, Ex. Sess., c. 1, s. 1; 1991, c. 436, s. 2; 2001-503, s. 2; 2006-201, s. 2(b); 2007-278, s. 1.)

§ 116-8. Chairman, vice-chairman and secretary.

The Board of Governors shall elect from its membership for two-year terms, and until their successors have been elected and qualified, a chairman, a vice-chairman and a secretary. No person may serve as chairman more than four years in succession. (1971, c. 1244, s. 1.)

§ 116-9. Meetings of Board of Governors.

The Board of Governors shall meet at stated times established by the Board, but not less frequently than six times a year. The Board of Governors shall also meet with the State Board of Education and the State Board of Community Colleges at least once a year to discuss educational matters of mutual interest and to recommend to the General Assembly such policies as are appropriate to encourage the improvement of public education at every level in this State; these joint meetings shall be hosted by the three Boards according to the schedule set out in G.S. 115C-11(b1). A quorum for the conduct of business shall consist of a majority of the members. (1971, c. 1244, s. 1; 1987 (Reg. Sess., 1988), c. 1102, s. 3.)

§ 116-10. Committees.

The Board of Governors shall have power to appoint from its own number committees which shall be clothed with such powers as the Board of Governors may confer. No committee may reverse a decision concerning policy taken by the Board of Governors at a regular meeting. (1971, c. 1244, s. 1.)

§ 116-11. Powers and duties generally.

The powers and duties of the Board of Governors shall include the following:

(1) The Board of Governors shall plan and develop a coordinated system of higher education in North Carolina. To this end it shall govern the 16 constituent institutions, subject to the powers and responsibilities given in this Article to the boards of trustees of the institutions, and to this end it shall maintain close liaison with the State Board of Community Colleges, the Community Colleges System Office and the private colleges and universities of the State. The Board, in consultation with representatives of the State Board of Community Colleges and of the private colleges and universities, shall prepare and from time to time revise a long-range plan for a coordinated system of higher education, supplying copies thereof to the Governor, the members of the General Assembly, and the institutions. Statewide federal or State programs that provide aid to institutions or students of post-secondary education through a State agency, except those related exclusively to the community college system, shall be administered by the Board pursuant to any requirements of State or federal statute in order to insure that all activities are consonant with the State's long-range plan for higher education.

(2) The Board of Governors shall be responsible for the general determination, control, supervision, management and governance of all affairs of the constituent institutions. For this purpose the Board may adopt such policies and regulations as it may deem wise. Subject to applicable State law and to the terms and conditions of the instruments under which property is acquired, the Board of Governors may acquire, hold, convey or otherwise dispose of, invest and reinvest any and all real and personal property, with the exception of any property that may be held by trustees of institutional endowment funds under the provisions of G.S. 116-36 or that may be held, under authority delegated by the Board of Governors, either by a board of trustees or by trustees of any other endowment or trust fund.

(3) The Board shall determine the functions, educational activities and academic programs of the constituent institutions. The Board shall also determine the types of degrees to be awarded. The powers herein given to the Board shall not be restricted by any provision of law assigning specific functions or responsibilities to designated institutions, the powers herein given superseding any such provisions of law. The Board, after adequate notice and after affording the institutional board of trustees an opportunity to be heard, shall have authority to withdraw approval of any existing program if it appears that the

program is unproductive, excessively costly or unnecessarily duplicative. The Board shall review the productivity of academic degree programs every two years, using criteria specifically developed to determine program productivity.

(3a) The Board of Governors shall direct each constituent institution to adopt a policy that authorizes a minimum of two excused absences each academic year for religious observances required by the faith of a student. The policy may require that the student provide written notice of the request for an excused absence a reasonable time prior to the religious observance. The policy shall also provide that the student shall be given the opportunity to make up any tests or other work missed due to an excused absence for a religious observance.

(4) The Board of Governors shall elect officers as provided in G.S. 116-14. Subject to the provisions of section 18 of this act [Session Laws 1971, Chapter 1244, section 18], the Board shall also elect, on nomination of the President, the chancellor of each of the constituent institutions and fix his compensation. The President shall make his nomination from a list of not fewer than two names recommended by the institutional board of trustees.

(4b) The Board of Governors shall encourage the constituent institutions to offer courses in American Sign Language as a modern foreign language.

(4c) The Board of Governors shall require each constituent institution to develop and implement a policy that recognizes the Cherokee language as a language for which a student may satisfy the foreign language course requirement for degree completion at the institution.

(5) The Board of Governors shall, on recommendation of the President and of the appropriate institutional chancellor, appoint and fix the compensation of all vice-chancellors, senior academic and administrative officers and persons having permanent tenure.

(5a) [Expired.]

(5b) The Board of Governors may by resolution provide that, until July 1, 1998, every president, vice-president, and other administrative officer of the University whom it elects and who is not subject to Chapter 126 of the General Statutes, and every chancellor, vice-chancellor, senior academic officer, senior administrative officer, and faculty member who serves a constituent institution or agency of the University and who is not subject to Chapter 126 of the General Statutes, shall retire on July 1 coincident with or next following his seventieth birthday, unless continued in service on a year-to-year basis in accordance with regulations adopted by the Board of Governors.

(6) The Board shall approve the establishment of any new publicly supported institution above the community college level.

(7) The Board shall set tuition and required fees at the institutions, not inconsistent with actions of the General Assembly.

(7a) The Board of Governors shall develop a uniform core set of notification principles regarding the tuition surcharge, including a process for each campus to notify students and parents at orientation and through each semester's tuition statements, and a process to provide appropriate advance notification to a student when the student is approaching the credit hour limit regarding the tuition surcharge. The Board of Governors shall direct each constituent institution to implement these procedures.

(8) The Board shall set enrollment levels of the constituent institutions.

(8a) The Board of Governors, after consultation with representatives from nonpublic schools, including representatives of nonpublic schools operated under Parts 1 and 3 of Article 39 of Chapter 115C of the General Statutes, and after taking into consideration comments received from the Joint Legislative Education Oversight Committee, shall adopt a policy regarding uniform admissions requirements for applicants from nonpublic schools lawfully operated under Article 39 of Chapter 115C of the General Statutes. The policy shall not arbitrarily differentiate between applicants based upon whether the applicant attended a public or a lawfully operated nonpublic school.

(8b) The Board of Governors shall adopt a policy that prohibits any constituent institution from soliciting or using information regarding the accreditation of a secondary school located in North Carolina that a person attended as a factor affecting admissions, loans, scholarships, or other educational activity at the constituent institution, unless the accreditation was conducted by a State agency. For purposes of this subdivision, the term 'accreditation' shall include certification or any other similar approval process.

(9) a. The Board of Governors shall develop, prepare and present to the Governor and the General Assembly a single, unified recommended budget for all of the constituent institutions of The University of North Carolina. The recommendations shall consist of requests in three general categories: (i) funds

for the continuing operation of each constituent institution, (ii) funds for salary increases for employees exempt from the North Carolina Human Resources Act and (iii) funds requested without reference to constituent institutions, itemized as to priority and covering such areas as new programs and activities, expansions of programs and activities, increases in enrollments, increases to accommodate internal shifts and categories of persons served, capital improvements, improvements in levels of operation and increases to remedy deficiencies, as well as other areas. The president may present to the General Assembly an updated estimate of tuition, fees, and other receipts by June 15 of each year to be included in the budget for the following fiscal year.

a1. The Board of Governors shall provide full documentation and justification of any enrollment change funding request at the time it is recommended. This documentation and justification shall include the most recent academic year's actual enrollment numbers in the same format in which the growth increase request is made. The actual enrollment numbers shall be the actual student credit hours (SCH) or full-time equivalencies (FTE).

b. Funds for the continuing operation of each constituent institution shall be appropriated directly to the institution. Funds for salary increases for employees exempt from the North Carolina Human Resources Act shall be appropriated to the Board in a lump sum for allocation to the institutions. Funds for the third category in paragraph a of this subdivision shall be appropriated to the Board in a lump sum for allocation to the institutions. The Board shall make allocations among the institutions in accordance with the Board's schedule of priorities and any specifications in the Current Operations Appropriations Act. When both the Board and the Director of the Budget deem it to be in the best interest of the State, funds in the third category may be allocated, in whole or in part, for other items within the list of priorities or for items not included in the list. Provided, nothing herein shall be construed to allow the General Assembly, except as to capital improvements, to refer to particular constituent institutions in any specifications as to priorities in the third category.

c. The Director of the Budget may, on recommendation of the Board, authorize transfer of appropriated funds from one institution to another to provide adjustments for over or under enrollment or may make any other adjustments among institutions that would provide for the orderly and efficient operation of the institutions.

d. Repealed by Session Laws 1987, c. 795, s. 27.

(9a) The Board of Governors shall report to the Joint Legislative Education Oversight Committee and the Office of State Budget and Management by March 1 of each year regarding the sum of facilities and administrative fees and overhead receipts for The University of North Carolina that are collected and expended by each constituent institution. The report shall include all of the following information:

a. The collection of facilities and administrative fees and overhead receipts by grant or program.

b. The use of facilities and administrative fees and overhead receipts showing expenditures by grant or program.

c. The sum of facilities and administrative fees and overhead receipts collected or expended by each constituent institution for maintenance and operation of facilities that were constructed with or at any time operated by funds from the General Fund.

(10) The Board shall collect and disseminate data concerning higher education in the State. To this end it shall work cooperatively with the Community Colleges System Office and shall seek the assistance of the private colleges and universities. It may prescribe for the constituent institutions such uniform reporting practices and policies as it may deem desirable.

(10a) The Board of Governors, the State Board of Community Colleges, and the State Board of Education, in consultation with nonprofit postsecondary educational institutions shall plan a system to provide an exchange of information among the public schools and institutions of higher education to be implemented no later than June 30, 1995. As used in this section, "institutions of higher education" shall mean (i) public higher education institutions defined in G.S. 116-143.1(a)(3), and (ii) those nonprofit postsecondary educational institutions as described in G.S. 116-280 that choose to participate in the information exchange. The information shall include:

a. The number of high school graduates who apply to, are admitted to, and enroll in institutions of higher education;

b. College performance of high school graduates for the year immediately following high school graduation including each student's: need for remedial coursework at the institution of higher education that the student attends; performance in standard freshmen courses; and continued enrollment in a subsequent year in the same or another institution of higher education in the State;

c. The progress of students from one institution of higher education to another; and

d. Consistent and uniform public school course information including course code, name, and description.

The Department of Public Instruction shall generate and the local school administrative units shall use standardized transcripts in an automated format for applicants to higher education institutions. The standardized transcript shall include grade point average, class rank, end-of-course test scores, and uniform course information including course code, name, units earned toward graduation, and credits earned for admission from an institution of higher education. The grade point average and class rank shall be calculated by a standard method to be devised by the institutions of higher education.

(10b) The Board of Governors of The University of North Carolina shall report to each community college and to the State Board of Community Colleges on the academic performance of that community college's transfer students.

(10c) The Board of Governors shall require each constituent institution to adhere fully to the Comprehensive Articulation Agreement between The University of North Carolina and the North Carolina Community College System that addresses the transfer of courses and academic credits between the two systems and the admission of transfer students. The Board of Governors shall further ensure that the agreement is applied consistently among the constituent institutions. The University of North Carolina and the North Carolina Community College System shall conduct biannual joint reviews of the Comprehensive Articulation Agreement to ensure that the agreement is fair, current, and relevant for all students and institutions and shall report their findings to the Joint Legislative Education Oversight Committee, including all revisions to the Comprehensive Articulation Agreement and reports of noncompliance by November 1 of each year. The University of North Carolina and the North Carolina Community College System shall also jointly develop an articulation agreement advising tool for students, parents, and faculty to simplify the course transfer and admissions process.

(11) The Board shall assess the contributions and needs of the private colleges and universities of the State and shall give advice and

recommendations to the General Assembly to the end that the resources of these institutions may be utilized in the best interest of the State.

(12)   The Board shall give advice and recommendations concerning higher education to the Governor, the General Assembly, and the boards of trustees of the institutions.

(12a)   Repealed by Session Laws 2013-226, s. 4, effective July 3, 2013, applicable beginning with the 2013-2014 school year.

(12b)   The Board of Governors of The University of North Carolina shall designate the UNC programs that will comprise the UNC Center for School Leadership Development. The Board of Governors shall submit to the Governor and the General Assembly a single, unified recommended budget for the continued operation and expansion of the programs in the Center for School Leadership Development.

(12c)   Repealed by Session Laws 2011-266, s. 1.41(b), effective June 23, 2011.

(12d)   The Board of Governors shall provide a comprehensive annual report on teacher education efforts at The University of North Carolina. The report shall include information about teacher education and recruitment, 2+2 initiatives, distance education programs focused on teacher education, and professional development programs for teachers and school administrators. The teacher education report shall be due on April 15 of each year to the Joint Legislative Education Oversight Committee and the State Board of Education.

(13)   The Board may delegate any part of its authority over the affairs of any institution to the board of trustees or, through the President, to the chancellor of the institution in any case where such delegation appears necessary or prudent to enable the institution to function in a proper and expeditious manner. The Board may delegate any part of its authority over the affairs of The University of North Carolina to the President in any case where such delegation appears necessary or prudent to enable The University of North Carolina to function in a proper and expeditious manner. Any delegation of authority may be rescinded by the Board at any time in whole or in part.

(13a)   The Board of Governors may authorize the President to purchase commercial insurance of any kind to cover all risks or potential liability of the University, the Board of Governors, boards of trustees, other administrative or oversight boards, the President, the University benefit plan administrators, and employees of the University relating to the management, direction, and administration of University employee benefit plans, including the risks and potential liability related to benefit plan investments managed by the University.

Members of the Board of Governors, boards of trustees, other administrative and oversight boards, and employees of the University shall be considered State employees for purposes of Articles 31 and 31A of Chapter 143 of the General Statutes. To the extent that the President purchases commercial liability insurance coverage in excess of one hundred fifty thousand dollars ($150,000) per claim for liability arising under Article 31 or 31A of Chapter 143 of the General Statutes, the provisions of G.S. 143-299.4 shall not apply. To the extent that the President purchases commercial insurance coverage for liability arising under Article 31 or 31A of Chapter 143 of the General Statutes, the provisions of G.S. 143-300.6(a) shall not apply.

The purchase of insurance by the President under this section shall not be construed to waive sovereign immunity or any other defense available to the University, the Board of Governors, boards of trustees, other administrative and oversight boards, the President, University benefit plan administrators, and employees of the University in an action or contested matter in any court, agency, or tribunal. The purchase of insurance by the President shall not be construed to alter or expand the limitations on claims or payments established in G.S. 143-299.2 or limit the right of the University, the Board of Governors, boards of trustees, other administrative or oversight boards, the President, University benefit plan administrators, and employees of the University to defense by the State as provided by G.S. 143-300.3.

(14) The Board shall possess all powers not specifically given to institutional boards of trustees. (1971, c. 1244, s. 1; 1979, c. 862, s. 8; c. 896, s. 13; 1979, 2nd Sess., c. 1130, s. 1; 1983, c. 163; c. 717, ss. 29, 30; c. 761, s. 113; 1983 (Reg. Sess., 1984), c. 1019, s. 2; 1985, c. 757, s. 152; 1985 (Reg. Sess., 1986), c. 955, ss. 23-27; 1987, c. 795, s. 27; 1991 (Reg. Sess., 1992), c. 880, ss. 2, 6; c. 1039, s. 25; 1993, c. 407, s. 2; 1993 (Reg. Sess., 1994), c. 677, s. 14; 1995, c. 288, s. 3; 1997-221, s. 12(b); 1997-240, s. 3; 1998-212, s. 11.12(a); 1999-84, s. 19; 2001-424, s. 31.4(b); 2005-276, s. 9.34(b); 2006-66, s. 9.17(a); 2006-95, s. 2.2; 2006-203, s. 40; 2007-154, s. 3(a); 2008-107, s. 9.8; 2008-204, s. 4.1; 2010-31, s. 9.3(a); 2010-112, s. 3; 2011-145, s. 9.18(g); 2011-266, s. 1.41(b); 2011-306, s. 1; 2012-142, ss. 9.4(a), (b), 9.15; 2013-72, s. 1; 2013-226, s. 4; 2013-322, s. 1; 2013-325, s. 2; 2013-360, s. 11.6(a); 2013-382, s. 9.1(c).)

§ 116-11.1. Transferred to G.S. 116-37 by Session Laws 1971, c. 1244, s. 6.

§ 116-11.2. Duties regarding programs in education administration.

The Board of Governors shall direct the constituent institutions with programs in education administration to revise the programs to reflect any increased standards required for programs approved by the State Board of Education, including new requirements for school-based leadership in the public schools. The Board of Governors shall monitor the programs and devise an assessment plan for all programs leading to certification in education administration. (1991, c. 689, s. 200(e).)

§ 116-12. Property and obligations.

All property of whatsoever kind and all rights and privileges held by the Board of Higher Education and by the Boards of Trustees of Appalachian State University, East Carolina University, Elizabeth City State University, Fayetteville State University, North Carolina Agricultural and Technical State University, North Carolina Central University, North Carolina School of the Arts, redesignated effective August 1, 2008, as the "University of North Carolina School of the Arts," Pembroke State University, redesignated effective July 1, 1996, as the "University of North Carolina at Pembroke", Western Carolina University and Winston-Salem State University, as said property, rights and privileges may exist immediately prior to July 1, 1972, shall be, and hereby are, effective July 1, 1972, transferred to and vested in the Board of Governors of the University of North Carolina. All obligations of whatsoever kind of the Board of Higher Education and of the Boards of Trustees of Appalachian State University, East Carolina University, Elizabeth City State University, Fayetteville State University, North Carolina Agricultural and Technical State University, North Carolina Central University, North Carolina School of the Arts, redesignated effective August 1, 2008, as the "University of North Carolina School of the Arts," Pembroke State University, redesignated effective July 1, 1996, as the "University of North Carolina at Pembroke", Western Carolina University and Winston-Salem State University, as said obligations may exist immediately prior to July 1, 1972, shall be, and the same hereby are, effective July 1, 1972, transferred to and assumed by the Board of Governors of the University of North Carolina. Any property, real or personal, held immediately prior to July 1, 1972, by a board of trustees of a constituent institution for the benefit of that institution or by the University of North Carolina for the benefit of any one or more of its six institutions, shall from and after July 1, 1972, be kept separate and distinct from other property held by the Board of Governors, shall continue to be held for the benefit of the institution or institutions that were previously the beneficiaries and shall continue to be held subject to the provisions of the respective instruments, grants or other means or process by which any property right was acquired. All property of whatsoever kind and all rights and privileges held by the Board of Trustees of the North Carolina School of Science and Mathematics, as said property, rights and privileges may exist immediately prior to July 1, 2007, shall be and hereby are, effective July 1, 2007, transferred to and vested in the Board of Governors of The University of North Carolina. All obligations of whatsoever kind of the Board of Trustees of the North Carolina School of Science and Mathematics as said obligations may exist immediately prior to July 1, 2007, shall be, and the same hereby are, effective July 1, 2007, transferred to and assumed by the Board of Governors of The University of North Carolina. In case a conflict arises as to which property, rights or privileges were held for the beneficial interest of a particular institution, or as to the extent to which such property, rights or privileges were so held, the Board of Governors shall determine the issue, and the determination of the Board shall constitute final administrative action. Nothing in this Article shall be deemed to increase or diminish the income, other revenue or specific property which is pledged, or otherwise hypothecated, for the security or liquidation of any obligations, it being the intent that the Board of Governors shall assume said obligations without thereby either enlarging or diminishing the rights of the holders thereof. (1971, c. 1244, s. 1; 1995 (Reg. Sess., 1996), c. 603, s. 4; 2006-66, s. 9.11(c); 2008-192, s. 4.)

§ 116-13. Powers of Board regarding property and services subject to general law.

(a) The power and authority granted to the Board of Governors with regard to the acquisition, operation, maintenance and disposition of real and personal property and services shall be subject to, and exercised in accordance with, the provisions of Chapters 143 and 146 of the General Statutes and related sections of the North Carolina Administrative Code, except when a purchase is being made that is not covered by a State term contract and either:

(1) The funds used to procure personal property or services are not moneys appropriated from the General Fund or received as tuition or, in the case of

multiple fund sources, moneys appropriated from the General Fund or received as tuition do not exceed thirty percent (30%) of the total funds; or

(2)   The funds used to procure personal property or services are contract and grant funds or, in the case of multiple fund sources, the contract and grant funds exceed fifty percent (50%) of the total funds.

When a special responsibility constituent institution makes a purchase under subdivision (1) or (2) of this subsection, the requirements of Chapter 143, Article 3 shall apply, except the approval or oversight of the Secretary of Administration or the State Purchasing Officer is not required, regardless of dollar value.

(b)   Special responsibility constituent institutions shall have the authority to purchase equipment, materials, supplies, and services from sources other than those certified by the Secretary of Administration on term contracts, subject to the following conditions:

(1)   The purchase price, including the cost of delivery, is less than the cost under the State term contract;

(2)   The items are the same or substantially similar in quality, service, and performance as items available under State term contracts;

(3)   The cost of the purchase shall not exceed the benchmark established under G.S. 116-31.10; and

(4)   The special responsibility constituent institution notifies the Department of Administration of purchases consistently being made under this provision so that State term contracts may be improved. (1971, c. 1244, s. 1; 2003-228, s. 1; 2013-234, s. 6.)

§ 116-13.1. Capital facilities; reports; chancellors may authorize certain repair, renovation, and maintenance projects.

(a)   The General Assembly finds that although The University of North Carolina is one of the State's most valuable assets, the current facilities of the University have been allowed to deteriorate due to decades of neglect and have unfortunately fallen into a state of disrepair because of inadequate attention to maintenance. It is the intent of the General Assembly to reverse this trend and to provide a mechanism to assure that the University's capital assets are adequately maintained. The General Assembly commits to responsible stewardship of these assets to protect their value over the years, as follows:

(1) The Board of Governors of The University of North Carolina shall require each constituent and affiliated institution to monitor the condition of its facilities and their needs or repair and renovation, and to assure that all necessary maintenance is carried out within funds available.

(2) Repealed by Session Laws 2012-142, s. 9.4(e), effective July 1, 2012.

(3) It is the intent of the General Assembly to assure that adequate oversight, funding, and accountability are continually provided so that the capital facilities of the University are properly maintained to preserve the level of excellence the citizens of this State deserve. To this end, the Joint Legislative Education Oversight Committee shall report to the General Assembly annually its recommendations for legislative changes to implement this policy.

(b) Equity in University Improvements. - The Board of Governors of The University of North Carolina shall continue to study and monitor any inequities in funding for capital improvements and facilities needs which may still exist on North Carolina's Public Historically Black Colleges and Universities and North Carolina's Historically American Indian University, the University of North Carolina at Pembroke, beyond the funding of the projects provided for in this act, and shall report annually to the Joint Legislative Commission on Governmental Operations on any remaining inequities found, including recommendations as to how those inequities should be addressed.

(c) Approval of Certain Repair and Maintenance Projects. - Notwithstanding G.S. 143C-8-7, the chancellor of a constituent institution may approve the expenditure of available operating funds in an amount not to exceed one million dollars ($1,000,000) per project for projects that are of a type listed in G.S. 143C-4-3(b) and that are for State facilities and related infrastructure that are supported from the General Fund. Funds contractually obligated to an approved project shall not revert at the end of the fiscal year and will remain available to fund the completion of the project. Projects approved pursuant to this subsection shall in all other respects accord with applicable laws governing capital improvement projects. The chancellor of a constituent institution shall report the approval of an expenditure under this subsection to the Office of State Budget and Management and to the Fiscal Research Division of the Legislative Services Commission within 60 days of the approval. (2000-3, ss. 1.1, 8; 2005-153, s. 2; 2011-145, s. 9.6C; 2012-142, s. 9.4(e); 2013-360, s. 36.10.)

§ 116-13.2. Report on University Fiscal Liabilities.

The Board of Governors shall report on an annual basis to the Joint Legislative Commission on Governmental Operations on:

(1)   Any financing of buildings or other facilities, regardless of the ownership of those buildings or other facilities, located on land owned by The University of North Carolina or the constituent institutions of The University of North Carolina; and

(2)   All fiscal liabilities or contingent liabilities, including payments for debt service or other contractual arrangements, of The University of North Carolina or any constituent institution. (2002-126, s. 9.16.)

§ 116-14. President and staff.

(a)   The Board shall elect a President of the University of North Carolina. The President shall be the chief administrative officer of the University.

(b)   The President shall be assisted by such professional staff members as may be deemed necessary to carry out the provisions of this Article, who shall be elected by the Board on nomination of the President. The Board shall fix the compensation of the staff members it elects. These staff members shall include a senior vice-president and such other vice-presidents and officers as may be deemed desirable. Provision shall be made for persons of high competence and strong professional experience in such areas as academic affairs, public service programs, business and financial affairs, institutional studies and long-range planning, student affairs, research, legal affairs, health affairs and institutional development, and for State and federal programs administered by the Board. In addition, the President shall be assisted by such other employees as may be needed to carry out the provisions of this Article, who shall be subject to the provisions of Chapter 126 of the General Statutes. The staff complement shall be established by the Board on recommendation of the President to insure that there are persons on the staff who have the professional competence and experience to carry out the duties assigned and to insure that there are persons on the staff who are familiar with the problems and capabilities of all of the principal types of institutions represented in the system. Subject to approval by the Board, the President may establish and abolish employment positions within the staff complement authorized by this subsection in the manner of and under the conditions prescribed by G.S. 116-30.4 for special responsibility constituent institutions.

(b1) The President shall receive General Fund appropriations made by the General Assembly for continuing operations of The University of North Carolina that are administered by the President and the President's staff complement established pursuant to G.S. 116-14(b) in the form of a single sum to Budget Code 16010 of The University of North Carolina in the manner and under the conditions prescribed by G.S. 116-30.2. The President, with respect to the foregoing appropriations, shall have the same duties and responsibilities that are prescribed by G.S. 116-30.2 for the Chancellor of a special responsibility constituent institution. The President may establish procedures for transferring funds from Budget Code 16010 to the constituent institutions for nonrecurring expenditures. The President may identify funds for capital improvement projects from Budget Code 16010, and the capital improvement projects may be established following the procedures set out in G.S. 143C-8-8 and G.S. 143C-8-9.

(b2) The President, in consultation with the State Auditor and the Director of the Office of State Human Resources, shall ascertain that the management staff and internal financial controls are in place and continue in place to successfully administer the additional authority authorized under G.S. 116-14(b1) and G.S. 116-30.3(e). All actions taken by the President pursuant to G.S. 116-14(b1) and G.S. 116-30.3(e) are subject to audit by the State Auditor.

(c) The President, with the approval of the Board, shall appoint an advisory committee composed of representative presidents of the private colleges and universities and may appoint such additional advisory committees as are deemed necessary or desirable. (1971, c. 1244, s. 1; 1999-237, s. 10.14(b); 2000-140, s. 26; 2006-203, s. 41; 2007-117, s. 1; 2013-382, s. 9.1(c).)

§ 116-15. Licensing of certain nonpublic post-secondary educational institutions.

(a1) The General Assembly of North Carolina in recognition of the importance of higher education and of the particular significance attached to the personal credentials accessible through higher education and in consonance with statutory law of this State making unlawful any "unfair or deceptive acts or practices in the conduct of any trade or commerce," hereby declares it the policy of this State that all institutions conducting post-secondary degree activity in this

State that are not subject to Chapter 115 or 115D of the General Statutes, nor some other section of Chapter 116 of the General Statutes shall be subject to licensure under this section except as the institution or a particular activity of the institution may be exempt from licensure by one or another provision of this section.

(a2) Definitions. - As used in this section the following terms are defined as set forth in this subsection:

(1) "Post-secondary degree". - A credential conferring on the recipient thereof the title of "Associate", "Bachelor", "Master", or "Doctor", or an equivalent title, signifying educational attainment based on (i) study, (ii) a substitute for study in the form of equivalent experience or achievement testing, or (iii) a combination of the foregoing; provided, that "post-secondary degree" shall not include any honorary degree or other so-called "unearned" degree.

(2) "Institution". - Any sole proprietorship, group, partnership, venture, society, company, corporation, school, college, or university that engages in, purports to engage in, or intends to engage in any type of post-secondary degree activity.

(3) "Post-secondary degree activity". - Any of the following is "post-secondary degree activity":

a. Awarding a post-secondary degree.

b. Conducting or offering study, experience, or testing for an individual or certifying prior successful completion by an individual of study, experience, or testing, under the representation that the individual successfully completing the study, experience, or testing will be awarded therefor, at least in part, a post-secondary degree.

(4) "Publicly registered name". - The name of any sole proprietorship, group, partnership, venture, society, company, corporation, school, college, or institution that appears as the subject of any Articles of Incorporation, Articles of Amendment, or Certificate of Authority to Transact Business or to Conduct Affairs, properly filed with the Secretary of State of North Carolina and currently in force.

(5) "Board". - The Board of Governors of The University of North Carolina.

(b) Required License. - No institution subject to this section shall undertake post-secondary degree activity in this State, whether through itself or through an agent, unless the institution is licensed as provided in this section to conduct post-secondary degree activity or is exempt from licensure under this section as hereinafter provided.

(c) Exemption from Licensure. - Any institution that has been continuously conducting post-secondary degree activity in this State under the same publicly registered name or series of publicly registered names since July 1, 1972, shall be exempt from the provisions for licensure under this section upon presentation to the Board of information acceptable to the Board to substantiate such post-secondary degree activity and public registration of the institution's names. Any institution that, pursuant to a predecessor statute to this subsection, had presented to the Board proof of activity and registration such that the Board granted exemption from licensure, shall continue to enjoy such exemption without further action by the Board.

(d) Exemption of Institutions Relative to Religious Education. - Notwithstanding any other provision of this section, no institution shall be subject to licensure under this section with respect to post-secondary degree activity based upon a program of study, equivalent experience, or achievement testing the institutionally planned objective of which is the attainment of a degree in theology, divinity, or religious education or in any other program of study, equivalent experience, or achievement testing that is designed by the institution primarily for career preparation in a religious vocation. This exemption shall be extended to any institution with respect to each program of study, equivalent experience, and achievement test that the institution demonstrates to the satisfaction of the Board should be exempt under this subsection.

(e) Post-secondary Degree Activity within the Armed Forces of the United States. - To the extent that an institution undertakes post-secondary degree activity on the premises of military posts or reservations located in this State for military personnel stationed on active duty there, or their dependents, the institution shall be exempt from the licensure requirements of this section.

(f) Standards for Licensure. - To receive a license to conduct post-secondary degree activity in this State, an institution shall satisfy the Board that the institution has met the following standards:

(1) That the institution is State-chartered. If chartered by a state or sovereignty other than North Carolina, the institution shall also obtain a

Certificate of Authority to Transact Business or to Conduct Affairs in North Carolina issued by the Secretary of State of North Carolina;

(2) That the institution has been conducting post-secondary degree activity in a state or sovereignty other than North Carolina during consecutive, regular-term, academic semesters, exclusive of summer sessions, for at least the two years immediately prior to submitting an application for licensure under this section, or has been conducting with enrolled students, for a like period in this State or some other state or sovereignty, post-secondary educational activity not related to a post-secondary degree; provided, that an institution may be temporarily relieved of this standard under the conditions set forth in subsection (i), below;

(3) That the substance of each course or program of study, equivalent experience, or achievement test is such as may reasonably and adequately achieve the stated objective for which the study, experience, or test is offered or to be certified as successfully completed;

(4) That the institution has adequate space, equipment, instructional materials, and personnel available to it to provide education of good quality;

(5) That the education, experience, and other qualifications of directors, administrators, supervisors, and instructors are such as may reasonably insure that the students will receive, or will be reliably certified to have received, education consistent with the stated objectives of any course or program of study, equivalent experience, or achievement test offered by the institution;

(6) That the institution provides students and other interested persons with a catalog or brochure containing information describing the substance, objectives, and duration of the study, equivalent experience, and achievement testing offered, a schedule of related tuition, fees, and all other necessary charges and expenses, cancellation and refund policies, and such other material facts concerning the institution and the program or course of study, equivalent experience, and achievement testing as are reasonably likely to affect the decision of the student to enroll therein, together with any other disclosures that may be specified by the Board; and that such information is provided to prospective students prior to enrollment;

(7) That upon satisfactory completion of study, equivalent experience, or achievement test, the student is given appropriate educational credentials by

the institution, indicating that the relevant study, equivalent experience, or achievement testing has been satisfactorily completed by the students;

(8) That records are maintained by the institution adequate to reflect the application of relevant performance or grading standards to each enrolled student;

(9) That the institution is maintained and operated in compliance with all pertinent ordinances and laws, including rules and regulations adopted pursuant thereto, relative to the safety and health of all persons upon the premises of the institution;

(10) That the institution is financially sound and capable of fulfilling its commitments to students and that the institution has provided a bond as provided in subsection (f1) of this section;

(11) That the institution, through itself or those with whom it may contract, does not engage in promotion, sales, collection, credit, or other practices of any type which are false, deceptive, misleading, or unfair;

(12) That the chief executive officer, trustees, directors, owners, administrators, supervisors, staff, instructors, and employees of the institution have no record of unprofessional conduct or incompetence that would reasonably call into question the overall quality of the institution;

(13) That the student housing owned, maintained, or approved by the institution, if any, is appropriate, safe, and adequate;

(14) That the institution has a fair and equitable cancellation and refund policy; and

(15) That no person or agency with whom the institution contracts has a record of unprofessional conduct or incompetence that would reasonably call into question the overall quality of the institution.

(f1) (1) A guaranty bond is required for each institution that is licensed. The Board may revoke the license of an institution that fails to maintain a bond pursuant to this subsection.

If the institution has provided a bond pursuant to G.S. 115D-95, the Board may waive the bond requirement under this subsection. The Board may not waive the bond requirement under this subsection if the applicant has provided an alternative to a guaranty bond under G.S. 115D-95(c).

(2) When application is made for a license or license renewal, the applicant shall file a guaranty bond with the clerk of the superior court of the county in which the institution will be located. The bond shall be in favor of the students. The bond shall be executed by the applicant as principal and by a bonding company authorized to do business in this State. The bond shall be conditioned to provide indemnification to any student, or his parent or guardian, who has suffered a loss of tuition or any fees by reason of the failure of the institution to offer or complete student instruction, academic services, or other goods and services related to course enrollment for any reason, including the suspension, revocation, or nonrenewal of an institution's license, bankruptcy, foreclosure, or the institution ceasing to operate.

The bond shall be in an amount determined by the Board to be adequate to provide indemnification to any student, or his parent or guardian, under the terms of the bond. The bond amount for an institution shall be at least equal to the maximum amount of prepaid tuition held at any time during the last fiscal year by the institution. The bond amount shall also be at least ten thousand dollars ($10,000).

Each application for a license shall include a letter signed by an authorized representative of the institution showing in detail the calculations made and the method of computing the amount of the bond, pursuant to this subdivision and the rules of the Board. If the Board finds that the calculations made and the method of computing the amount of the bond are inaccurate or that the amount of the bond is otherwise inadequate to provide indemnification under the terms of the bond, the Board may require the applicant to provide an additional bond.

The bond shall remain in force and effect until cancelled by the guarantor. The guarantor may cancel the bond upon 30 days notice to the Board. Cancellation of the bond shall not affect any liability incurred or accrued prior to the termination of the notice period.

(g) Review of Licensure. - Any institution that acquires licensure under this section shall be subject to review by the Board to determine that the institution continues to meet the standard for licensure of subsection (f), above. Review of such licensure by the Board shall always occur if the institution is legally reconstituted, or if ownership of a preponderance of all the assets of the institution changes pursuant to a single transaction or agreement or a recognizable sequence of transactions or agreements, or if two years has elapsed since licensure of the institution was granted by the Board.

Notwithstanding the foregoing paragraph, if an institution has continued to be licensed under this section and continuously conducted post-secondary degree activity in this State under the same publicly registered name or series of publicly registered names since July 1, 1979, or for six consecutive years, whichever is the shorter period, and is accredited by an accrediting commission recognized by the Council on Post-Secondary Accreditation, such institution shall be subject to licensure review by the Board every six years to determine that the institution continues to meet the standard for licensure of subsection (f), above. However, should such an institution cease to maintain the specified accreditation, become legally reconstituted, have ownership of a preponderance of all its assets transferred pursuant to a single transaction or agreement or a recognizable sequence of transactions or agreements to a person or organization not licensed under this section, or fail to meet the standard for licensure of subsection (f), above, then the institution shall be subject to licensure review by the Board every two years until a license to conduct post-secondary degree activity and the requisite accreditation have been restored for six consecutive years.

(h) Denial and Revocation of Licensure. - Any institution seeking licensure under the provisions of this section that fails to meet the licensure requirements of this section shall be denied a license to conduct post-secondary degree activity in this State. Any institution holding a license to conduct post-secondary degree activity in this State that is found by the Board of Governors not to satisfy the licensure requirements of this section shall have its license to conduct post-secondary degree activity in this State revoked by the Board; provided, that the Board of Governors may continue in force the license of an institution deemed by the Board to be making substantial and expeditious progress toward remedying its licensure deficiencies.

(i) Regulatory Authority in the Board. - The Board shall have authority to establish such rules, regulations, and procedures as it may deem necessary or appropriate to effect the provisions of this section. Such rules, regulations, and procedures may include provision for the granting of an interim permit to conduct post-secondary degree activity in this State to an institution seeking licensure but lacking the two-year period of activity prescribed by subsection (f)(2), above.

(j) Enforcement Authority in the Attorney General. - The Board shall call to the attention of the Attorney General, for such action as he may deem appropriate, any institution failing to comply with the requirements of this section.

(k) Severability. - The provisions of this section are severable, and, if any provision of this section is declared unconstitutional or invalid by the courts, such declaration shall not affect the validity of the section as a whole or any provision other than the provision so declared to be unconstitutional or invalid. (1971, c. 1244, s. 1; 1973, c. 1331, s. 3; 1975, c. 268; 1977, c. 563, ss. 1-4; 1979, c. 896, s. 13; 1979, 2nd Sess., c. 1130, s. 1; 1983 (Reg. Sess., 1984), c. 1006; 1989 (Reg. Sess., 1990), c. 824, s. 2; 1997-456, s. 27; 2011-183, s. 81.)

§ 116-16. Tax exemption.

The lands and other property belonging to the University of North Carolina shall be exempt from all kinds of public taxation. (Const., art. 5, s. 5; 1789, c. 306, s. 3; P.R.; R.S., vol. 2, p. 428; Code, s. 2614; Rev., s. 4262; C.S., s. 5783; 1971, c. 1244, s. 2.)

§ 116-17. Purchase of annuity or retirement income contracts for faculty members, officers and employees.

Notwithstanding any provision of law relating to salaries and/or salary schedules for the pay of faculty members, administrative officers, or any other employees of universities, colleges, constituent institutions, and other institutions of higher learning as named and set forth in this Article, and other State agencies qualified as educational institutions under section 501(c)(3) of the United States Internal Revenue Code, the governing boards of any such universities, colleges, constituent institutions, and other institutions of higher learning may authorize the business officer or agent of same to enter into annual contracts with any of the faculty members, administrative officers and employees of said institutions which provide for a reduction in salary below the total established compensation or salary schedule for a term of one year. The financial officer or agent shall use the funds derived from the reduction in the salary of the faculty member, administrative officer or employee to purchase a nonforfeitable annuity or retirement income contract for the benefit of said faculty member, administrative officer or employee of said universities, colleges and institutions. A faculty member, administrative officer or employee who has agreed to a salary reduction for this purpose shall not have the right to receive the amount of the salary reduction in cash or in any other way except the annuity or retirement income contract. Funds used for the purchase of an annuity or retirement income contract shall not be in lieu of any amount earned by the faculty member, administrative officer or employee before his election for a salary reduction has become effective. The agreement for salary reductions referred to herein shall be effected under any necessary regulations and procedures adopted by the various governing boards of the various institutions and on forms prepared by said governing boards. Notwithstanding any other provision of this section or law, the amount by which the salary of any faculty member, administrative officer or employee is reduced pursuant to this section shall not be excluded, but shall be included, in computing and making payroll deductions for social security and retirement system purposes, and in computing and providing matching funds for retirement system purposes.

In lieu of the annuity and related contracts provided for under this section, interests in custodial accounts pursuant to Section 401(f), Section 403(b)(7), and related sections of the Internal Revenue Code of 1986 as amended may be purchased for the benefit of qualified employees under this section with the funds derived from the reduction in the salaries of such employees. (1965, c. 365; 1971, c. 1244, s. 3; 1989, c. 526, s. 3; 2006-66, s. 9.11(d).)

§ 116-17.1. Dependent care assistance program.

The Board of Governors of The University of North Carolina is authorized to provide eligible employees of constituent institutions a program of dependent care assistance as available under Section 129 and related sections of the Internal Revenue Code of 1986, as amended. The Board of Governors may authorize constituent institutions to enter into annual agreements with employees who elect to participate in the program to provide for a reduction in salary. With the approval of the Director of the Budget, savings in the employer's share of contributions under the Federal Insurance Contributions Act on account of the reduction in salary may be used to pay some or all of the administrative expenses of the program. Should the Board of Governors decide to contract with a third party to administer the terms and conditions of a program of dependent care assistance, it may select a contractor only upon a thorough and completely competitive procurement process. (1989, c. 458, s. 3; 1991 (Reg. Sess., 1992), c. 1044, s. 14(d); 1993, c. 561, s. 42; 1993 (Reg. Sess., 1994), c. 769, s. 7.28A; 1997-443, s. 33.20(a); 1999-237, s. 28.27(a).)

§ 116-17.2. Flexible Compensation Plan.

Notwithstanding any other provisions of law relating to the salaries of employees of The University of North Carolina, the Board of Governors of The University of North Carolina is authorized to provide a plan of flexible compensation to eligible employees of constituent institutions for benefits available under Section 125 and related sections of the Internal Revenue Code of 1986 as amended. This plan shall not include those benefits provided to employees under Articles 1, 3B, and 6 of Chapter 135 of the General Statutes nor any vacation leave, sick leave, or any other leave that may be carried forward from year to year by employees as a form of deferred compensation. If a plan of flexible compensation is offered, then a TRICARE supplement shall be offered. In providing a plan of flexible compensation, the Board of Governors may authorize constituent institutions to enter into agreements with their employees for reductions in the salaries of employees electing to participate in the plan of flexible compensation provided by this section. With the approval of the Director of the Budget, savings in the employer's share of contributions under the Federal Insurance Contributions Act on account of the reduction in salary may be used to pay some or all of the administrative expenses of the program. Should the Board of Governors decide to contract with a third party to administer the terms and conditions of a plan of flexible compensation as provided by this section, it may select such a contractor only upon a thorough and completely advertised competitive procurement process. (1989 (Reg. Sess., 1990), c. 1059, s. 3; 1991 (Reg. Sess., 1992), c. 1044, s. 14(h); 1993, c. 561, s. 42; 1993 (Reg. Sess., 1994), c. 769, s. 7.28A; 1997-443, s. 33.20(a); 1999-237, s. 28.27(a); 2013-292, s. 3.)

§ 116-18. Information Center established.

The Board of Governors of the University of North Carolina, with the cooperation of other concerned organizations, shall establish, as a function of the Board, an Educational Opportunities Information Center to provide information and assistance to prospective college and university students and to the several institutions, both public and private, on matters regarding student admissions, transfers and enrollments. The public institutions shall cooperate with the Center by furnishing such nonconfidential information as may assist the Center in the performance of its duties. Similar cooperation shall be requested of the private institutions in the State.

An applicant for admission to an institution who is not offered admission may request that the institution send to the Center appropriate nonconfidential information concerning his application. The Center may, at its discretion and with permission of the applicant, direct the attention of the applicant to other institutions and the attention of other institutions to the applicant. The Center is authorized to conduct such studies and analyses of admissions, transfers and enrollments as may be deemed appropriate. (1971, c. 1086, s. 1; c. 1244, s. 4.)

§ 116-19: Repealed by Session Laws 2011-145, s. 9.18(c), effective July 1, 2012.

§ 116-20: Repealed by Session Laws 2011-145, s. 9.18(c), effective July 1, 2012.

§ 116-21: Repealed by Session Laws 2011-145, s. 9.18(c), effective July 1, 2012.

§ 116-21.1: Repealed by Session Laws 2011-145, s. 9.18(c), effective July 1, 2012.

§ 116-21.2: Repealed by Session Laws 2011-145, s. 9.18(c), effective July 1, 2012.

§ 116-21.3: Repealed by Session Laws 2011-145, s. 9.18(c), effective July 1, 2012.

§ 116-21.4: Repealed by Session Laws 2011-145, s. 9.18(c), effective July 1, 2012.

§ 116-21.5: Repealed by Session Laws 2009-451, s. 9.15(a), effective July 1, 2009.

§ 116-21.6: Repealed by Session Laws 2011-145, s. 9.14, effective July 1, 2011.

§ 116-22: Repealed by Session Laws 2011-145, s. 9.18(c), effective July 1, 2012.

§§ 116-22.1 through 116-25. Transferred to §§ 116A-3 to 116A-7 by Session Laws 1971, c. 1135, s. 2.

§ 116-25.1. Semester limitation on eligibility for The University of North Carolina need-based financial aid grants.

(a) Except as otherwise provided by this section, a student shall not receive a grant from The University of North Carolina Need-Based Financial Aid Program for more than 10 full-time academic semesters, or its equivalent if enrolled part-time, unless the student is enrolled in a program officially designated by the Board of Governors as a five-year degree program. If a student is enrolled in such a five-year degree program, then the student shall not receive a need-based grant from The University of North Carolina Need-Based Financial Aid Program for more than 12 full-time academic semesters or its equivalent if enrolled part-time.

(b) Upon application by a student, the constituent institution may grant a waiver to the student who may then receive a grant for the equivalent of one additional full-time academic semester if the student demonstrates that any of the following have substantially disrupted or interrupted the student's pursuit of a degree: (i) a military service obligation, (ii) serious medical debilitation, (iii) a short-term or long-term disability, or (iv) other extraordinary hardship. The Board of Governors shall establish policies and procedures to implement the waiver provided by this subsection. (2011-145, s. 9.11(a); 2013-360, s. 11.15(d).)

§ 116-26. Transferred to § 116-43 by Session Laws 1971, c. 1244, s. 17.

§ 116-27. Repealed by Session Laws 1971, c. 1244, s. 1.

§ 116-28: Repealed by Session Laws 1963, c. 448, s. 7.

§ 116-29: Repealed by Session Laws 1963, c. 448, s. 7.

§ 116-29.1. University Cancer Research Fund.

(a) Fund. - The University Cancer Research Fund is established as a special revenue fund in the Office of the President of The University of North Carolina. Allocations from the fund shall be made in the discretion of the Cancer Research Fund Committee and shall be used only for the purpose of cancer research under UNC Hospitals, the Lineberger Comprehensive Cancer Center, or both.

(b) Effective July 1 of each calendar year, the funds remitted to the University Cancer Research Fund by the Secretary of Revenue from the tax on tobacco products other than cigarettes pursuant to G.S. 105-113.40A are appropriated for this purpose.

(c) Cancer Research Fund Committee. - The Cancer Research Fund Committee shall consist of five ex officio members and two appointed members. The five ex officio members shall consist of the following: (i) one member shall be the Chancellor of the University of North Carolina at Chapel Hill, (ii) one member shall be the Director of the Lineberger Comprehensive Cancer Center, (iii) one member shall be the Dean of the School of Medicine at The University of North Carolina, (iv) one member shall be the Dean of the School of Pharmacy at The University of North Carolina, and (v) one member shall be the Dean of the School of Public Health at The University of North Carolina. The remaining two members shall be appointed by a majority vote of the standing members of the Committee and shall be selected from persons holding a leadership position in a nationally prominent cancer program.

If any of the specified positions cease to exist, then the successor position shall be deemed to be substituted in the place of the former one, and the person holding the successor position shall become an ex officio member of the Committee.

(d) Chair. - The chair shall be the Chancellor of the University of North Carolina at Chapel Hill.

(e) Quorum. - A majority of the members shall constitute a quorum for the transaction of business.

(f) Meetings. - The Committee shall meet at least once in each quarter and may hold special meetings at any time and place at the call of the chair or upon the written request of at least a majority of its members.

(g) Report. - By November 1 of each year, the Cancer Research Fund Committee shall provide to the Joint Legislative Education Oversight Committee and to the Office of State Budget and Management an annual financial report which shall include the following components:

(1) Accounting of expenditures of State funds related to strategic initiatives, development of infrastructure, and ongoing administrative functions.

(2) Accounting of expenditures of extramural funds related to strategic initiatives, development of infrastructure, and ongoing administrative functions.

(3) Measures of impact to the State's economy in the creation of jobs, intellectual property, and start-up companies.

(4) Other performance measures directly related to the investment of State funds.

(5) Accounting of any fund balances retained by the Fund, along with information about any restrictions on the use of these funds. (2007-323, s. 6.23(b); 2009-451, s. 27A.5(e); 2010-31, s. 9.12; 2011-145, ss. 6.11(c), 9.4; 2013-360, s. 6.4(d).)

§ 116-29.5: Repealed by Session Laws 2009-209, s. 3, effective June 29, 2009.

§ 116-30: Transferred to § 116-40 by Session Laws 1971, c. 1244, s. 9.

Part 2A. Fiscal Accountability and Flexibility.

§ 116-30.01: Recodified as G.S. 115C-296.4 by Session Laws 2006-66, s. 9.17(c), effective January 1, 2007.

§ 116-30.1. Special responsibility constituent institutions.

The Board of Governors of The University of North Carolina, acting on recommendation made by the President of The University of North Carolina after consultation by him with the State Auditor, may designate one or more constituent institutions of The University as special responsibility constituent institutions. That designation shall be based on an express finding by the Board of Governors that each institution to be so designated has the management staff and internal financial controls that will enable it to administer competently and responsibly all additional management authority and discretion to be delegated to it. The Board of Governors, on recommendation of the President, shall adopt rules prescribing management staffing standards and internal financial controls and safeguards, including the lack of any significant findings in the annual financial audit by the State Auditor's Office, that must be met by a constituent institution before it may be designated a special responsibility constituent institution and must be maintained in order for it to retain that designation. These rules shall not be designed to prohibit participation by a constituent institution because of its size. These rules shall establish procedures for the President and his staff to review the annual financial audit reports, special reports, electronic data processing reports, performance reports, management letters, or any other report issued by the State Auditor's Office for each special responsibility constituent institution. The President shall take immediate action regarding reported weaknesses in the internal control structure, deficiencies in the accounting records, and noncompliance with rules and regulations. In any instance where significant findings are identified, the President shall notify the Chancellor of the particular special responsibility constituent institution that the institution must make satisfactory progress in resolving the findings, as determined by the President of The University, after consultation with the State Auditor, within a three-month period commencing with the date of receipt of the published financial audit report, any other audit report, or management letter. If satisfactory progress is not made within a three-month period, the President of The University shall recommend to the Board of Governors at its next meeting that the designation of the particular institution as a special responsibility constituent institution be terminated until such time as the exceptions are resolved to the satisfaction of the President of The University of North Carolina, after consultation with the State Auditor. However, once the designation as a special responsibility constituent institution has been withdrawn by the Board of Governors, reinstatement may not be effective until the beginning of the following fiscal year at the earliest. Any actions taken by the Board of Governors with respect to withdrawal or reinstatement of an institution's status as a special responsibility constituent institution shall be reported immediately to the Joint Legislative Education Oversight Committee.

The rules established under this section shall include review by the President, after consultation with the State Auditor, the Director of the Office of State Human Resources, and the Director of the Division of State Purchasing and Contracts in ascertaining whether or not a constituent institution has the management staff and internal financial controls to administer the additional authorities authorized under G.S. 116-30.2, 116-30.4, and 143-53.1. Such review and consultation must take place no less frequently than once each biennium. (1991, c. 689, s. 206.2(a); 1993 (Reg. Sess., 1994), c. 591, s. 10(a); 1996, 2nd Ex. Sess., c. 18, s. 7.4(k); 1997-71, s. 1; 2013-382, s. 9.1(c).)

§ 116-30.2. Appropriations to special responsibility constituent institutions.

(a) All General Fund appropriations made by the General Assembly for continuing operations of a special responsibility constituent institution of The University of North Carolina shall be made in the form of a single sum to each budget code of the institution for each year of the fiscal period for which the appropriations are being made. Notwithstanding G.S. 143C-6-4 and G.S.120-76(8), each special responsibility constituent institution may expend monies from the overhead receipts special fund budget code and the General Fund monies so appropriated to it in the manner deemed by the Chancellor to be calculated to maintain and advance the programs and services of the institutions, consistent with the directives and policies of the Board of Governors. Special responsibility constituent institutions may transfer appropriations between budget codes. These transfers shall be considered certified even if as a result of agreements between special responsibility constituent institutions. The preparation, presentation, and review of General Fund budget requests of special responsibility constituent institutions shall be conducted in the same manner as are requests of other constituent institutions. The quarterly allotment procedure established pursuant to G.S. 143C-6-3 shall apply to the General Fund appropriations made for the current operations of each special responsibility constituent institution. All General Fund monies so appropriated to each special responsibility constituent institution shall be recorded, reported, and audited in the same manner as are General Fund appropriations to other constituent institutions.

(b) Repealed by Session Laws 2006-66, s. 9.11(f), effective July 1, 2007.(1991, c. 689, s. 206.2(a); 1993 (Reg. Sess., 1994), c. 591, s. 10(a); c. 769, s. 17.6(c); 1996, 2nd Ex. Sess., c. 18, s. 7.4(i); 1997-443, s. 10.8; 2001-449, s. 1; 2004-124, s. 9.6; 2006-66, ss. 9.8, 9.11(e), (f); 2006-203, s. 42.)

§ 116-30.3. Reversions.

(a) Of the General Fund current operations appropriations credit balance remaining at the end of each fiscal year in each budget code of a special responsibility constituent institution, except for the budget code of the Area Health Education Centers of the University of North Carolina at Chapel Hill, any amount of the General Fund appropriation for that fiscal year may be carried forward by the institution to the next fiscal year and is appropriated for one-time expenditures that will not impose additional financial obligations on the State. Of the General Fund current operations appropriations credit balance remaining in the budget code of the Area Health Education Centers of the University of North Carolina at Chapel Hill, any amount of the General Fund appropriation for that fiscal year may be carried forward in that budget code to the next fiscal year and is appropriated for one-time expenditures that will not impose additional financial obligations on the State. However, the amount carried forward under this section shall not exceed two and one-half percent (2 1/2%) of the General Fund appropriation. The Director of the Budget, under the authority set forth in G.S. 143C-6-2 shall establish the General Fund current operations credit balance remaining in each budget code of each institution.

(b)   Repealed by Session Laws 1998-212, s. 11(b).

(c)   Repealed by Session Laws 1998-212, s. 11(a).

(d)   Repealed by Session Laws 1998-212, s. 11(b).

(e)   Notwithstanding G.S. 143C-1-2 of the General Fund current operations appropriations credit balance remaining in Budget Code 16010 of the Office of General Administration of The University of North Carolina, any amount of the General Fund appropriation for that fiscal year may be carried forward in that budget code to the next fiscal year and is appropriated for one-time expenditures that will not impose additional financial obligations on the State. However, the amount carried forward under this subsection shall not exceed two and one-half percent (2 1/2%) of the General Fund appropriation. The Director of the Budget, under the authority set forth in G.S. 143C-6-2, shall establish the General Fund current operations credit balance remaining in Budget Code 16010 of the Office of General Administration of The University of North Carolina. The funds shall not be used to support positions. (1991, c. 689, s. 206.2(a); 1993 (Reg. Sess., 1994), c. 591, s. 10(a); 1995, c. 507, s. 15.16; 1997-443, s. 10.19; 1998-212, s. 11(a), (b); 1999-237, s. 10.14(a); 2006-203, s. 43.)

§ 116-30.3A. Availability of excess receipts.

Notwithstanding the provisions of Chapter 143C of the General Statutes, receipts within The University of North Carolina realized in excess of budgeted levels shall be available, up to a maximum of ten percent (10%) above budgeted levels, for each Budget Code, in addition to appropriations to support the operations generating the receipts as approved by the Director of the Budget. Notwithstanding the provisions of Chapter 143C of the General Statutes, receipts within The University of North Carolina Health Care System realized in excess of budgeted levels shall be available above budgeted levels, for each Budget Code, in addition to appropriations to support the operations generating the receipts as approved by the Director of the Budget. (2006-203, s. 4.)

§ 116-30.3B. Energy conservation savings.

(a) In addition to the funds carried forward under G.S. 116-30.3, the General Fund current operations appropriations credit balance remaining at the end of each fiscal year for utilities of a constituent institution that is energy savings realized from implementing an energy conservation measure shall be carried forward by the institution to the next fiscal year. Sixty percent (60%) of the energy savings realized shall be utilized for energy conservation measures by that institution. The use of funds under this section shall be limited to onetime capital and operating expenditures that will not impose additional financial obligations on the State. The Director of the Budget, under the authority set forth in G.S. 143C-6-2, shall establish the General Fund current operations credit balance remaining in each budget code of each institution.

(b) It is the intent of the General Assembly that appropriations to the Board of Governors on behalf of a constituent institution not be reduced as a result of the institution's realization of energy savings. Instead, the General Assembly intends that the amount of appropriations be determined as if no energy savings had been realized. The Director of the Budget shall not decrease the recommended continuation budget requirements for utilities for constituent institutions by the amount of energy savings realized from implementing energy conservation measures, including savings achieved through a guaranteed energy savings contract.

(c) Constituent institutions shall submit annual reports on the use of funds authorized pursuant to this section as required under G.S. 143-64.12.

(d) As used in this section, "energy savings," "guaranteed energy savings contract," and "energy conservation measure" have the same meaning as in G.S. 143-64.17. (2010-196, s. 1; 2011-145, s. 9.6D(c).)

§ 116-30.4. Position management.

The Chancellor of a special responsibility constituent institution, when he finds that to do so would help to maintain and advance the programs and services of the institution, may establish and abolish positions, acting in accordance with:

(1)   State personnel policies and procedures if these positions are subject to the North Carolina Human Resources Act and if the institution is operating under the terms of a Performance Agreement or a Decentralization Agreement authorized under Chapter 126 of the General Statutes; or

(2)   Policies and procedures of the Board of Governors if these positions are exempt from the North Carolina Human Resources Act.

The results achieved by establishing and abolishing positions pursuant to the conditions set forth in subdivision (1) of this section shall be subject to postauditing by the Office of State Human Resources. Implementation of personnel actions shall be subject to the availability of funds within the institution's current budget to fund the full annualized costs of these actions. (1991, c. 689, s. 206.2(a); 1993 (Reg. Sess., 1994), c. 591, s. 10(a); 2013-382, s. 9.1(c).)

§ 116-30.5. Impact on education.

The Board of Governors shall require each special responsibility constituent institution to include in its institutional effectiveness plan those assessment measures that are determined by the Board to be measures that will assure some standard measure of student learning and development in general undergraduate education at the special responsibility constituent institutions. The intent of this requirement is to measure the impact of G.S. 116-30.1 through G.S. 116-30.5, establishing and administering special responsibility constituent institutions, and their implementation on undergraduate student learning and development. (1991, c. 689, s. 206.2(a); 1993 (Reg. Sess., 1994), c. 591, s. 10(a).)

§ 116-30.6: Repealed by Session Laws 2007-322, s. 6, effective July 30, 2007.

§ 116-30.7. Biennial projection of enrollment growth for The University of North Carolina.

By October 15 of each even-numbered year, the General Administration of The University of North Carolina shall provide to the Joint Education Legislative Oversight Committee and to the Office of State Budget and Management a projection of the total student enrollment in The University of North Carolina that is anticipated for the next biennium. The enrollment projection shall be divided into the following categories and shall include the projected growth for each year of the biennium in each category at each of the constituent institutions: undergraduate students, graduate students (students earning master's and doctoral degrees), first professional students, and any other categories deemed appropriate by General Administration. The projection shall also distinguish between on-campus and distance education students. The projections shall be considered by the Director of the Budget when determining the amount the Director proposes to fund as the continuation requirement for the enrollment increase in the university system pursuant to G.S. 143C-3-5(b). (2008-107, s. 9.15; 2009-451, s. 9.11.)

§ 116-30.8. Special responsibility constituent institutions: annual audit by State Auditor.

Each special responsibility constituent institution shall be audited annually by the State Auditor. The audit shall be provided to the Chancellor and Board of Trustees of the special responsibility institution, and the Board of Governors of The University of North Carolina. The audit shall also be included in the State's Comprehensive Annual Financial Report (CAFR).

The Board of Governors of The University of North Carolina shall ensure that all special responsibility constituent institutions are audited in accordance with this section. (2011-145, s. 9.16; 2012-142, s. 17.2; 2013-373, s. 2.)

§ 116-30.9: Reserved for future codification purposes.

§ 116-30.10: Reserved for future codification purposes.

§ 116-30.11: Reserved for future codification purposes.

§ 116-30.12: Reserved for future codification purposes.

§ 116-30.13: Reserved for future codification purposes.

§ 116-30.14: Reserved for future codification purposes

§ 116-30.15: Reserved for future codification purposes.

§ 116-30.16: Reserved for future codification purposes.

§ 116-30.17: Reserved for future codification purposes.

§ 116-30.18: Reserved for future codification purposes

§ 116-30.19: Reserved for future codification purposes.

Part 2B. Private, Nonprofit Corporations.

§ 116-30.20. Establishment of private, nonprofit corporations.

The Board of Governors of The University of North Carolina shall encourage the establishment of private, nonprofit corporations to support the constituent institutions of The University of North Carolina and The University System. The President of The University of North Carolina and the chancellors of the constituent institutions may assign employees to assist with the establishment and operation of a nonprofit corporation and may make available to the corporation office space, equipment, supplies, and other related resources; provided, the sole purpose of the corporation is to support The University of North Carolina or one or more of its constituent institutions.

The board of directors of each such private, nonprofit corporation shall secure and pay for the services of The University System's internal auditors or employ a certified public accountant to conduct an audit of the financial accounts of the corporation. The board of directors shall transmit to the Board of Governors a copy of the annual financial audit report of the private, nonprofit corporation. (2005-276, s. 9.22.)

Part 3. Constituent Institutions.

§ 116-31. Membership of the boards of trustees.

(a)   All persons who, as of June 30, 1972, are serving as trustees of the regional universities and of the North Carolina School of the Arts, redesignated effective August 1, 2008, as the "University of North Carolina School of the Arts," except those who may have been elected to the Board of Governors, shall continue to serve for one year beginning July 1, 1972, and the terms of all such trustees shall continue for the period of one year.

(b)   Effective July 1, 1972, a separate board of trustees shall be created for each of the following institutions: North Carolina State University at Raleigh, the University of North Carolina at Asheville, the University of North Carolina at Chapel Hill, the University of North Carolina at Charlotte, the University of North Carolina at Greensboro, and the University of North Carolina at Wilmington. For the period commencing July 1, 1972, and ending June 30, 1973, each such board shall be constituted as follows:

(1)   Twelve or more persons elected prior to July 1, 1972, by and from the membership of the Board of Trustees of the University of North Carolina, and

(2)   The president of the student government of the institution, ex officio.

(c)   If any vacancy should occur in any board of trustees during the year beginning July 1, 1972, the Governor may appoint a person to serve for the balance of the year.

(d)   Except as provided in G.S. 116-65, effective July 1, 1973, each of the 16 institutions of higher education set out in G.S. 116-2(4) shall have board of trustees composed of 13 persons chosen as follows:

(1)   Eight elected by the Board of Governors,

(2)   Four appointed by the Governor, and

(3)   The president of the student government ex officio.

The Board of Trustees of the North Carolina School of Science and Mathematics shall be established in accordance with G.S. 116-233.

(e)   From and after July 1, 1973, the term of office of all trustees, except the ex officio member, shall be four years, commencing on July 1 of odd-numbered years. In every odd-numbered year the Board of Governors shall elect four persons to each board of trustees and the Governor shall appoint two persons to each such board.

(f)   In electing boards of trustees to serve commencing July 1, 1973, the Board of Governors shall designate four persons for four-year terms and four for two-year terms. The Governor, in making appointments of trustees to serve commencing July 1, 1973, shall designate two persons for four-year terms and two for two-year terms.

(g)   From and after July 1, 1973, any person who has served two full four-year terms in succession as a member of a board of trustees shall, for a period of one year, be ineligible for election or appointment to the same board but may be elected or appointed to the board of another institution.

(h)   No member of the General Assembly or officer or employee of the State, The University of North Carolina, or any constituent institution shall be eligible for election or appointment as a trustee. No spouse of a member of the General Assembly, or of an officer or employee of a constituent institution may be a trustee of that constituent institution. Any trustee who is elected or appointed to the General Assembly or who becomes an officer or employee of the State, The University of North Carolina, or any constituent institution or whose spouse is elected or appointed to the General Assembly or becomes an officer or employee of that constituent institution shall be deemed thereupon to resign from his membership on the board of trustees.

(i)   No person may serve simultaneously as a member of a board of trustees and as a member of the Board of Governors. Any trustee who is elected or appointed to the Board of Governors shall be deemed to resign as a trustee effective as of the date that his term commences as a member of the Board of Governors.

(j)   From and after July 1, 1973, whenever any vacancy shall occur in the membership of a board of trustees among those appointed by the Governor, it shall be the duty of the secretary of the board to inform the Governor of the existence of such vacancy, and the Governor shall appoint a person to fill the unexpired term, and whenever any vacancy shall occur among those elected by the Board of Governors, it shall be the duty of the secretary of the board to inform the Board of Governors of the existence of the vacancy, and the Board of Governors shall elect a person to fill the unexpired term. Whenever a member shall fail, for any reason other than ill health or service in the interest of the State or nation, to be present for three successive regular meetings of a board of trustees, his place as a member shall be deemed vacant. (1971, c. 1244, s. 1; 2006-66, s. 9.11(g); 2007-278, s. 2; 2008-192, s. 5.)

§ 116-31.10. Powers of Board regarding certain purchasing contracts.

(a) Notwithstanding G.S. 143-53.1 or G.S. 143-53(a)(2), the expenditure benchmark for a special responsibility constituent institution with regard to competitive bid procedures and the bid value benchmark shall be an amount not greater than five hundred thousand dollars ($500,000). The Board shall set the benchmark for each institution from time to time. In setting an institution's benchmark in accordance with this section, the Board shall consider the institution's overall capabilities including staff resources, purchasing compliance reviews, and audit reports. The Board shall also consult with the Director of the Division of Purchase and Contract and the Director of the Budget prior to setting the benchmark.

(b) Each institution with an expenditure benchmark greater than two hundred fifty thousand dollars ($250,000) shall comply with this subsection for any purchase greater than the institution's benchmark set by the Board but not greater than five hundred thousand dollars ($500,000). This institution shall submit to the Division of Purchase and Contract for that Division's approval or other action deemed necessary by the Division a copy of all offers received and the institution's recommendation of award or other action. Notice of the Division's decision shall be sent to that institution. The institution shall then proceed with the award of contract or other action recommended by the Division. (1997-412, s. 1; 2003-312, s. 1; 2011-145, s. 9.6F(a).)

§ 116-31.11. Powers of Board regarding certain fee negotiations, contracts, and capital improvements.

(a) Notwithstanding G.S. 143-341(3) and G.S. 143-135.1, the Board shall, with respect to the design, construction, or renovation of buildings, utilities, and other property developments of The University of North Carolina requiring the estimated expenditure of public money of two million dollars ($2,000,000) or less:

(1) Conduct the fee negotiations for all design contracts and supervise the letting of all construction and design contracts.

(2) Develop procedures governing the responsibilities of The University of North Carolina and its affiliated and constituent institutions to perform the duties of the Department of Administration and the Director or Office of State Construction under G.S. 133-1.1(d) and G.S. 143-341(3).

(3) Develop procedures and reasonable limitations governing the use of open-end design agreements, subject to G.S. 143-64.34 and the approval of the State Building Commission.

(4) Use existing plans and specifications for construction projects, where feasible. Prior to designing a project, the Board shall consult with the Department of Administration on the availability of existing plans and specifications and the feasibility of using them for a project.

(b) The Board may delegate its authority under subsection (a) of this section to a constituent or affiliated institution if the institution is qualified under guidelines adopted by the Board and approved by the State Building Commission and the Director of the Budget.

(c) The University shall use the standard contracts for design and construction currently in use for State capital improvement projects by the Office of State Construction of the Department of Administration.

(d) A contract may not be divided for the purpose of evading the monetary limit under this section.

(e) Notwithstanding any other provision of this Chapter, the Department of Administration shall not be the awarding authority for contracts awarded pursuant to this section.

(f) The Board of Governors shall annually report to the State Building Commission the following:

(1) A list of projects governed by this section.

(2) The estimated cost of each project along with the actual cost.

(3) The name of each person awarded a contract under this section.

(4) Whether the person or business awarded a contract under this section meets the definition of "minority business" or "minority person" as defined in G.S. 143-128.2(g). (1997-412, s. 1; 2001-496, s. 8(a); 2005-300, ss. 1, 2; 2006-217, s. 2.)

§ 116-31.12. (Effective until June 30, 2015) Acquisition and disposition of real property by lease.

Notwithstanding G.S. 143-341(4), and in addition to the powers granted in G.S. 116-198.34(5), the Board of Governors may authorize the constituent institutions and the General Administration to acquire or dispose of real property by lease if the lease is for a term of not more than 10 years. The Board of Governors shall establish a policy for acquiring and disposing of an interest in real property for the use of The University of North Carolina and its constituent institutions by lease. This policy may delegate authorization of the acquisition or disposition of real property by lease to the boards of trustees of the constituent institutions or to the President of The University of North Carolina. The Board of Governors shall submit all initial policies adopted pursuant to this section to the State Property Office for review prior to adoption by the Board. Any subsequent changes to these policies adopted by the Board of Governors shall be submitted to the State Property Office for review. Any comments by the State Property Office shall be submitted to the President of The University of North Carolina. After the acquisition or disposition of an interest in real property by lease, The University of North Carolina shall promptly file a report concerning the acquisition or disposition to the Secretary of Administration. Acquisitions and dispositions of an interest in real property by lease pursuant to this section shall not be subject to the provisions of Article 36 of Chapter 143 of the General Statutes or to the provisions of Article 6 or 7 of Chapter 146 of the General Statutes. (2007-322, s. 9; 2012-142, s. 9.10(a); 2013-360, s. 11.10(b); 2013-363, s. 3.12.)

§ 116-31.12. (Effective June 30, 2015) Acquisition of real property by lease.

Notwithstanding G.S. 143-341(4), the Board of Governors may authorize the constituent institutions and the General Administration to acquire real property by lease if the lease is for a term of not more than 10 years. The Board of Governors shall establish a policy for acquiring an interest in real property for the use of The University of North Carolina and its constituent institutions by lease. This policy may delegate authorization of the acquisition of real property by lease to the boards of trustees of the constituent institutions or to the President of The University of North Carolina. The Board of Governors shall submit all initial policies adopted pursuant to this section to the State Property Office for review prior to adoption by the Board. Any subsequent changes to these policies adopted by the Board of Governors shall be submitted to the

State Property Office for review. Any comments by the State Property Office shall be submitted to the President of The University of North Carolina. After the acquisition of an interest in real property by lease, The University of North Carolina shall promptly file a report concerning the acquisition to the Secretary of Administration. Acquisitions of an interest in real property by lease pursuant to this section shall not be subject to the provisions of Article 36 of Chapter 143 of the General Statutes or to the provisions of Article 6 of Chapter 146 of the General Statutes. (2007-322, s. 9.)

§ 116-32. Officers and meetings of the boards of trustees.

At the first meeting after June 30 of each year each board of trustees shall elect from its membership a chairman, a vice-chairman and a secretary. Each board of trustees shall hold not less than three regular meetings a year and may hold such additional meetings as may be deemed desirable. (1971, c. 1244, s. 1.)

§ 116-33. Powers and duties of the boards of trustees.

Each board of trustees shall promote the sound development of the institution within the functions prescribed for it, helping it to serve the State in a way that will complement the activities of the other institutions and aiding it to perform at a high level of excellence in every area of endeavor. Each board shall serve as advisor to the Board of Governors on matters pertaining to the institution and shall also serve as advisor to the chancellor concerning the management and development of the institution. The powers and duties of each board of trustees, not inconsistent with other provisions of this Article, shall be defined and delegated by the Board of Governors. (1971, c. 1244, s. 1.)

§ 116-33.1. Board of trustees to permit recruiter access.

If a board of trustees provides access to its buildings and campus and the student information directory to persons or groups which make students aware of occupational or educational options, the board of trustees shall provide access on the same basis to official recruiting representatives of the military forces of the State and of the United States for the purpose of informing students of educational and career opportunities available in the military. (1981, c. 901, s. 3.)

§ 116-33.2. Cooperative Extension Service employees.

The Board of Trustees of North Carolina State University shall adopt personnel policies governing the employment of the employees of the North Carolina Cooperative Extension Service who are exempted from certain provisions of Chapter 126 of the General Statutes pursuant to G.S. 126-5(c1)(9a). (2007-195, s. 2.)

§ 116-34. Duties of chancellor of institution.

(a) The chancellor shall be the administrative and executive head of the institution and shall exercise complete executive authority therein, subject to the direction of the President. He shall be responsible for carrying out policies of the Board of Governors and of the board of trustees. As of June 30 of each year he shall prepare for the Board of Governors and for the board of trustees a detailed report on the operation of the institution for the preceding year.

(b) It shall be the duty of the chancellor to attend all meetings of the board of trustees and to be responsible for keeping the board of trustees fully informed on the operation of the institution and its needs.

(c) It shall be the duty of the chancellor to keep the President, and through him the Board of Governors, fully informed concerning the operations and needs of the institution. Upon request, he shall be available to confer with the President or with the Board of Governors concerning matters that pertain to the institution.

(d) Subject to policies prescribed by the Board of Governors and by the board of trustees, the chancellor shall make recommendations for the appointment of personnel within the institution and for the development of educational programs. (1971, c. 1244, s. 1.)

§ 116-35. Electric power plants, campus school, etc.

Institutions operating electric power plants and distribution systems as of October 30, 1971, are authorized to continue such operation and, after furnishing power to the institution, to sell any excess current to the people of the community at a rate or rates approved by the Utilities Commission. Any net profits derived from the operation, or any proceeds derived from the lease or sale, of such power plants and distribution systems are appropriated and shall be paid into the permanent endowment fund held for the institution as provided for in G.S. 116-36. Institutions operating or authorized to operate, as of October 30, 1971, water or sewer distribution systems, may continue to do so. Each of the institutions now operating a campus laboratory or demonstration school may continue to do so under the presently existing plan of operation, consistent with the appropriations made therefor. The provisions of this section shall not apply to the University Enterprises of the University of North Carolina at Chapel Hill, which shall continue to be governed in all respects as provided in Chapters 634 and 723 of the Session Laws of 1971, G.S. 116-41.1 through 116-41.12, and other applicable legislation. (1971, c. 1244, s. 1; 2006-203, s. 43.1.)

§ 116-36. Endowment fund.

(a) The board of trustees of each constituent institution shall establish and maintain, pursuant to such terms and conditions, uniformly applicable to all constituent institutions, as the Board of Governors of the University of North Carolina may from time to time prescribe, an endowment fund for the constituent institution.

(b) It is not the intent of this section that the proceeds from any endowment fund shall take the place of State appropriations or any part thereof, but it is the intent of this section that those proceeds shall supplement the State appropriations to the end that the institution may improve and increase its functions, may enlarge its areas of service, and may become more useful to a greater number of people.

(c) Pursuant to the foregoing subsections and consistent with the powers and duties prescribed in this section, each board of trustees shall appoint an investment board to be known as "The Board of Trustees of the Endowment Fund of _____" (here shall be inserted the name of the constituent institution).

(d) The trustees of the endowment fund may receive and administer as part of the endowment fund gifts, and devises and any other property of any kind that may come to them from the Board of Governors of the University of North Carolina or that may come to the trustees of the endowment fund from any other source, excepting always the monies received from State appropriations and from tuition and fees collected from students and used for the general operation of the institution.

(e) The trustees of the endowment fund shall be responsible for the prudent investment of the fund in the exercise of their sound discretion, without regard to any statute or rule of law relating to the investment of funds by fiduciaries but in compliance with any lawful condition placed by the donor upon that part of the endowment fund to be invested.

(f) In the process of prudent investment of the fund or to realize the statutory intent of the endowment, the board of trustees of the endowment fund may expend or use interest and principal of gifts, and devises; provided that, the expense or use would not violate any condition or restriction imposed by the original donor of the property which is to be expended or used. To realize the statutory intent of the endowment fund, the board of trustees of the endowment fund may transfer interest or principal of the endowment fund to the useful possession of the constituent institution; provided that, the transfer would not violate any condition or restriction imposed by the original donor of the property which is the subject of the proposed transfer.

(g) The trustees of the endowment fund shall have the power to buy, sell, lend, exchange, lease, transfer, or otherwise dispose of or to acquire (except by pledging their credit or violating a lawful condition of receipt of the corpus into the endowment fund) any property, real or personal, with respect to the fund, in either public or private transaction, and in doing so they shall not be subject to the provisions of Chapters 143, 143C, and 146 of the General Statutes; provided that, any expense or financial obligation of the State of North Carolina created by any acquisition or disposition, by whatever means, of any real or personal property of the endowment fund shall be borne by the endowment fund unless authorization to satisfy the expense or financial obligation from some other source shall first have been obtained from the Director of the Budget.

(h) The Board of Governors of the University of North Carolina shall establish and maintain in a manner not inconsistent with the provisions of this section or with regulations established under this section an endowment fund for all endowment funds now held or hereafter acquired by the University of North

Carolina for the benefit of the University as a whole, or for the joint benefit of any two or more constituent institutions of the University.

(i)   The Board of Governors of the University of North Carolina shall establish and maintain in a manner not inconsistent with the provisions of this section or with regulations established under this section an endowment fund for all endowment funds now held or hereafter acquired for the benefit of the University of North Carolina Press.

(i1)   The Board of Governors of the University of North Carolina shall establish and maintain in a manner not inconsistent with the provisions of this section or with regulations established under this section an endowment fund for all endowment funds now held or hereafter acquired for the benefit of the University of North Carolina Center for Public Television.

(j)   Any gift or devise of real or personal property to a constituent institution of the University of North Carolina or to the University of North Carolina or to the University of North Carolina Press or to the University of North Carolina Center for Public Television shall be presumed, nothing to the contrary appearing, a gift or devise, as the case may be, to the endowment fund of the respective institution or agency.

(k)   Whenever any property of an endowment fund authorized by this section is disposed of or otherwise transferred from the endowment fund, any instrument of transfer shall indicate that the donor, grantor, seller, lessor, lender, or transferor, as the case may be, is the board of trustees of the endowment fund.

(l)   The proceeds and funds described by this section are appropriated and may be used only as provided by this section.

(m)   Chapter 36E of the General Statutes applies to an endowment fund authorized by this section. (1971, c. 1244, s. 1; 1977, c. 506; 1979, c. 649, ss. 2, 3; 1983, c. 717, s. 31; 1985 (Reg. Sess., 1986), c. 955, ss. 28, 29; 2006-203, ss. 44, 44.1; 2009-8, s. 5; 2011-284, s. 83(a), (b), (c).)

§ 116-36.1. Regulation of institutional trust funds.

(a) The Board is responsible for the custody and management of the trust funds of the University of North Carolina and of each institution. The Board shall adopt uniform policies and procedures applicable to the deposit, investment, and administration of these funds which shall assure that the receipt and expenditure of such funds is properly authorized and that the funds are appropriately accounted for. The Board may delegate authority, through the president, to the respective chancellors of the institutions when such delegation is necessary or prudent to enable the institution to function in a proper and expeditious manner.

(b) Trust funds and investment earnings thereon, are available for expenditure by each institution without further authorization from the General Assembly.

(c) Repealed by Session Laws 2011-145, s. 9.6E(a), effective July 1, 2011.

(d) Trust funds are subject to the oversight of the State Auditor pursuant to Article 5A of Chapter 147 of the General Statutes but are not subject to the provisions of the State Budget Act except for capital improvements projects which shall be authorized and executed in accordance with G.S. 143C-8-8 and G.S. 143C-8-9.

(e) Each institution shall submit such reports or other information concerning its trust fund accounts as may be required by the Board.

(f) Trust funds or the investment income therefrom shall not take the place of State appropriations or any part thereof, but any portion of these funds available for general institutional purposes is appropriated and shall be used to supplement State appropriations to the end that the institution may improve and increase its functions, may enlarge its areas of service, and may become more useful to a greater number of people.

(g) As used in this section, "trust funds" means:

(1) Monies, or the proceeds of other forms of property, received by an institution as gifts or devises that are neither presumed nor designated to be gifts or devises to the endowment fund of the institution;

(2) Moneys received by an institution pursuant to grants from, or contracts with, the United States government or any agency or instrumentality thereof;

(3) Moneys received by an institution pursuant to grants from, or contracts with, any State agencies, any political subdivisions of the State, any other states or nations or political subdivisions thereof, or any private entities whereby the institution undertakes, subject to terms and conditions specified by the entity providing the moneys, to conduct research, training or public service programs, or to provide financial aid to students;

(4) Moneys collected by an institution to support extracurricular activities of students of the institution;

(5) Moneys received from or for the operation by an institution of activities established for the benefit of scholarship funds or student activity programs;

(6) Moneys received from or for the operation by an institution of any of its self-supporting auxiliary enterprises, including institutional student auxiliary enterprise funds for the operation of housing, food, health, and laundry services;

(7) Moneys received by an institution in respect to fees and other payments for services rendered by medical, dental or other health care professionals under an organized practice plan approved by the institution or under a contractual agreement between the institution and a hospital or other health care provider;

(8) The net proceeds from the disposition effected pursuant to Chapter 146, Article 7, of any interest in real property owned by or under the supervision and control of an institution if the interest in real property had first been acquired by gift or devise or through expenditure of monies defined in this subsection (g) as "trust funds," except the net proceeds from the disposition of an interest in real property first acquired by the institution through expenditure of monies received as a grant from a State agency;

(9) Moneys received from the operation and maintenance of institutional forests and forest farmlands, provided, that such moneys shall be used, when used, by the institution for support of forest-related research, teaching, and public service programs;

(10) Moneys received from an activity authorized by G.S. 66-58(b)(8)m., n., and o.;

(11) Moneys deposited to the State Education Assistance Authority Fund pursuant to G.S. 116-209.3;

(12) Any other moneys collected by an institution as student fees previously approved by the Board of Governors.

(h) The Board may authorize, through the President, that the chancellors may deposit or invest each institution's available trust fund cash balances in interest-bearing accounts and other investments as may be authorized by the Board in the exercise of its sound discretion, without regard to any statute or rule of law relating to the investment of funds by fiduciaries.

(i) The cash balances on hand as of June 30, 1978, and all future receipts accruing thereafter, of funds identified in this section are hereby appropriated to the use of the University of North Carolina and its constituent institutions. (1977, 2nd Sess., c. 1136, s. 30; 1981, c. 529; 1983, c. 913, s. 19; 1989 (Reg. Sess., 1990), c. 936, s. 1(c); 2005-397, s. 3; 2006-203, s. 45; 2011-145, s. 9.6E(a); 2011-284, s. 84; 2012-142, s. 9.9.)

§ 116-36.2. Regulation of special funds of individual institutions.

(a) Notwithstanding Chapter 143C or any provisions of law other than Article 5A of Chapter 147 of the General Statutes, the chancellor of each institution is responsible for the custody and management of the special funds of that institution. The Board shall adopt uniform policies and procedures applicable to the administration of these funds which shall assure that the receipt and expenditure of such funds is properly authorized and that the funds are appropriately accounted for. The special funds of individual institutions regulated by this section are appropriated and may be used only as authorized by this section.

(b) As used in this section, "special funds of individual institutions" means:

(1) Moneys received from or for the operation by an institution of its program of intercollegiate athletics;

(2) Moneys held by an institution as fiscal agent for individual students, faculty, staff members, and organizations. (1977, 2nd Sess., c. 1136, s. 31; 1983, c. 913, s. 19; 2006-203, s. 46.)

§ 116-36.3: Repealed by Session Laws 1989 (Reg. Sess., 1990), c. 936, s. 1(b).

§ 116-36.4. Vending facilities.

Each institution shall provide to the director of the Budget and the State Auditor such information as they may from time to time require concerning the use of net proceeds from operations of vending facilities for the previous fiscal year under G.S. 116-36.1. Net proceeds are appropriated and may be used only as authorized by the Board of Governors, but this section does not authorize expenditures for purposes not otherwise authorized by law.(1983 (Reg. Sess., 1984), c. 1034, s. 172; 1987, c. 738, s. 233(b); 1993, c. 406, s. 1; 1995, c. 507, s. 15.7; 2006-203, s. 46.1.)

§ 116-36.5. Centennial Campus trust fund; Horace Williams Campus trust fund; Millennial Campuses' trust funds.

(a) All moneys received through development of the Centennial Campus of North Carolina State University at Raleigh, from whatever source, including the net proceeds from the lease or rental of Centennial Campus real property, shall be placed in a special, continuing, and nonreverting trust fund having the sole and exclusive use for further development of the Centennial Campus, including its operational development. This fund shall be treated in the manner of institutional trust funds as provided in G.S. 116-36.1, and, like the institutional trust funds, is exempt from Chapter 143C, except for Article 8 of Chapter 143C of the General Statutes. This fund shall be deemed an additional and alternative method of funding the Centennial Campus and not an exclusive one. For purposes of this section the term "Centennial Campus" is defined by G.S. 116-198.33(4). To the extent that any general, special, or local law is inconsistent with this section, it is declared inapplicable to this section.

(b) All moneys received through development of the Horace Williams Campus of the University of North Carolina at Chapel Hill, from whatever source, including the net proceeds from the lease or rental of Horace Williams Campus real property, shall be placed in a special, continuing, and nonreverting trust fund having the sole and exclusive use for further development of the Horace Williams Campus, including its operational development. This fund shall be treated in the manner of institutional trust funds as provided in G.S. 116-36.1, and, like the institutional trust funds, is exempt from Chapter 143C, except for Article 8 of Chapter 143C of the General Statutes. This fund shall be deemed an additional and alternative method of funding the Horace Williams Campus and not an exclusive one. For purposes of this section the term "Horace Williams Campus" is defined by G.S. 116-198.33(4a). To the extent that any general, special, or local law is inconsistent with this section, it is declared inapplicable to this section.

(c) All moneys received through development of a Millennial Campus of a constituent institution of The University of North Carolina as defined by G.S. 116-198.33(4b), from whatever source, including the net proceeds from the lease or rental of real property on a Millennial Campus, shall be placed in a special, continuing, and nonreverting trust fund having the sole and exclusive use for further development of that Millennial Campus, including its operational development. This fund shall be treated in the manner of institutional trust funds as provided in G.S. 116-36.1, and, like the institutional trust funds, is exempt from Chapter 143C, except for Article 8 of Chapter 143C of the General Statutes. This fund shall be deemed an additional and alternative method of funding the Millennial Campus and not an exclusive one. To the extent that any general, special, or local law is inconsistent with this section, it is declared inapplicable to this section.

(d) The moneys described by this section are appropriated and may be used only as provided by this section.(1987, c. 790, s. 1; 1998-159, s. 1; 1999-234, s. 1; 2000-177, ss. 1, 2; 2006-203, s. 47.)

§ 116-36.6. East Carolina University School of Medicine; Medicare receipts.

The East Carolina University School of Medicine shall request, on a regular basis consistent with the State's cash management plan, funds earned by the School from Medicare reimbursements for education costs. Upon receipt, these funds are appropriated and shall be allocated as follows:

(1) The portion of the Medicare reimbursement generated through the effort and expense of the School of Medicine's Medical Faculty Practice Plan shall be transferred to the appropriate Medical Faculty Practice Plan account within the School of Medicine. The Medical Faculty Practice Plan shall assume responsibility for any of these funds that subsequently must be refunded due to final audit settlements.

(2) Repealed by Session Laws 2005-276, s. 9.26(a).

(2a) Funds that were received pursuant to this section prior to July 1, 2005, and that were transferred to a special fund account on deposit with the State Treasurer are appropriated to the Brody School of Medicine at East Carolina University and may be expended by the Brody School of Medicine for the family medicine center and for purposes consistent with its stated mission.

(3) Repealed by Session Laws 2005-276, s. 9.26(a). (1995, c. 507, s. 15.4; 2005-276, s. 9.26(a); 2006-203, s. 47.1.)

§ 116-37. University of North Carolina Health Care System.

(a) Creation of System. -

(1) There is hereby established the University of North Carolina Health Care System, effective November 1, 1998, which shall be governed and administered as an affiliated enterprise of The University of North Carolina in accordance with the provisions of this section, to provide patient care, facilitate the education of physicians and other health care providers, conduct research collaboratively with the health sciences schools of the University of North Carolina at Chapel Hill, and render other services designed to promote the health and well-being of the citizens of North Carolina.

(2) As of November 1, 1998, all of the rights, privileges, liabilities, and obligations of the board of directors of the University of North Carolina Hospitals at Chapel Hill, not inconsistent with the provisions of this section, shall be transferred to and assumed by the board of directors of the University of North Carolina Health Care System.

(3) The University of North Carolina Hospitals at Chapel Hill and the clinical patient care programs established or maintained by the School of Medicine of the University of North Carolina at Chapel Hill shall be governed by the board of directors of the University of North Carolina Health Care System.

(4) With respect to the provisions of subsections (d), (e), (f), (h), (i), (j), and (k) of this section, the board of directors may adopt policies that make the authorities and responsibilities established by one or more of said subsections applicable to the University of North Carolina Hospitals at Chapel Hill, to the

clinical patient care programs of the School of Medicine of the University of North Carolina at Chapel Hill, to both, or to other persons or entities affiliated with or under the control of the University of North Carolina Health Care System.

(5) To effect an orderly transition, the policies and procedures of the clinical patient care programs of the School of Medicine of the University of North Carolina at Chapel Hill and of the University of North Carolina Hospitals at Chapel Hill effective as of October 31, 1998, shall remain effective in accordance with their terms until changed by the Board of Directors of the University of North Carolina Health Care System.

(b) Board of Directors. - The board of directors of the University of North Carolina Health Care System is hereby restructured effective November 1, 2012:

(1) The board of directors shall be composed of 24 members as follows:

a. Eight members ex officio shall be the President of The University of North Carolina (or the President's designee); the Chief Executive Officer of the University of North Carolina Health Care System; the Chancellor of the University of North Carolina at Chapel Hill and one additional administrative officer of the University of North Carolina at Chapel Hill designated by the Chancellor; the President of the University of North Carolina Hospitals; the President of the UNC Faculty Physicians; and two members of the faculty of the School of Medicine of the University of North Carolina at Chapel Hill designated by the Dean of the School of Medicine. If the Dean of the School of Medicine of the University of North Carolina at Chapel Hill does not also hold one of the positions designated as an ex officio member of the board, the Dean shall serve in one of the positions reserved for a member of the faculty.

b. Sixteen members at large shall be appointed for four-year terms, commencing on November 1 of the year of appointment. Twelve of the members at large shall be appointed by the Board of Governors after consultation with the President of The University of North Carolina. Four of the members at large shall be appointed by the board of directors.

c. The initial class of at-large members shall be composed of the following individuals:

1. The persons who hold the appointed memberships on the board of directors as of October 31, 2012, and whose terms do not expire on that date.

The terms of membership for these at-large members will expire on the last day of October of the year in which their term would have expired.

2. Three persons appointed by the Board of Governors after consultation with the President of The University of North Carolina whose terms will commence on November 1, 2012, and will expire on October 31, 2016.

3. One person appointed by the board of directors whose term will commence on November 1, 2012, and will expire on October 31, 2016.

The Board of Governors shall appoint successor at-large members for those members whose terms end on October 31, 2013, October 31, 2014, and four of the five members whose terms end on October 31, 2016. The board of directors shall appoint successor at-large members for those members whose terms end on October 31, 2015, and one of the five members whose terms end on October 31, 2016.

d. All at-large positions shall be filled by the appointment of persons from the business and professional public at large who have special competence in business management, hospital administration, health care delivery, or medical practice or who otherwise have demonstrated dedication to the improvement of health care in North Carolina, and who are neither members of the Board of Governors, members of the board of trustees of a constituent institution of The University of North Carolina, nor officers or employees of the State. No member may be appointed to more than two full four-year terms in succession, including members serving as of June 30, 2012. Any vacancy in an unexpired term shall be filled by the appointing authority for the balance of the term remaining.

(2) The board of directors, with each ex officio and at-large member having a vote, shall elect a chairman only from among the at-large members, for a term of two years. Notwithstanding the foregoing limitation, the Chancellor of the University of North Carolina at Chapel Hill may serve as Chairman. No person shall be eligible to serve as chairman for more than three terms in succession.

(3) The board of directors of the University of North Carolina Health Care System shall meet at least every 60 days and may hold special meetings at any time and place within the State at the call of the chairman. Board members, other than ex officio members, shall receive the same per diem and reimbursement for travel expenses as members of the State boards and commissions generally.

(4)   In meeting the patient-care, educational, research, and public-service goals of the University of North Carolina Health Care System, the board of directors is authorized to exercise such authority and responsibility and adopt such policies, rules, and regulations as it deems necessary and appropriate, not inconsistent with the provisions of this section or the policies of the Board of Governors or, to the extent the board's actions affect employees of the University of North Carolina at Chapel Hill, the policies of the University of North Carolina at Chapel Hill. The board may authorize any component of the University of North Carolina Health Care System, including the University of North Carolina Hospitals at Chapel Hill, to contract in its individual capacity, subject to such policies and procedures as the board of directors may direct. The board of directors may enter into formal agreements with the University of North Carolina at Chapel Hill with respect to the provision of clinical experience for students and for the provision of maintenance and supporting services. The board's action on matters within its jurisdiction is final, except that appeals may be made, in writing, to the Board of Governors with a copy of the appeal to the Chancellor of the University of North Carolina at Chapel Hill. The board of directors shall keep the Board of Governors and the board of trustees of the University of North Carolina at Chapel Hill fully informed about health care policy and recommend changes necessary to maintain adequate health care delivery, education, and research for improvement of the health of the citizens of North Carolina.

(c)   Officers. -

(1)   The executive and administrative head of the University of North Carolina Health Care System shall have the title of "Chief Executive Officer." The board of directors, the board of trustees, and the Chancellor of the University of North Carolina at Chapel Hill, following such search process as the boards and the Chancellor deem appropriate, shall identify two or more persons as candidates for the office, who, pursuant to criteria agreed upon by the boards and the Chancellor, have the qualifications for both the positions of Chief Executive Officer of the University of North Carolina Health Care System and Vice-Chancellor for Medical Affairs of the University of North Carolina at Chapel Hill. The names of the candidates so identified, once approved by the board of directors and the board of trustees, shall be forwarded by the Chancellor to the President of The University of North Carolina, who if satisfied with the quality of one or more of the candidates, will nominate one as Chief Executive Officer, subject to selection by the Board of Governors. The individual serving as Chief Executive Officer shall have complete executive and administrative authority to formulate proposals for, recommend the adoption of, and implement policies

governing the programs and activities of the University of North Carolina Health Care System, subject to all requirements of the board of directors. That same individual, when serving as Vice-Chancellor for Medical Affairs, shall have all authorities, rights, and responsibilities of a vice-chancellor of the University of North Carolina at Chapel Hill.

(2) The executive and administrative head of the University of North Carolina Hospitals at Chapel Hill shall have the title of "President of the University of North Carolina Hospitals at Chapel Hill."

(3) The board of directors shall elect, on nomination of the Chief Executive Officer, the President of the University of North Carolina Hospitals at Chapel Hill, and such additional administrative and professional staff employees of the University of North Carolina Health Care System as may be deemed necessary to assist in fulfilling the duties of the office of the Chief Executive Officer, all of whom shall serve at the pleasure of the Chief Executive Officer.

(d) Personnel. - Employees of the University of North Carolina Health Care System shall be deemed to be employees of the State and shall be subject to all provisions of State law relevant thereto; provided, however, that except as to the provisions of Articles 5, 6, 7, and 14 of Chapter 126 of the General Statutes, the provisions of Chapter 126 shall not apply to employees of the University of North Carolina Health Care System, and the policies and procedures governing the terms and conditions of employment of such employees shall be adopted by the board of directors; provided, that with respect to such employees as may be members of the faculty of the University of North Carolina at Chapel Hill, no such policies and procedures may be inconsistent with policies established by, or adopted pursuant to delegation from, the Board of Governors of The University of North Carolina.

(1) The board of directors shall fix or approve the schedules of pay, expense allowances, and other compensation and adopt position classification plans for employees of the University of North Carolina Health Care System.

(2) The board of directors may adopt or provide for rules and regulations concerning, but not limited to, annual leave, sick leave, special leave with full pay or with partial pay supplementing workers' compensation payments for employees injured in accidents arising out of and in the course of employment, working conditions, service awards and incentive award programs, grounds for dismissal, demotion, or discipline, other personnel policies, and any other measures that promote the hiring and retention of capable, diligent, and

effective career employees. However, an employee who has achieved career State employee status as defined by G.S. 126-1.1 by October 31, 1998, shall not have his or her compensation reduced as a result of this subdivision. Further, an employee who has achieved career State employee status as defined by G.S. 126-1.1 by October 31, 1998, shall be subject to the rules regarding discipline or discharge that were effective on October 31, 1998, and shall not be subject to the rules regarding discipline or discharge adopted after October 31, 1998.

(3) The board of directors may prescribe the office hours, workdays, and holidays to be observed by the various offices and departments of the University of North Carolina Health Care System.

(4) The board of directors may establish boards, committees, or councils to conduct hearings upon the appeal of employees who have been suspended, demoted, otherwise disciplined, or discharged, to hear employee grievances, or to undertake any other duties relating to personnel administration that the board of directors may direct.

The board of directors shall submit all initial classification and pay plans and other rules and regulations adopted pursuant to subdivisions (1) through (4) of this subsection to the Office of State Human Resources for review upon adoption by the board. Any subsequent changes to these plans, rules, and policies adopted by the board shall be submitted to the Office of State Human Resources for review. Any comments by the Office of State Human Resources shall be submitted to the Chief Executive Officer and to the President of The University of North Carolina.

(e) Finances. - The University of North Carolina Health Care System shall be subject to the provisions of the State Budget Act, except for trust funds as provided in G.S. 116-36.1 and G.S. 116-37.2. The Chief Executive Officer, subject to the board of directors, shall be responsible for all aspects of budget preparation, budget execution, and expenditure reporting. All operating funds of the University of North Carolina Health Care System may be budgeted and disbursed through special fund codes, maintaining separate auditable accounts for the University of North Carolina Hospitals at Chapel Hill and the clinical patient care programs of the School of Medicine of the University of North Carolina at Chapel Hill. All receipts of the University of North Carolina Health Care System may be deposited directly to the special fund codes, and except for General Fund appropriations, all receipts of the University of North Carolina Hospitals at Chapel Hill may be invested pursuant to G.S. 116-37.2(h). General

Fund appropriations for support of the University of North Carolina Hospitals at Chapel Hill shall be budgeted in a General Fund code under a single purpose, "Contribution to University of North Carolina Hospitals at Chapel Hill Operations" and be transferable to a special fund operating code as receipts.

(f) Finances - Patient/Health Care System Benefit. - The Chief Executive Officer of the University of North Carolina Health Care System, or the Chief Executive Officer's designee, may expend operating budget funds, including State funds, of the University of North Carolina Health Care System for the direct benefit of a patient, when, in the judgment of the Chief Executive Officer or the Chief Executive Officer's designee, the expenditure of these funds would result in a financial benefit to the University of North Carolina Health Care System. Any such expenditures are declared to result in the provision of medical services and create charges of the University of North Carolina Health Care System for which the health care system may bill and pursue recovery in the same way as allowed by law for recovery of other health care systems' charges for services that are unpaid.

These expenditures shall be restricted (i) to situations in which a patient is financially unable to afford ambulance or other transportation for discharge; (ii) to afford placement in an after-care facility; (iii) to assure availability of a bed in an after-care facility after discharge from the hospitals; (iv) to secure equipment or other medically appropriate services after discharge; or (v) to pay health insurance premiums. The Chief Executive Officer or the Chief Executive Officer's designee shall reevaluate at least once a month the cost-effectiveness of any continuing payment on behalf of a patient.

To the extent that the University of North Carolina Health Care System advances anticipated government entitlement benefits for a patient's benefit, for which the patient later receives a lump-sum "back-pay" award from an agency of the State, whether for the current admission or subsequent admission, the State agency shall withhold from this back pay an amount equal to the sum advanced on the patient's behalf by the University of North Carolina Health Care System, if, prior to the disbursement of the back pay, the applicable State program has received notice from the University of North Carolina Health Care System of the advancement.

(g) Reports. - The Chief Executive Officer and the President of The University of North Carolina jointly shall report by September 30 of each year on the operations and financial affairs of the University of North Carolina Health Care System to the Joint Legislative Commission on Governmental Operations.

The report shall include the actions taken by the board of directors under the authority granted in subsections (d), (h), (i), and (j) of this section.

(h) Purchases. - Notwithstanding the provisions of Articles 3, 3A, and 3C of Chapter 143 of the General Statutes to the contrary, the board of directors shall establish policies and regulations governing the purchasing requirements of the University of North Carolina Health Care System. These policies and regulations shall provide for requests for proposals, competitive bidding, or purchasing by means other than competitive bidding, contract negotiations, and contract awards for purchasing supplies, materials, equipment, and services which are necessary and appropriate to fulfill the clinical, educational, research, and community service missions of the University of North Carolina Health Care System. The board of directors shall submit all initial policies and regulations adopted pursuant to this subsection to the Division of Purchase and Contract for review upon adoption by the board. Any subsequent changes to these policies and regulations adopted by the board shall be submitted to the Division of Purchase and Contract for review. Any comments by the Division of Purchase and Contract shall be submitted to the Chief Executive Officer and to the President of The University of North Carolina.

(i) Property. - The board of directors shall establish rules and regulations for acquiring or disposing of any interest in real property for the use of the University of North Carolina Health Care System. These rules and regulations shall include provisions for development of specifications, advertisement, and negotiations with owners for acquisition by purchase, gift, lease, or rental, but not by condemnation or exercise of eminent domain, on behalf of the University of North Carolina Health Care System. This section does not authorize the board of directors to encumber real property. The board of directors shall submit all initial policies and regulations adopted pursuant to this subsection to the State Property Office for review upon adoption by the board. Any subsequent changes to these policies and regulations adopted by the board shall be submitted to the State Property Office for review. Any comments by the State Property Office shall be submitted to the Chief Executive Officer and to the President of The University of North Carolina. After review by the Attorney General as to form and after the consummation of any such acquisition, the University of North Carolina Health Care System shall promptly file a report concerning the acquisition or disposition with the Governor and Council of State. Acquisitions and dispositions of any interest in real property pursuant to this section shall not be subject to the provisions of Article 36 of Chapter 143 of the General Statutes or the provisions of Chapter 146 of the General Statutes.

(j) Property - Construction. - Notwithstanding G.S. 143-341(3) and G.S. 143-135.1, the board of directors shall adopt policies and procedures with respect to the design, construction, and renovation of buildings, utilities, and other property developments of the University of North Carolina Health Care System requiring the expenditure of public money for:

(1) Conducting the fee negotiations for all design contracts and supervising the letting of all construction and design contracts.

(2) Performing the duties of the Department of Administration, the Office of State Construction, and the State Building Commission under G.S. 133-1.1(d), Article 8 of Chapter 143 of the General Statutes, and G.S. 143-341(3).

(3) Using open-end design agreements.

(4) As appropriate, submitting construction documents for review and approval by the Department of Insurance and the Division of Health Service Regulation of the Department of Health and Human Services.

(5) Using the standard contracts for design and construction currently in use for State capital improvement projects by the Office of State Construction of the Department of Administration.

The board of directors shall submit all initial policies and procedures adopted under this subsection to the Office of State Construction for review upon adoption by the board. Any subsequent changes to these policies and procedures adopted by the board shall be submitted to the Office of State Construction for review. Any comments by the Office of State Construction shall be submitted to the Chief Executive Officer and to the President of The University of North Carolina.

(k) Patient Information. - The University of North Carolina Health Care System shall, at the earliest possible opportunity, specifically make a verbal and written request to each patient to disclose the patient's social security number, if any. If the patient does not disclose that number, the University of North Carolina Health Care System shall deny benefits, rights, and privileges of the University of North Carolina Health Care System to the patient as soon as practical, to the maximum extent permitted by federal law or federal regulations. The University of North Carolina Health Care System shall make the disclosure to the patient required by Section 7(b) of P.L. 93-579. This subsection is supplementary to G.S. 105A-3(c). (1971, c. 762, s. 1; c. 1244, s. 6; 1981, c.

859, s. 41.5; 1983, c. 717, s. 32; 1985 (Reg. Sess., 1986), c. 955, ss. 30, 31; 1989, c. 141, s. 1; 1991, c. 550, s. 2; c. 689, s. 206.2(d); 1993 (Reg. Sess., 1994), c. 591, s. 10(a); 1998-212, s. 11.8(a); 1999-252, s. 4(a); 2005-417, s. 3; 2006-203, s. 47.2; 2007-182, s. 1; 2007-306, s. 1; 2010-31, s. 9.11; 2011-145, s. 9.6E(b); 2012-174, s. 1; 2013-382, s. 9.1(c).)

Vision Books Order Form

Fax Orders: 1-980-299-5965

Phone Orders: 1-704-898-0770

E-mail Orders: www.visionbooks.org

Mail Orders: Vision Books, LLC
                  P.O. Box 42406
                  Charlotte, NC 28215

Shipp To:
Name_____
Address_____
City_____State_____Zip_____
Phone_____Fax_____
Email_____@_____

Bill To: We can bill a third party on your behalf.
Name_____
Address_____
City_____State_____Zip_____
Phone____(_____)_____Fax_____
Email_____@_____

Pamphlet Number ($15.00 Each)	Qty	Total Cost
_____	_____	_____
_____	_____	_____
_____	_____	_____
_____	_____	_____
_____	_____	_____
_____	_____	_____
_____	_____	_____
<u>Full Volume Set 1-92</u>	<u>92 Pamphlets</u>	<u>1,380.00</u>

Free Shipping Shipping & Handling on Full Volume Orders
Add $1.00 Shipping & Handling per pamphlet $_____

Total Cost $_____

Thank you for your support. Management!

DID YOU ENJOY THIS BOOK?

Vision Books, LLC would like to hear from you! If you or someone you know has been fasely imprisoned, we would like to hear your story. If the 'North Carolina Criminal Law and Procedure' has had an effect in your life or if you have suggestions, we would like to hear from you. Send your letters to:

Vision Books, LLC
Attn: Staff Writers
P.O. Box 42406
Charlotte, NC 28215
Email: staff@visionbooks.org

Order Additional Copies:

Fax Orders:	1-980-299-5965
Phone Orders:	1-704-898-0770
E-mail Orders:	www.visionbooks.org
Mail Orders:	Vision Books, LLC P.O. Box 42406 Charlotte, NC 28215

www.ingramcontent.com/pod-product-compliance
Lightning Source LLC
Chambersburg PA
CBHW051636170526
45167CB00001B/217